Knights of St John

Knights of St John
A history to the
Siege of Vienna, 1688

Augusta Theodosia Drane

Knights of St John
*A history to the
Siege of Vienna, 1688*
by Augusta Theodosia Drane

First published under the title
*The Knights of St John: With the Battle of
Lepanto and Siege of Vienna*

Leonaur is an imprint
of Oakpast Ltd

Copyright in this form © 2009 Oakpast Ltd

ISBN: 978-1-84677-656-4 (hardcover)
ISBN: 978-1-84677-655-7 (softcover)

http://www.leonaur.com

Publisher's Notes

In the interests of authenticity, the spellings, grammar and place names used have been retained from the original editions.

The opinions of the authors represent a view of events in which he was a participant related from his own perspective, as such the text is relevant as an historical document.

The views expressed in this book are not necessarily those of the publisher.

Contents

Preface	7
Commencement of the Order	11
The Knights of Limisso	30
Progress of the Turks	48
Character of D'Aubusson	73
Bajazet and Djem	94
Ill Success of Turkish Troops	115
Departure From Rhodes	130
Exploits of Knights in Africa	145
Arrival of the Turkish Fleet	159
St John's Day	175
The Battle of Lepanto	199
Vienna: The Siege	234
The Relief	255

Preface

In this little volume it has not been attempted to give a complete history of the Order of Knights Hospitallers, even from the comparatively late date from which the narrative begins; nor, indeed, has it been thought necessary, in a publication of such slight pretensions, to enter into a full and detailed description of the several great sieges around which the chief interest of the story gathers. All that the writer has endeavoured to do is, to present the reader with as vivid a picture of events so memorable in the annals of the world as could be conveyed in a rapid and an elaborate sketch. Other incidents and circumstances having an important bearing on the general contest between the Moslem and the Christian have been interwoven with the staple of the narrative, either for the purpose of linking together the principal facts, or of giving them that position and prominence which belongs to them.

The determined courage and heroic devotion of the Knights of St. John have commanded the admiration of every noble and generous mind, whatever may have been its religious convictions or prejudices. At Acre, at Smyrna, at Rhodes, and lastly at Malta, these brave champions of the faith occupied what for the time being was the outpost of Christendom. At times almost annihilated, they rose again before the eyes of their enemies with more than recovered strength; abandoned, or but tardily and grudgingly succoured by the powers of Europe,—who were too much engaged with their own political quarrels, and too deeply absorbed by their own selfish and immediate interests, to look to the future or unite against the common foe,—they confronted single-handed the enormous hosts of the infidels in their descents upon Europe, arrested their triumphant march towards the West, retreated from one position only to rally in another, and renew a contest which in appearance was hopeless; and at length, when all seemed lost, by sheer fortitude and perseverance they baffled and beat back the barbarian invader in the very pride of his strength, so that he never dared to approach their stronghold again.

So much is patent on the very face of history, and is acknowledged by all. But few, save they who share the faith of these brave men, seem to discern wherein the secret of their strength lay, and what it was that lent such force to their arms, endued them with that dauntless courage, that irresistible energy, and that tenacity of purpose, which enabled them to dare and to do and to suffer as they did. Some, knowing not how else to characterise it, give it the name of "attachment to their order,"—an indefinable something corresponding to what the world calls honour, or *esprit de corps*. Doubtless the Knights of St. John, as sworn companions in arms, vowed to fight and to die in the same great cause, felt themselves bound to each other by no ordinary tie, and were ever ready to sacrifice their lives for the sake of their brethren; but it was not in this that their strength lay. It lay in the simple power of divine faith, in a religious devotion as humble as it was ardent, and a burning enthusiasm for the cause of God in the world.

This it was that elevated their valour to a supernatural virtue, and gave them the calm intrepid bearing and the indomitable spirit of martyrs. They were dutiful sons of holy Church, and as such they fought in her defence; always and every where they demeaned themselves as veritable soldiers of the Cross, faithful followers of Jesus, devout clients of Mary. And in this was included what can never be separated from it—a true-hearted and loyal obedience to the successor of St. Peter. The Knights of St John were ever the devoted subjects of the Holy See. It was as the Pope's militia that they performed those wondrous deeds of arms which have gained them the respect and sympathy of writers who can scarcely allude to the occupant of Peter's chair without an expression of contempt; and if to them, and to those other noble warriors whose exploits are related in the following pages, belong the credit and the renown of having stemmed the advancing tide of Ottoman invasion, it is to the Popes in the first place that the glory is due.

Europe owes to the Sovereign Pontiffs a heavy debt of gratitude for the indefatigable zeal with which they never ceased to sound the note of alarm, and to urge the Christian powers, not only to oppose the farther progress of the Turkish arms, but to drive back the barbarian hordes into the regions from which they had emerged; a debt all the heavier that each respite and each success was obtained almost against the will of those for whom it was won, and with an apparent unconsciousness, on their part, of the imminence of the danger or the nature of the calamity with which they were threatened. If the Turk retreated from Malta in shame and confusion,—if at Lepanto he lost the prestige of his naval superiority,—if Vienna defied his beleaguering hosts and sent him flying from her walls, never again to return,—it was the Vicar of Christ who thus foiled him and smote him, and who, from the height of his throne on the Vatican hill, pronounced that irreversible word, "Thus far shalt thou come, and no farther."

Every check, every failure, every defeat the infidels encountered, originated with Rome. D'Aubusson, L'Isle Adam, La Valette, Don John of Austria, Sobieski,—all were but the lieutenants of the Pope; and that Europe was not delivered over to a blasphemous apostasy, and desolated and trodden down by the foulest tyranny which the world has ever known, may justly be attributed, in the good providence of God, to the untiring vigilance and the energetic and persevering hostility of the old man who reigns at Rome, and who never dies.[1]

---

1. The reader will not need to be reminded of the striking summary given by Dr. Newman, in his *Lectures on the Turks* (pp. 181-188), of the successive measures, spiritual and otherwise, taken by the Popes, from the 11th to the 18th century, to rouse Christendom to a common crusade against the Ottomans, and to mark each victory obtained over them as a *fait accompli* in the commemorations of the Church.

The writer had relied chiefly on the works of the Abbé Vertot and Mr. Taafe for the sketch of the Order of Knights Hospitallers. It may be proper, however, to state, that since the manuscript came into the editor's hands it has been carefully compared with the text of various approved authors who have either previously or subsequently written on the subject, and to the results of whose labours reference is made in the notes. The account of the Battle of Lepanto is mainly founded on the history recently published by Don Cajetan Rosell, and the *Life of St. Pius V.* by Maffei; and the story of the Siege and Relief of Vienna is taken for the most part from Salvandy's *Life of John Sobieski,* and that by the Abbé Coyer.

E. H. T.

CHAPTER 1

Commencement of the Order

The order of the Knights Hospitallers of St. John [1] dates its origin from that heroic period of Christian chivalry when Jerusalem opened her gates to the arms of Godfrey de Bouillon. Whether or not its mixed military and religious character were coeval with its first establishment, or whether its singular constitution came to be gradually developed, as it was added to by successive masters, is a point of little consequence for us to decide. It is certain that at a very early period after its foundation it is to be found with both these characters united; and whilst the Hospital of St. John exercised that admirable charity which was the first condition of the order's existence, the knights were winning on every field of Palestine the title bestowed on them by their Moslem enemies of the "heroes of the Christian armies."

It is not our present purpose to set before, the reader any account of those achievements of the order in the Holy Land, which properly belong to the wars of the Crusades, and cannot be separated from the history of that period: but, before taking up the narrative from the day when, driven from the walls of Acre, the shattered remnant of its heroic legions was tossing in a single *bark* on the waters of the Levant, as yet without a home in Europe,—a few remarks seem necessary, both to explain its constitution as a religious body, and its position at the moment when our story of its fortunes begins.

---
1. St. John the Baptist, the patron of the Order.

At the period when the military orders first sprang into existence, the road to the Holy Land was, as everyone knows, the highway of Europe; and year by year crowds of pilgrims of all ranks came flocking to the Holy City, encountering innumerable perils on the way, and often arriving at their journey's end in a state of extreme suffering and destitution. Now the object of the Order of St. John may very briefly be described if we say, that its members took on themselves the office of administering the hospitality of Christ: "Servants of the poor of Christ" was the title that they assumed; and this name of Christ's poor was applied indiscriminately to all pilgrims and crusaders.

The ceremonies attendant on the reception of a knight had a peculiar significance, and strikingly illustrate the spirit of the order. The postulant presented himself with a lighted taper in his hand, and carrying his naked sword to be blessed by the priest. He had previously prepared himself by a general confession and the reception of holy communion. After blessing the sword, the priest returned it to him with these words:

> Receive this holy sword in the name of the Father, and of the Son, and of the Holy Ghost, amen; and use it for thy own defence, and that of the Church of God, to the confusion of the enemies of Jesus Christ and of the Christian faith, and take heed that no human frailty move thee to strike any man with it unjustly.

Then he replaced it in the sheath, the priest saying as he girded himself:

> Gird thyself with the sword of Jesus Christ; and remember that it is not with the sword, but with faith, that the saints have conquered kingdoms.

The knight then once more drew his sword, whilst these words were addressed to him:

> Let the brilliancy of this sword represent to thee the brightness of faith; let its point signify hope, and its hilt charity. Use it for the Catholic faith, for justice, and for

the consolation of widows and orphans: for this is the true faith and justification of a Christian knight.

Then he brandished it thrice in the name of the Holy Trinity, and the brethren proceeded to give him his golden spurs, saying:

Seest thou these spurs? They signify that as the horse fears them when he swerves from his duty, so shouldst thou fear to depart from thy post or from thy vows.

Then the mantle was thrown over him, and as they pointed to the cross of eight points embroidered on the left side, they said:

We wear this white cross as a sign of purity; wear it also within thy heart as well as outwardly, and keep it without soil or stain. The eight points are the signs of the eight beatitudes, which thou must ever preserve: *viz.* 1. spiritual joy; 2. to live without malice; 3. to weep over thy sins; 4. to humble thyself to those who injure thee; 5. to love justice; 6. to be merciful; 7. to be sincere and pure of heart; and 8. to suffer persecution.

Then he kissed the cross, and the mantle was fastened, whilst the ministering knight continued:

Take this cross and mantle in the name of the Holy Trinity, for the repose and salvation of thy soul, the defence of the Catholic faith, and the honour of our Lord Jesus Christ; and I place it on the left side near thy heart, that thou mayst love it, and that thy right hand may defend it, charging thee never to abandon it, since it is the standard of our holy faith. Shouldst thou ever desert the standard, and fly when combating the enemies of Jesus Christ, thou wilt be stripped of this holy sign, according to the statutes of the order, as having broken the vow thou hast taken, and shalt be cut off from our body as an unsound member.

On the mantle were embroidered all the instruments of the

Passion; each of them was pointed out to the new-made knight, with the words:

> In order that thou mayst put all thy hope in the passion of Jesus Christ, behold the cord whereby He was bound; see, too, His crown of thorns; this is the column to which He was tied; this is the lance which pierced His side; this is the sponge with which He was drenched with gall; these are the whips that scourged Him; and this the cross on which He suffered. Receive, therefore, the yoke of the Lord, for it is easy and light, and will give rest to thy soul; and I tie this cord about thy neck in pledge of the servitude thou hast promised. We offer thee nothing but bread and water, a simple habit and of little worth. We give thee and thy parents and relatives a share in the good works performed by the order, and by our brethren now and hereafter, throughout the whole world. Amen.

He was then received to the kiss of peace.

We find no mention of serving the sick in the formula of the vow, but the obligation of hospitality was indispensable. The grand master even took the title of the "guardian of the poor of Christ," and the knights were wont (according to Michaud) to call the poor and sick "our masters." We find various notices of their even undertaking the charge of deserted children,—a charge which seems to speak volumes for the loving tenderness of these soldiers of the faith. The succour of the sick formed, therefore, but one portion of the duties embraced by their rule under the name of hospitality; these guests of Christ had to be protected on their journey, as well as guarded and entertained on their arrival; and thus the military defence of the Holy City itself came naturally to be first among the acts, of hospitality to which the order devoted itself, and which included at the same time the tending of the sick, the care of orphan children, the entertainment of strangers, the ransom of captives, and the daily clothing and support of the vast multitudes whom every day brought to the gates of their "Xenodochia," as the large hospital of the order was styled.

A chronicler, writing in the year 1150, and describing what he had himself seen in his youth, says, that you might behold all these offices of charity going on at the same time: the knights mounting their horses to ride out to battle; the pilgrims crowding to the halls of the hospital; and the infirmary full of sick and wounded Christians, who were served and tended with the utmost care. The necessary expenses of so vast an undertaking readily account for the large endowments granted to the order in every Christian country; their lands and revenues were not held as furnishing the means of luxury to themselves, but were the funds ungrudgingly contributed by Christendom for the support of her pilgrims, and the defence of the sepulchre of her Lord; and thus the knights were made the holders and administrators of a mighty trust of charity.

To carry out the full design of their foundation, they extended their views far beyond the territory of Jerusalem; hospitals were founded in all the principal maritime states of Europe, which were considered as affiliated to the mother-house, where pilgrims were received and helped forward on their journey, and furnished with escorts and protection in times of danger. These houses afterwards became the commanderies of the order, and had, of course, their own communities of knights; for all did not reside at the principal seat of government, though, as we shall afterwards find, they were liable to be summoned thither at any moment, either to assist at elections, or to reinforce the troops actually engaged in war.

In these hospitals the knights led a strict community life, much of their time being given to active works of charity; a circumstance to which is doubtless owing the superiority which the order of St. John always preserved over that of the Templars as a religious body; for by their peculiar constitution, the military spirit could never become exclusive among them, but was always tempered and restrained by their obligation to the duties of Christian hospitality.

St. Bernard, in his *Exhortation to the Knights of the Temple* has left us a picture of a military religious order, whose original was doubtless in part taken from the houses of the Hospitallers, who preceded the Templars by some years in their foundation.

"They live," he says, "in a happy yet frugal manner, having neither wives nor children; and calling nothing their own—not even their own wills: they are never idle; but when not actually marching to the field against the infidels, they mend their arms or the harness of their horses, or engage in various pious exercises under the orders of their chief. Never does an insolent word, or the least murmur, or immoderate laughter, pass without severe correction. They detest all games of chance, and never engage in the chase, or in useless visits; they avoid with horror shows and buffoonery, together with songs and conversation of a light or dangerous character; they are little studious of their dress; their faces are brown with exposure to the sun, and their aspect is stern and severe. When the hour of combat approaches, they arm themselves with faith within and with steel without,—no useless ornament glitters on their armour or that of their horses; their arms are their only decoration, and they use them valiantly in the greatest dangers, without fearing either the numbers or the strength of the barbarians, for their confidence is in the God of Armies; and in fighting for His cause they seek either certain victory or a holy and honourable death."

The various duties of the order were not all discharged by the same members of the community. Their body was divided into three classes: the knights, always of noble birth, in whom the government of the order was vested; the clergy, or chaplains of St. John, whose duties were purely ecclesiastical, and who also acted as almoners; and the brothers servants-at-arms, a large and very important class, who assisted the knights both in war and in the hospitals, and may be considered as something between squires and lay brothers,—for they did not act in a menial capacity, and though never eligible to the rank of knights, they were treated almost on an equality, and had votes for the election of master. All these classes were bound by the three essential vows of religion; but, although religious, the knights never bore the priestly character, as has been sometimes represented.

Many instances, however, occur of ecclesiastics having previously seen military service as knights of the order before assuming the sacerdotal character. Even the military powers of the knights themselves had their limitations: they were bound to a strict neutrality in all wars among Christian nations, and could take arms only in defence of religion, and against its enemies; when not so engaged, they were to devote themselves to the care of the sick and poor: and this neutrality was not only the rule, but the invariable practice of the order, as their history amply testifies.

So long as the Holy City remained in the hands of the Christians, it continued to be the principal residence of the Knights of St. John of Jerusalem; and their large hospital, able to contain above 2000 guests, lay exactly opposite the Holy Sepulchre. It is of this hospital that Innocent II. speaks in words which so perfectly describe the character of the institute that we will insert them, as the best means of conveying a notion to the reader of the design of its foundation, and the manner of its fulfilment.

> "How pleasing to God," he says, "and how venerable to man, is at least one spot on earth! How commodious, how useful a refuge is that which the Hospitallers' house of hospitality in Jerusalem affords to all poor pilgrims who face the various dangers by land and sea, with the pious and devout wish to visit the Sacred City and our Lord's sepulchre, as is well known to the whole universe! There, indeed, are the indigent assisted, and every sort of humane attention is shown to the weak fatigued by their numerous labours and dangers. There they are refreshed and recover their strength; so that they are enabled to visit the sacred places which have been sanctified by our Saviour's corporeal presence.

"Nor do the brethren of that house hesitate to expose their lives for their brothers in. Jesus Christ; but with infantry and cavalry, kept for that special purpose, and supported by their own money, they defend the faithful fearlessly from the Paynims, both in going and returning. It is these Hospitallers who are the instruments by which the Omnipotent preserves His Church in the East from the defilements of the infidels."

This was written in 1130: the following year witnessed the death of Baldwin II., and was succeeded by sorrowful times for Palestine. Those who came after him, and bore in turn the title of kings of Jerusalem, were but little fitted for the kingdom whose sceptre was a sword. Under Guy of Lusignan the cause of the Crusaders became well-nigh desperate; and on the fatal field of Tiberias, after a combat which lasted three days, the flower of the Christian army was cut to pieces, and the king himself was taken prisoner. When he recovered his freedom, it was to mourn over a yet greater disaster; for Jerusalem itself had fallen (a.d. 1187), and, eighty-eight years after the triumphant entry of Godfrey de Bouillon, was once more in the hands of the Moslems. The news of that event, which is said to have caused the death of the reigning Pope, immediately roused the sovereigns of Europe to prepare for a fresh crusade.

Nevertheless it was marked by one circumstance equally honourable to the Christians and to their enemies. Saladin, we are told, was so touched by the reports brought him of the charity exercised at the hospital of St. John, that he gave permission for the Hospitallers to remain in the city one year undisturbed, that the sick and wounded under their charge might be perfectly restored before removal In 1191 the forces of France and England were united before the walls of Acre; and the third crusade may be said to have opened by the capitulation of that city, when it fell into the hands of Richard *Cœur de Lion*. The Hospitallers were foremost in the glorious campaign that followed. It lasted little more than a year; but when the English monarch again embarked for Europe he showed his gratitude and esteem for the Order of St. John by bestowing on them the city of Acre as a free donation; and thus the knights came for the first time to have a fixed residence and sovereignty, and gave their name to the city, which has ever since been known as St. Jean d'Acre. It is here, then, that our narrative finds them, the sovereigns of a city which in all ages seems destined to be the battle-field for East and West, and which in its very aspect appears to claim for itself the right never to sink into insignificance.

Beautiful as it is, even in our own day, it was yet more beautiful when, seven centuries ago, it was the Christian capital of the East. Its snow-white palaces sparkled like jewels against the dark woods of Carmel which rose towards the south. To the east there stretched away the glorious plain, over which the eye might wander till it lost itself in the blue outlines of hills on which no Christian eye could gaze unmoved; for they hid in their bosom the village of Nazareth and the waters of Tiberias, and had been trodden all about by the feet of One whose touch had made them holy ground. That rich and fertile plain, now marshy and deserted, but then a very labyrinth of fields and vineyards, circled Acre also to the north; but there the eye was met by a new boundary,—the snowy summits of a lofty mountain range whose bases were clothed with cedar; while all along the lovely coast broke the blue waves of that mighty sea whose shores are the empires of the world.

There lay Acre among her gardens; the long rows of her marble houses, with their flat roofs, forming terraces odorous with orange-trees, and rich with flowers of a thousand hues, which silken awnings shaded from the sun. You might walk from one end of the city to the other on these terraced roofs, and never once descend into the streets; and the streets themselves were wide and airy, their shops brilliant with the choicest merchandise of the East, and thronged with the noblest chivalry of Europe. It was the gayest, gallantest city in existence; its gilded steeples stood out against the mountains, or above the horizon of those bright waters that tossed and sparkled in the flood of southern sunshine, and in the fresh breeze that kissed them from the west;

every house was rich with painted glass,—for this art, as yet rare in Europe, is spoken of by all writers as lavishly employed in Acre, and was perhaps first brought from thence by the Crusaders; every nation had its street, inhabited by its own merchants and nobles, and no less than twenty crowned heads kept up within the city-walls their palaces and courts.

The emperor of Germany, and the kings of England, France, Sicily, Spain, Portugal, Denmark, and Jerusalem, had each their residence there; while the Templars and the Teutonic order had establishments as well as the Hospitallers, and on a scarcely less sumptuous scale. But it was the great Xenodochia of the latter which was the glory of the place; it rivalled in size, and in the magnificence of its arrangements, the first hospital of Jerusalem; and with a grand and noble magnanimity, not only Christians, but Moslems and Saracens were received within its walls. Its fame became poetical, and it had its legends. Saladin, it is said, hearing of the surprising things done in the hospital of Acre, came in the disguise of a poor man, and feigning sickness, was entertained with a marvellous hospitality:

> "For," says the French chronicler, "the infirmarian came to him, and asked him what he would eat; but he answered, 'The only thing I can eat, and do intensely desire, it were madness even to name.'
>
> "'Do not hesitate in the least, dear brother,' replied the infirmarian; 'for a sick man here is given whatsoever he fancies, if gold can buy it; ask, therefore, for what you will, and you shall have it.'
>
> "'It is the foot of Moriel, the grand master's horse,' answered the pretended invalid; 'they say he will not take a thousand *bezants* for him; nevertheless, if that be not cut off in my presence, I can never eat a morsel more.'
>
> "So the infirmarian went and told all to the master, and he marvelled greatly. 'Well, since it be so, take my horse,' he said; 'better that all my horses were dead than a man.' So the horse was led to the side of the sick man's bed, and the groom armed himself with a hatchet, and prepared to

strike off the fore-foot of the beautiful and noble steed. "'Hold now,' cried Saladin, 'for I am satisfied, and will be content with mutton.' Then Moriel was loosed again, and led back to his stable, and the grand master and his brethren were right glad thereof. So, when the *soldan* had eaten and drunk, he arose and returned to his country, and sent thence a charter sealed with his own seal, which ran as follows: 'Let all men know that I, Saladin, *soldan* of Babylon, give and bequeath to the hospital of Acre a thousand bezants of gold, to be paid every year, in peace or war, unto the grand master, be he who he may, in gratitude for the wonderful charity of himself and of his order.'"

We have called this a legendary tale; but though, indeed, it reads more like fable than reality, it would not be out of harmony with the romantic and adventurous spirit of its hero, and might be truth, but that the death of the great *soldan* occurred in the very year when the Christians took possession of Acre. Nevertheless it may instance the kind of reputation enjoyed at that time by the Hospitallers of St. John.

The term of their residence in Acre was scarce a hundred years;—a period marked by the Latin conquest of Constantinople, and several fresh crusades, one of which brought St. Louis to the port of Acre after his gallant army had been destroyed in Egypt. This was in 1254. A few years later, and the last crusading prince who ever left the shores of Europe came thither in the person of Edward I. of England; and there, in 1271, befell the romantic incident of his attempted assassination, and the heroic devotion of his wife Eleanor.

Meanwhile, in spite of every effort, Palestine was being lost to the Christian arms; one by one, every town and castle fell into the hands of the infidels, and the Christians of Syria were driven to take refuge behind the forts of Acre, almost the last citadel whereon the banner of the Cross still waved untouched. Its day, however, was coming, and each new conquest of Kelaoun, the new sultan of the Saracens, drew the circle of its enemies closer and closer round its walls.

Marcab fell, then Tripoli, which had been Christian near two hundred years; and the advancing steps of the victors were marked at each successive triumph by enormities and crimes, the recital of which could create only horror and disgust. Acre knew herself doomed; but in vain did she look to Europe for help in her extremity; the crusading spirit was extinct; and De Lorgue, the grand master of the Hospitallers, after a fruitless journey to the courts of Europe, returned to die of a broken heart in his own city, whose catastrophe he saw was not far distant.

It was hastened by a breach of truce committed by some of the garrison; but ere it came, Sir John de Villiers, the new grand master, addressed a circular to all the knights of the order, summoning then to Acre to join him in its defence; and he himself set out on a fresh embassy, which proved as useless as his predecessor's. He, too, returned disconsolate and alone; and before those whom he had addressed could came to his assistance, Melec Seraf, the son of Kelaoun, was encamped beneath the walls of the devoted city (a.d. 1291). The resources of the Christians were very small: not much above two hundred of the knights of St. John, and about as many of the Templars, were to be found in the garrison; for most of the members of both orders had fallen at Tripoli, and the reinforcements from Europe had not yet arrived. There were mercenary troops of all nations, but the entire force underarms amounted to no more than 12,000 men; for, large as was the population of Acre, it was mostly of the mercantile class.

Of the troops, 500 were from Cyprus, brought thence by Henry, who bore the empty title of king of Jerusalem; but the succour was small in point or numbers, and for fidelity scarcely to be depended upon, and the king's reputation for courage was none of the highest The port of Acre, it must be remembered, was still open, which enabled the greater part of the inhabitants to embark with their families and effects, and take flight before the siege began: of those that remained, many were engaged in the defence; but faction and disunion sadly weakened their ranks, and the Hospitallers, though nominally masters of the city, had little power to maintain order and discipline among the various nations and parties that made up its population. By common consent, Peter de Beaujeu, grand master of the Templars, was elected governor of the city; and whatever may be said of the jealousies of the two orders, it is certain that the most perfect union existed between them during the whole of this memorable siege.

The Sultan Kelaoun had expired at Cairo whilst actively preparing to set out for Acre. Before his death he exacted a solemn promise from his son never to celebrate has funeral until he should have taken the Christian city, and put all its inhabitants to the sword. Melec Seraf took the oath with right good will, and sent a host of sappers and miners before him to prepare the ground; and everyday during the long month of March the Christians had watched the ground from Carmel to the seashore broken up by new entrenchments, and the camp filling with the reinforcements that were constantly coming in, not from Egypt alone, but from Arabia and the provinces of the Euphrates, till the vast plain glittered with the multitudes that covered it; their golden targets and polished lance-points resembling (says Michaud)

> the shining stars on a serene night; and on the hosts' advancing, it was like a forest for the multitude of the lances held aloft:

And well it might be, for they were more than 400,000 fighting men, and they covered the entire plain. A little before sunset, the sultan rode out, surrounded by his officers, to survey his thirty miles of entrenchments filled with troops whose arms had as yet been found irresistible; and when he compared his host of combatants with the contemptible size of the city, the weakness of whose defenders was well known to him, it seemed to him that the very idea of resistance was somewhat laughable, and he gave orders for a peremptory summons to surrender; but there was neither answer nor movement on the part of the Christians, and the night passed in silence on both sides.

The rosy dawn was streaking the sky just above those low hills that rose dark against the eastern horizon, when the silence was broken by a hideous crash. The smoke and dust cleared away, and you might see a mass of crumbling ruins where but a moment before rose the stately ramparts of the city.

Then a loud cry from the ranks of the Saracens, a pell-mell charge towards the spot, and a pause as they reached the verge of a wide, deep ditch which a curve in the ground till then had concealed from view. There was a bloody struggle on its edge; and the infidels were forced to retire, leaving five thousand corpses on the ruined breach. But what were five thousand men to such a host as theirs? Such a repulse hardly seemed a check; and the word sped rapidly through the ranks of the cavalry to charge and force their way to the foot of the breach, which was manned by the Christians, and defended by several large instruments of war.

So the horsemen came on at a gallop; and even the besieged gazed on the gallant sight with admiration as they beheld that line of warriors sweeping forwards on their Arab chargers, their arms and *cuirasses*, and even the harness of their horses, glittering in gold; for they were the flower of the sultan's troops. But their gallantry was powerless to carry them over that yawning terrible abyss—not a blow could they level at their adversaries; whilst a shower of stones and arrows from the engines on the walls rolled horses and riders in the dust by scores.

For five days were these scenes renewed, and always with the same result; cavalry and infantry never flinching from the orders of the sultan, which sent them to certain destruction, but continuing to rush on with a desperate courage, only to be driven back upon their ranks, leaving half their numbers dead upon the field.

The sultan was greatly enraged at his repeated failures; but satisfied at length that the city was not yet to be carried by assault, he yielded to the persuasions of his *emirs*, and commanded the ditch to be filled up. This was a work of time; for, first it had to be drained of the water, and then huge camel-loads of earth and stone were thrown into it by thousands; and still, as day after day went on, it scarcely seemed to fill, and the month of April passed without his finding himself a step nearer to the end of his toil.

He became impatient, and without waiting for the work to be finished, gave fresh orders for the assault. The ditch was but half filled; and when the first line of the Saracens rushed to the edge, they were once more obliged to fall back in confusion, baffled and unable to cross, for it was still a full yard deep, and the horses refused to enter.

Then followed a scene, which perhaps has never had its equal in the chronicles of war or of fanaticism; yet, strange and incredible as the facts may seem, they are related by all historians—some being the eye-witnesses of what they describe. There was among the sultan's troops a body of men known by the name of Chages, a kind of new sect among the Moslems, who surpassed all their comrades in their terrible and bloody devotion to the cause of Islam.

To them Melec Seraf now turned: "You who call yourselves the chosen of the Prophet," he cried, "show now your faith by deeds, and throw yourselves into yonder ditch as a bridge for the Mamelukes." Without a moment's hesitation the Chages obeyed the call, and with a mad enthusiasm flung themselves into the chasm by hundreds, while the others urged their horses over the quivering bridge of human bodies.

To us it seems a strange idea to storm a breach with cavalry; but the Saracen and his horse were rarely parted, and many succeeded in clambering with their chargers up the ruined wall only to find their labour useless, for a new one had risen behind the old, strongly and skilfully erected, and defended by the Hospitallers themselves, with their marshal, Claremont, at their head.

But though the horsemen were easily driven back, the miners of the sultan soon found their way to the foundation of the new defence: down it came, and with it many a tower and battlement beside; among them was the principal fortress of the city, which the infidels were wont to call "the Cursed Tower," from the mischief their men received beneath its walls.

One assault now followed close upon another, and just when pressed the hardest, the Christians were deserted by their Cypriot allies. King Henry had had to sustain the shock of one day's assault, and that was enough for him; under pretext that his men required repose, he got the Teutonic knights to take his post during the night, promising again, to relieve them when morning dawned. But that dawn only showed the sails of his vessels sinking in the horizon; he had taken advantage of the night to embark unperceived, and was far on his way to Cyprus when the battle recommenced.

That day the Saracens were well-nigh in possession of the town; for in one of their furious charges at the breach, they not only carried it with the slaughter of all its defenders, but penetrated to the very heart of the town. There was hard fighting hand to hand in the crowded streets, and the combat lasted two entire days, until at length Claremont, at the head of a handful of knights, drove the intruders back again to their trenches; whilst some of them were seen to seize their antagonists in their brawny arms and hurl them headlong over the battlements. One of these men, a Norman of prodigious size, leapt from his horse and threw three of the Saracens over one after another, like so many dogs; but as he was struggling with a fourth, a stone from a war-engine struck him to the ground.

Another attack;—this time, however, in a different direction: the great gate of St. Anthony was assaulted by a picked corps of Mamelukes; but there, too, they were met by the Hospitallers and the Templars, with the two grand masters at their head.

These brave men seemed to be in all parts of the town at one and the same time, and their presence animated their followers to prodigies of valour. Alas! their valour availed but little, and at most could but gain a brief delay; fresh enemies swarmed in the place of those who fell, while every loss on the part of the Christians was irreparable, and their numbers were reduced to a scanty handful. Sir John de Villiers was already badly wounded, when the master of the Templars thus addressed him: "The town is lost, as things now stand," he said; "you must try a sortie that will draw them off awhile, and give us time to complete some fresh defences." Villiers, wounded as he was, did his best to carry out this order, and gathering together all his men who were yet able to mount, he rode out to the enemy's camp, his whole body not consisting of above 500 in number.

Bravely did the little company fall on the Saracen host, which they thought to take by surmise; but they were met by all the cavalry of the sultan, and after a desperate struggle, re-entered the town with half their number missing. Bad news, too, met them on their return; Beaujeu had been struck, as it was feared, by a poisoned arrow, and half the town was already in possession of the enemy; with daylight they could look for nothing but one last death-struggle, and the loss of all; and a council of the surviving knights of the three orders was hastily summoned, together with certain of the citizens and the gallant old patriarch of Jerusalem, who, though he might long since have secured his safety by flight, had chosen to remain to encourage his children by his presence.

There was indeed little to debate, for all were of one mind; they knew well enough that they had only to choose between death and night,—but of the last they never thought; the port was indeed open, and there was yet time; but Acre was all Palestine to its defenders, and each one felt that to die on its battlements was to die in the cause of Christ.

For such a death they therefore prepared as became the cross they wore; the holy sacrifice was offered, and each one received what to far the greater number was the last *viaticum*; they gave the kiss of peace each one to his neighbour, old grudges were made up where any existed, and those who had lived in jealousy or enmity shook one another by the hand, and swore to stand together and die as friends.

It is said that Beaujeu, before the last combat began, forced his way to the sultan's tent to propose conditions of truce; which might have been accepted but for the unwillingness shown by the renegades in the Saracen army to listen to terms of peace, whether or not this be true, the attempt was certainly of no avail; for it was still night when the Moslems broke into the city by the great gate of St. Anthony, their way lighted up by the terrible gleam of the Greek fire, and a frightful carnage followed in the streets.

Beaujeu fell in the front of the defenders, and Claremont too, the gallant marshal of the Hospitallers, was cut to pieces by a thousand blows. The day broke cold and gloomy over the city, which was the scene, not of one, but of innumerable combats. Every house was defended and stormed; every square was a rallying post and a battle-ground; the streets were piled high with dead and dying, and were slippery with blood.

At length it was all over: a rush towards the port carried soldiers and populace together in one dense and crowded mass, pursued and massacred by the Mamelukes, as they swept along treading one another under in the crush. Of all that multitude, not half ever reached the vessels; for the Saracens were amongst them, slaughtering them as they stood, the Greek fire fell thick over the shipping, and the crowded boats that left the shore were burnt or sunk before they reached the vessels' sides. Sixty thousand Christians fell, it is said, in that short but horrible massacre.

A whole convent of nuns of the order of St. Clare, to save themselves from the brutal violence of the conquerors, following the example of their courageous superior, mutilated their features in the most frightful manner; so that the Pagan soldiery no sooner beheld these spouses of Christ all bleeding and ghastly, than, seized with disgust and fury, they fell upon them and slaughtered them without mercy.[2] As to the Hospitallers, there

---

2. Roger of Wendover, in his *Flowers of History*, relates a similar instance of admirable courage on the part of the nuns of Coldingham in Berwickshire, when the country was invaded by the merciless Danes in the year 870. Assembling all the sisters, the holy abbess addressed them, and having obtained from them a promise of implicit obedience to her maternal commands, she "took a razor, and with it cut off her nose, together with her upper lip unto the teeth, presenting herself a horrible spectacle to those who stood by. (Carried forward next page.)

were but six left alive, and these made a gallant retreat under cover of a shower of arrows, and gained the carrack, or galley of the order, in which they made their way towards Cyprus.

The Templars finding it impossible to cut their way through the masses of their enemies, threw themselves into a tower, and held it for some days against all assaults. It was the last struggle of despair: the tower was soon mined, and scaled by thousands of the Saracens; but as they crowded to the ladders, the walls gave way, and falling with a hideous crash, buried Christians and Moslems in their ruins. It is said that ten Templars escaped previous to the catastrophe, and found their way to Cyprus; but all that remained in the city, whether soldiers or citizens, were put to the sword; and for days the slaughter lasted, till there were none left to be slain.

The fall of Acre was quickly followed by that of Tyre, and all the smaller towns along the Syrian coast. Nicopolis held out for two years longer, thanks to a little garrison of Hospitallers; but at length an earthquake accomplished what the Saracen arms could not effect, and city and garrison were buried under one heap of ruins. Thus the Cross was overthrown forever in Syria; and the order that was created for its defence was compelled to seek another home.

Filled with admiration at this heroic deed, the whole community followed her example, and each did the like to themselves. With the morrow's dawn came those most cruel tyrants, to disgrace the holy women dedicated to God, and to pillage and burn the monastery; but on beholding the abbess and all the sisters so frightfully mutilated and stained with their own blood from the sole of their foot unto their head, they retreated in haste from the spot, thinking a moment too long for tarrying there. But as they were retiring, the leaders ordered their wicked followers to set fire and burn the monastery, with all its buildings and its holy inmates. Which being done, the holy abbess and all the holy virgins with her attained the glory of martyrdom."

Chapter 2

The Knights of Limisso

The little handful of knights whom we left covered with wounds in their single galley, directed their course towards Cyprus, which was looked on in those days as a resting-place on the road between Europe and Syria, and had been conquered years before, and granted to Guy de Lusignan by Richard *Cœur de lion* in the beginning of his short crusade. The island was still held, together with the title of King of Jerusalem, by one of the descendants of De Lusignan, and seemed a fitting place of refuge for the soldiers of the Gross. We have said that there were but six who found their way alive out of Acre, of whom the grand master was one; but their numbers were soon increased, for knights flocked in from every country in answer to the circular which had been sent before the siege began; and Villiers soon found himself surrounded by a numerous and well-appointed body of his order. King Henry had granted the town of Limisso to him and the Templars as their temporary place of residence; and here a chapter of the Hospitallers was held to consider what best was to be done in the emergency.

Never since the first day of their foundation had such an assembly been seen; for scarcely a man had remained in Europe, but all had hastened when the summons reached them, and had met in Cyprus on their road to Acre, though too late to proceed further on their way. The first act of Villiers was to submit himself to the judgement of the chapter, for the fact of his leaving Acre alive; and then a resolute vote was passed, in spite of all their losses, never to abandon the cause for which their order had been first created, just two centuries before; but to sacrifice their lives for the Holy Land whenever and however they might be called; and for this purpose, to fortify Limisso as they should best be able, as being nearer to the shores of Syria than any other residence which it was then in their power to choose.

The spirit of the order must still have been very fresh and vigorous; for though Limisso was old and half in ruins from the continual attacks of the Saracen pirates, and there were neither fortifications, nor even accommodation sufficient for the knights, yet their first care was directed to preparing some establishment for the reception of the poor and of the pilgrims. The Xenodochia of Jerusalem and of Acre could not indeed be thought of; but still the order might not exist without its hospital. The next step was one whose future results they themselves perhaps scarcely contemplated: it was the refitting of the galley which had brought them from Acre, and which they determined to keep in repair to assist them against the pirates; at the same time they also resolved by degrees to build other vessels, that the pilgrims who still found their way to the holy places, in spite of the presence of the infidels, might be protected on their journey by sea, since they could have their escort on land no longer.

This was the origin of their celebrated navy, which afterwards contributed more than any other single power to defend the coasts of Europe, and restrain the Moslems within their own shores. It was from the corsairs of Barbary and Egypt that the Christians suffered so much during the three centuries that followed; for not only was every vessel that plied on the Mediterranean subject to their attacks, but the towns and villages on the coasts of France and Italy were constantly ravaged, and their inhabitants carried into captivity; nor as yet had there arisen any maritime power bold and warlike enough to protect the highway of the sea. Very soon there appeared in all the chief ports of Europe little vessels of various sizes and construction, armed and manned by the soldiers of the Cross, collecting pilgrims and escorting them on their way to the Syrian shores, and guarding them, a few months later, on their return. The corsairs, accustomed to make an easy prey of the pilgrims, were not long in attacking these new galleys; out they found a different resistance from what they had expected; and few years passed without the Hospitallers bringing some of the captured vessels of the Saracens into the ports of Cyprus; so that their little fleet gradually grew considerable, and the flag of St. John soon came to be feared and respected in every sea.

Here we can scarcely avoid observing, on the one hand, an example of that wonderful spirit of adaptation to be found in all the elder religious orders of the Church, which enabled them to take new shapes and assume new duties, according as the purposes for which they were originally instituted changed and shifted with the age; and, on the other hand, the wonders of God's providence, which is ever bringing good out of evil, and turning what men call the disasters and failures of the Church to her greater glory. The Hospitallers, whilst fixed within the boundaries of Palestine, were able, indeed, to discharge a great work of charity, but one whose limits were necessarily prescribed; the very defeat, however, which drove them out of Syria, and seemed even to threaten their extinction, became the means of opening to them a new sphere of action, in which they may be said to have become the protectors of all Christendom.

The numbers they rescued from captivity, or saved from falling into a bondage often worse than death, are beyond calculation; and if the crusades, though failing in their primary object, yet kept the Moslems at bay during two centuries, and thus saved Europe from that inundation of infidelity which overwhelmed the eastern nations, the maritime power of the Knights of St. John contributed in no small degree to the same end, when the old crusading enthusiasm had faded and died away.

As may be imagined, it was not with indifference that Melec Seraf, the conqueror of Acre, watched the resurrection to new life of an order he had thought to destroy. Its new enterprises and repeated successes against the commanders of his galleys stung him most sensibly; and he prepared a powerful flotilla to be despatched against Limisso, for the purpose of exterminating the insolent Hospitallers and razing their citadel to the ground. God, however, watched over His own cause.

A civil war broke out in the sultan's own dominions; he himself fell in the first engagement; and his successor had too much on his hands to be in a condition to pursue a distant expedition: thus the knights were saved from an attack against which they possessed scarcely any defences, and their naval power, instead of being crushed in its infancy, had time to strengthen and increase.

The residence of the order at Limisso lasted for about eighteen years; during which period the temporary success of the Tartars, under their great *khan*, Gazan, seemed at one time to give hopes of a re-establishment of the Christian power in Palestine. Gazan, though not a Christian himself, was always solicitous for the alliance of the Christian sovereigns. He had Christians from the Asiatic provinces among his troops, and to please them is said to have even placed the cross upon his banners. The better to pursue his hostilities against the Saracens, he entered into a league with the kings of Armenia and Cyprus, and the orders of the Hospitallers and Templars; and at the head of their united forces made himself master of Syria. Once more did the Christian knights find themselves within the walls of the Holy City; and whilst gazing on the ruins of their old home, or on the grassy mounds which were all that remained to show the fate of their brethren of Nicopolis, they doubtless thought the day was come for the Cross once more to triumph, and that they should behold the hospital of Jerusalem rise from its ashes in all its ancient splendour. But Gazan was recalled to his own dominions; and the forces of the Christians were too weak to hold the country they had conquered.

The ambassadors of the *khan* were seen indeed at the court of Rome; and had Boniface VIII., who then filled the Papal See, been able to unite the European powers in a fresh crusade, it is probable that a greater advantage might have been obtained than had ever yet attended their arms,—for the Saracens had lost the prestige of success; but the pontiff was engaged in a quarrel with the most powerful of those princes who would naturally have lent their aid to such an enterprise, and whilst France was governed by Philip le Bel no undertaking preached by Boniface could look for support from that nation. The whole plan, therefore, fell to the ground; and the Hospitallers, whose continuance in Cyprus gave rise to many jealousies on the part of the sovereigns of the island, began to see the necessity of abandoning their hopes of returning to Palestine, and of looking out for some other settlement in the neighbourhood of its shores, where their independence might be undisputed.

There were many plans afloat at this time for the union of the two great military orders under one head; plans which, originating with Clement V., the successor of Boniface, may perhaps have been intended as a means of avoiding the more violent measures for the suppression of the Templars forced on him later by the French king. Molay was then grand master of the Templars, and William de Villaret of the Hospitallers: both were summoned to France, where the pontiff then resided, under pretext of conferring on the practicability of a new crusade; but Molay alone obeyed; Villaret excused his delay by alleging the urgent necessity which lay on him to provide for the settlement of his order. He had already fixed on the island of Rhodes as the place most adapted for his purpose: it was but a short distance from Palestine, provided with an excellent port, and capable of being strongly fortified; whilst the circumstances of its existing government seemed to justify the attempt at conquest. It was nominally subject to the Greeks; but in the decay of their empire the lords of Gualla had assumed the real sovereignty of the island; and, the better to protect their independence against the court of Constantinople, had introduced a population of Turks and Saracens, whose lawless piracies they connived at and encouraged.

The ports of Rhodes offered a sure refuge for the vessels of the corsairs when pursued by the galleys of the Hospitallers, or of other Christian powers; and the island had come to have a bad reputation, as little else than a nest of robbers. Villaret, therefore, felt little doubt that his plan for erecting Rhodes into a sovereignty for his order would meet with no opposition from the European princes on the ground of justice: so, after reconnoitring the island, and coming to the conclusion that the enterprise was beyond his strength without the assistance of a larger force than he then possessed, he prepared to set out for Europe, both in obedience to the pontifical summons, and also for the purpose of collecting the requisite reinforcements. But he died before putting his proposed voyage into execution; and the knights immediately elected in his room his brother Fulk de Villaret, as being fully possessed of his most secret designs, and the best capable of bringing them to a successful termination.

Fulk therefore hastened to France early in the spring of 1307, to lay the plan before the Pope and the French king; Molay had already preceded him, and was at Poitiers (then the residence of the papal court) at the very time of his visit. The storm had not yet broken over the head of the Templars, and the designs against them were kept a close secret; yet it is probable that there were even then sufficient tokens of ill-will and approaching disgrace to impress the grand master of the Hospitallers with the belief, that France was just then no safe quarters for the representative of either of the military orders.

Nevertheless, it would seem that Clement at least entered favourably into his views; and though the real object of the enterprise was kept a secret, yet the proposal for a fresh expedition against the infidels, when publicly proclaimed, was received with such enthusiasm, that Villaret soon found himself furnished with men and money sufficient for his purpose. The money was principally contributed by the women of Genoa, who sold their jewels to supply the means of this new crusade, as it was termed; the troops were chiefly from Germany; and thus provided, he hastened to return to Cyprus, where he arrived in the August of the same year.

Two months later Molay was arrested, and that terrible tragedy was enacted which ranks the suppression of the Templars among the great crimes of history. Its relation forms no part of our subject; for whilst every fresh investigation serves only to add new evidence of the innocence of the accused, and to increase the infamy of their enemies, there has never been an attempt to involve the Hospitallers in the charges brought against them. Yet it can scarcely be doubted that they too were included in the original design of the French king; and that, had Villaret withdrawn his knights to Europe, and, like Molay, put himself within the power of his enemies, the fate of both orders would have been alike. But Providence ordered it otherwise; and at the very time when the Templars were being tortured and massacred in France, the brilliant fame acquired by the Hospitallers in Rhodes placed them in a position of safety beyond the grasp of Philip.

Villaret's movements were conducted with the greatest secrecy; he remained at Cyprus only long enough to take on board his vessels those of the knights who still remained in the island, and then directed his course towards the coast of Asia Minor. Even they, as well as the rest of the troops, were persuaded that the expedition was about to be directed against Syria, and the real object was suspected by none. Anchoring in the port of Myra, the grand master despatched a secret embassy to the Greek Emperor Andronicus to solicit tine formal investiture of Rhodes, under condition of rendering him military service against the infidels. A compliance with this request would have been every way advantageous to the emperor's interest; but the old jealousy of the Latins was too strong, and he rejected the proposal with disdain.

His reply, however, made little difference in the course of events; without waiting for the return of his ambassador, Villaret publicly announced his real design; and taking the Rhodians by surprise; he disembarked his troops and military stores with scarcely a show of resistance. In spite of this first success, however, he found himself encompassed by many difficulties: the corsairs assembled in great numbers from the neighbouring islands at the first intelligence of the Christians landing; and a desultory war began, which lasted for four years with various success. The inhabitants, assisted by a body of troops despatched by the Greek emperor, threw themselves into the city of Rhodes, whose strength of position enabled them to hold out against repeated assaults. On the other hand, the German and French volunteers gradually dropped away, and left the knights unsupported; so that their numbers were considerably reduced, and they, in their turn, were obliged to stand on the defensive. But for the capacity and unwearied exertions of their grand master, they might have found themselves in a critical position; but whilst he succeeded in raising fresh levies in Europe, he found means also to inspire his followers with an enthusiasm which never failed them, in spite of every reverse.

No details have been left by contemporary historians of the final struggle; we know only that it was most bloody; and that before the banner of the order was planted on the walls of Rhodes, many of the bravest among the knights were cut to pieces. Villaret, however, found himself in the end master of the city and of the whole island; and such of the Saracens as escaped alive, took to their vessels, and were the first to spread the news of their defeat along the coasts and among the islands of the Archipelago.

The universal joy and admiration excited throughout Europe by the intelligence of the event, was a testimony of the benefit which all felt would accrue to the Christian cause by the establishment of an independent sovereignty in those seas, which had hitherto been entirely at the command of the infidels; and the title of "Knights of Rhodes" was not so much assumed by the order as accorded to them by the unanimous voice of all nations.

The first act of the grand master, after the surrender of the capital, and the submission of the Christian inhabitants to their new sovereigns, was to order the restoration of the city fortifications, that they might be put in a thorough state of defence; after which he proceeded to visit the surrounding group of islets, which readily acknowledged his authority. The territories now subject to the order included, besides the larger island of

Rhodes, nine others, some scarcely more than fortified rocks, yet serving as outposts of defence, and all of them inhabited. Others were richly wooded and productive, and were granted on a kind of feudal tenure to certain of the knights who had most distinguished themselves in the late war; of these the most considerable was Cos, or Lango, which afterwards, under the rule of its new masters, rose to an important position among the islands of the Archipelago.

In the midst of these surrounding islets, not twenty miles distant from the Asiatic coast, lay Rhodes—a fairy island on a fairy ocean; and the soft southern breeze, as it swept over her fields, carried far over the waters the scent of those roses which bloomed through all the year, and from which she derived her name. The very rocks were garlanded with them; beds of flowering myrrh perfumed the air; and tufts of laurel-roses adorned the margins of the rivulets with their gaudy blossoms.

It is scarcely strange that Rhodes should in old times have been the school of art; for men caught, as it were naturally, the painter's inspiration amidst scenes of such enchanting loveliness. She was made, indeed, to be a home of peace; her skies were ever cloudless and untroubled; her woods stood thick with fruit-trees, and the velvet of her sloping lawns sparkled with a thousand flowers. Her beauty was neither stern nor grand,— it was entirely pastoral; and if you wandered inland round her entire circuit, which was scarcely thirty miles, one verdant landscape everywhere met your eye, woods and gardens breaking the sameness of those lovely pastures; while all round, between the hills and through the foliage of the trees, you caught the blue line of the sea, whose music, as it murmured on the shore, was never absent from your ears.

In old times, as we have said, Rhodes had had her celebrity; she had taught eloquence to Rome, and had claimed the empire of the seas; but all her greatness had vanished under Greek misrule and the barbarism of her Saracen masters; and when the knights took possession of their new territory, they found nothing left of ancient Rhodes but her beauty and her name.

There were, however, great resources, and these, under their hands, were not long in developing. The forests furnished wood, and the island of Syma skilful carpenters for ship-building; and these latter had the art of constructing galleys so light and swift that no vessel on the eastern seas could match them with either sail or oar. So on the summit of a high mountain in Syma a watch-tower was built, and the inhabitants bound themselves to keep a look-out over the ocean, and send the first news to Rhodes by their swiftest galley of the approach of hostile fleets; and by their skill the navy of the order rapidly increased in magnitude and excellence.

Then there was Lero, with her quarries of rich marble, which supplied a commerce of herself; and Nisara, whose ships were known in every city on the southern coasts, and whose inhabitants had retained something of their old fame as artists, and encouraged by a free and generous government, soon filled their towns with palaces that vied with those of Genoa;—with rich columns, and statues, and marble fountains, all brought together in a lavish profusion, and bespeaking the noble tastes of her merchant lords.

There were plenty of ports and harbours on these island coasts, and a population of maritime habits, accustomed to live on the sea, or well-nigh in it; in short, everything contributed to point out naval and commercial enterprise as the road to the future greatness of Rhodes.

The first enemy who threatened the safety of the knights in their new home was one of whom they were hereafter to hear more. The Tartar Othman was beginning to lay the foundation of the Turkish empire, and had established himself in Bithynia and other Asiatic provinces, which he had conquered from the Greeks. It was to him that the Saracens of Rhodes fled for refuge after being finally driven out of the island; and he very willingly undertook their cause, and despatched a considerable force, which besieged the knights in their city before they had time to restore the walls or raise fresh fortifications in place of those they had destroyed.

Nevertheless, in spite of their defenceless position, Othman received his first defeat; and, obliged to retire with considerable loss, he contented himself with plundering the neighbouring islands, from whence he kept up a desultory warfare which lasted for some time longer. In 1315, however, the knights were enabled, with the assistance, as it is said, of Amadeus of Savoy, to expel their Turkish neighbours, and commence the work of rebuilding and fortifying. So soon as this was completed, Villaret bent all his endeavours to the restoration of commerce: the port of Rhodes was thrown open to all nations, and many of the Latin Christians who had been driven from the Holy Land, and were scattered about in various parts of Greece, hastened to enrol themselves under the banner of St. John, which protected all alike—Greek and Latin, mercantile or military; and out of these various elements the new state rapidly rose to opulence and renown.

Its opulence was perhaps a doubtful good, to some at least among the knights, who after their long hardships and sufferings were tempted to make their restoration to better fortunes the excuse for a life of ease find indulgence. The relaxation was far from universal; and from the description left us of the general state of their dominions, it is evident that a wise and enlightened policy directed their government, and that the abuses, such as they were, were confined to a minority.

But unhappily the grand master himself was of the number; hero and man of genius as he had proved himself to be, after winning the applause of all Europe and a name among the great men of the time, he was not strong enough to withstand his own success, and his luxury and neglect of duty soon raised the voice of the order against him. His irregularities must have been great, for rarely is a successful chief unpopular among his followers; yet the discontent even spread into revolt, and the majority of the knights, after solemnly deposing Villaret from his authority, chose Maurice de Pagnac in his room,—a man of stern and austere character, and a zealous advocate of discipline.

The matter ended in the interference of the Pope, John XXII., who summoned the rival grand masters to Avignon, where Villaret was obliged to retire on a rich commandery of the order; and Pagnac soon after dying, Helion de Villeneuve was elected on the recommendation, or nomination, of the pontiff.

On his return to Rhodes from Montpellier, where he had convened a general chapter for the reform of abuses, matters began to mend; laws were passed obliging the residence of all the principal officers of the order at the seat of government; all the islands were strongly fortified, and such a spirit infused into the little commonwealth, that many built and maintained war-galleys for defence against the infidels at their own expense, in addition to those kept up by the government; and, in spite of the vast expenses rendered necessary by the circumstances of the time, the chief glory of Rhodes and her knightly sovereigns lay in the happiness of those who lived beneath their rule.

They were still worthy of their ancient title, "Servants of the poor of Christ;" "for," says Vertot, "there was, not a poor man in all the territories of the order:" there were employment and support for all; and for the sick there was the large find magnificent hospital, where soul as well as body was cared for, and where the grand master's example of charity animated and kept alive the fervour of primitive discipline in the hearts of his knights.

Yet the Hospitallers had their enemies; those who had plundered and destroyed one order, and given it up to centuries of defamation, would willingly have done the same by its survivor. It was said of them that they never gave alms;—scarcely an accusation, had it even been true, if indeed they kept their subjects from the need of almsgiving, but false, unless we leave out of sight the hospital and its vast system of charity daily dispensed in grand and lavish profusion.

And that they did not spare themselves in their exertions to meet the expenses of that system, is evident from the law made about that time limiting the table of the knights to a single dish. The Hospitallers had been nominally declared heirs to the unfortunate Templars; yet, save the odium attaching to the suspicion of possessing enormous wealth, they gained little by the decree; for in almost every country, with the exception of England, the property of the suppressed order found its way into the royal coffers.

Villeneuve, and the grand masters who succeeded him, were unsparing in their efforts to maintain the primitive and religious character of the order; and though, doubtless, there were abuses to reform, yet if we read the repeated remonstrances addressed to them from the pontiffs, the accusations do not come to much.

> "There is a general feeling," writes Clement V., "that you do not make a very good use of your money; it is said you keep fine horses, are superbly dressed, keep dogs and birds of prey, and neglect the defence of Christendom."

It must be allowed that these charges are somewhat vague. The real crime of the Hospitallers in the eyes of those who incessantly endeavoured to poison the minds of the pontiffs against them, was their supposed wealth, which their accusers longed to sequestrate, and which, though greatly exaggerated, was made the pretence for throwing on them the chief burden of the Turkish war. During its long continuance they bore a part which should at least have acquitted them from the charge of slothfulness in the cause of Christendom.

A new league having been formed against the infidels between the Pope, the king of Cyprus, the republic of Venice, and the Order of St. John, it was Biandra prior of Lombardy who led their forces in the attack on Smyrna, which he carried, sword in hand, at the head of his knights. Later, when the league was falling to pieces, it was revived by the grand master Deodato de Gozon. This Deodato was a very hero of romance—a second St. George, were we to credit the popular story of his combat with the dragon.[3]

---

3. The legend is as follows: "A huge serpent, or crocodile,—for it is described as an amphibious animal,—had taken up its abode in a cavern on the brink of a marsh situated at the base of Mount St. Stephen, about two miles from the city, from whence it sallied forth frequently in search of prey. Not only cattle, but even men, became its victims; and the whole island trembled at its voracity. (c/f next page)

In his own day he deserved to receive the title of the "Magnanimous." Immediately on his election he sailed in quest of the Turkish fleet, which he found at the little isle of Embro, near the mouth of the Dardanelles. Falling on it by surprise, he gained a brilliant victory, and captured 118 of the enemy's vessels; and on returning from this exploit, he found the ambassadors of the king of Armenia awaiting him at Rhodes, to implore his assistance against the Egyptian Saracens.

The king was a Greek schismatic; and at a time when the jealousies between Greek and Latin were at their height, many might have hesitated to risk the success of such an enterprise. Not so, however, with Deodato the Magnanimous: "full of zeal," says Vertot, "and animated with the true spirit of his institute, he would not abandon the Christians to the fury of the barbarians." So a powerful force was despatched to Armenia; nor did it return till the last of the Saracen invaders was driven from the country.

Yet at the very time of these achievements, whilst, the treasury of the order was being exhausted by its disinterested exertions, and its blood was flowing freely on every coast of the Archipelago, the old murmurs were being repeated, and rep-

---

Knight after knight, ambitious of the renown of slaying such a monster, stole singly and secretly to its haunt, and never returned. The creature was covered with scales, which were proof against the keenest arrows and darts: and at length the grand master held it his duty to forbid the knights from courting so unequal an encounter. Deodato de Gozon, a knight of Provence, alone failed to respect this prohibition, and resolved to deliver the island from the monster, or perish. Having often reconnoitred the beast from a distance, he constructed a model of it of wood or pasteboard, and habituated two young bull-dogs to throw themselves under its belly on a certain cry being given, while he himself, mounted and clad in armour, assailed it with his lance.

Having perfected his arrangements, he bestrode his charger, and rode down privately into the marsh, leaving several confidential attendants stationed in a spot from whence they could behold the combat. The monster no sooner beheld him approach, than it ran, with open mouth and eyes darting fire, to devour him. Gozon charged it with his lance; but the impenetrable scales turned aside the weapon; and his steed, terrified at the fierce hissing and abominable effluvium of the creature, became so ungovernable that he had to dismount and trust to his good sword and his dogs. But the scales of the monster were as proof against his falchion as his lance. (c/f next page)

resentations were constantly made at the papal court that the knights were idling away their time in their luxurious palaces, employed in the amassing of vast treasures, and the enjoyment of a life of ease.

Nor was this all: not a post or embassy from Europe but brought them a fresh budget of advice. Rhodes was unfit for the residence of the order; they ought to be somewhere on the mainland; they should be in the Morea, which the Turks were threatening to overrun; and above all, why did they not return to the Holy Land.

This last suggestion was seriously propounded in an embassy despatched from Rome, at whose head appeared one of their own brethren! Heredia, grand prior of Castile,—a man of consummate abilities, but who, for the gratification of his boundless ambition, had separated himself from the interests of the order, and had succeeded in gaining extraordinary influence in the councils of the Pontiff, Innocent VI.

This continual interference from authorities in Europe, to whom the real state of affairs was wholly unknown, caused the grand masters much embarrassment, which was increased by the

---

With a slap of its tail it dashed him to the earth, and was just opening its voracious jaws to devour him, helmet, *hauberk*, spurs and all, when his faithful dogs gripped it tightly with their teeth in a vulnerable part of the belly.
On this the knight quickly sprang to his feet, and thrust his sword up to the hilt in a place which had no scales to defend it.
"The monster, rearing itself in agony, fell with a tremendous hiss on the knight, and again prostrated him in the dust; and though it instantly gasped its last, so prodigious was its size that Gozon would have been squeezed to death, had not his attendants, seeing the object of their terror deprived of life, made haste to his assistance. They found their master in a swoon; but after they had with great difficulty drawn him from under the serpent, he began to breathe again, and speedily recovered. The fame of this achievement being bruited in the city, a multitude of people hurried forth to meet him. He was conducted in triumph to the grand master's palace; but that dignitary, heedless of popular acclamation, sternly demanded wherefore he had violated his orders, and commanded him to be carried to prison. At a subsequent meeting of the council he proposed that the culprit should atone for his disobedience with his life; but this severe sentence was mitigated to a deprivation of the habit of the order. To this degradation he was forced to submit; but in a little time the grand master relented, and not only restored him to his former rank, but loaded him with favours."
Sutherland's *Knights of Malta*, vol. 1. pp.

internal dissensions which rose out of the new division of the order into languages. This division had gradually been adopted for the convenience it afforded in several ways, but was only formally acknowledged in the grand chapter held under Helion de Villeneuve in 1322.

Each language then, had its inn, as it was called, where the knights met for meals in common, and to debate in their own tongue. But the evil effects of this arrangement was soon felt in the growth of national jealousies, and the unity of the order was severely injured by it.

To it may be attributed the failure and disappointment of many a noble plan: as when the heroic Raymund Beranger, grand master of the order in 1365, after a bold and successful enterprise against Alexandria, which he took by surprise, entirely destroying the piratical fleet of the Saracens, addressed letters to all the powers of Christendom to implore their assistance against the threatened invasion of his island by the sultan of Babylon, and appealed at the same time to the order in every country of Europe to pay up the arrears owing from the different commanderies and priories, and unite together to avert so imminent a danger.

Not only were the letters disregarded, but the jealousies between the languages of Provence and Italy reached such a height that Beranger, worn out with sorrow and disappointment, was only prevented from resigning in disgust by the authority of Gregory XI., who finally took the adjustment of the whole question into his own hands.

On the death of Beranger, in 1374, Robert de Juillac, grand prior of France, was chosen as his successor. He was at his priory at the time of his election, and setting out for Rhodes, he presented himself at Avignon on his road, to offer homage to the pope. The devotion of the grand masters to the Holy See through all their difficulties is very striking; and on no occasion did they offer a more noble example of religious obedience than on the present.

Smyrna was still in the hands of the Christians; its Venetian governor was half-merchant, half-soldier; and complaints were addressed to the papal court on the part of the archbishop and inhabitants, that, in consequence of his devotion to his commercial engagements and frequent voyages to Italy, the place was left without defence, and almost without a garrison. Gregory decided on committing the care of the city to the Hospitallers; and when Juillac appeared at Avignon, the first intelligence that reached his ears was that, in addition to every other difficulty and embarrassment, the defence of Smyrna was to be given into his hands. In vain he represented that Smyrna was a forlorn hope, isolated in the midst of the Turkish dominions, and too far from Italy to receive any succours from thence in case of siege.

> "The situation of the city," replied the pontiff "in the heart of the infidel's own country, is the very cause of my entrusting it to your order; for the Turks will not advance farther so long as they have so considerable an enemy at home; and I therefore charge you under pain of excommunication, to despatch the necessary garrison immediately on your return to Rhodes."

When this injunction was communicated to the council of the order assembled in the island on the arrival of the grand master, there was but one feeling as to the nature of the commission entrusted to them.

> "All were very well aware," says Vertot, "that it was to send the knights to certain death; nevertheless they took the part of obedience, and many of them even generously offered themselves for a service whose dangers and glory were equally certain. For it was not to be supposed that the Turks, whose power daily increased, would long leave the knights in peaceable possession of a place which was in the very centre of their dominions."

For twenty-seven years, therefore, did the Hospitallers succeed in holding Smyrna triumphantly against the Turks; and its noble defence is said to have delayed the fall of Constantinople, and possibly to have saved the rest of Christendom by drawing away the attack of the infidels from other quarters. The event, therefore, amply vindicated the sagacity of Pope Gregory, yet not the less does it elevate the obedience of the knights to the dignity of a sacrifice.

CHAPTER 3

Progress of the Turks

From the period of the first settlement of the order at Rhodes the war with the Turks, though desultory, had been continual. The Turkish empire, which, under its first Sultan Othman, already included many of the provinces of Asia Minor, extended itself into Europe in the reign of his son Orchan. Disputes at Constantinople between the rival emperors, John Palæologus and Cantacuzenus, led to the unhappy policy adopted by the latter of sailing in the Turks to his aid. Orchan (to whom Cantacuzenus had given his daughter in marriage) did not fail to seize so favourable an opportunity of enlarging his conquests; his son Solyman crossed the Hellespont; and speedily making himself master of the northern provinces of the Greek empire, even endeavoured to gain a footing in the Morea. Orchan's son Amurath,—for Solyman had died in the midst of his career,—followed up his father's victories with still greater success; and Palæologus, who in vain strove to resist the advances of the Turks, was compelled gradually to yield all his possessions to their arms, with the exception of Constantinople, Thessalonica, the Morea, and a few islands.

Adrianople (at no great distance from the walls of Constantinople itself) became the metropolis of the Ottoman dominion in Europe (a.d. 1301), and the danger of the latter city became daily more and more imminent; for whilst, on the one side, Asia was in the hands of the infidels, they were, on the other. masters of all the Macedonian cities and provinces, and from their position at Adrianople were able to attack and overrun the Bulgarian and Servian principalities; and thus the capital of the Greek emperors was gradually surrounded on all sides by the victorious Moslem. Two defences alone of any strength remained to the Christian arms on the shores of the Archipelago: they were the island of Rhodes and the devoted garrison of Smyrna.

The divisions and dissensions of that unhappy time no doubt contributed in a great degree to the rapid extension of the Turkish conquests: First and foremost, and that which lay at the root of all the rest, was the disastrous schism which ensued on the death of Gregory XI., when a pope and an anti-pope claimed the obedience of the nations. Christendom, thus divided against itself, had no time to give to the danger that threatened it from without; the western powers, engaged in contesting the pretensions of two rival claimants of the papal chair, were unable to unite against the common foe. The Christian world was, in fact, bereft of its directing head; the popes had ever been the life and soul of the crusades against the infidel; and when their voice was dumb, or gave, or at least seemed to give, an uncertain sound, who could prepare himself for the battle?

As regarded the, order of the Knights Hospitallers, the evil was unmitigated. Our purpose in the present sketch, being less to offer a continuous, history of the order of St. John than to recount their struggles with the Moslems, we must pass rapidly over the period during which Heredia, the prior of Castile, was grand master, and redeemed his previous disloyal conduct, by a government of remarkable disinterestedness and devotion. Brave he was even to daring.

At the siege of Patras he mounted the breach, sword in hand, careless whether his knights followed him or not, and flinging himself with all the ardour of a young soldier. into the midst of the Turks, encountered the governor; in single combat and laid him dead at the foot of the wall he had been defending. At Corinth, which was, the next point of attack, he fell into an ambush and was taken prisoner. The order offered the restitution of Patras, together with a large sum of money, for his ransom, and three of the grand priors even engaged to remain as hostages in his place until the conditions were fulfilled: but though the Turks consented, Heredia magnanimously rejected the proposal.

> "Leave me, my dear brothers," he said, "leave me, worn out as I am with years and toil, to die in my chains, and reserve yourselves who are young and active for the service of God and His Church."

As for the money, he would not hear of its being paid out of the treasury of the order; it should come from his own family, whom his ambition had enriched. One would have thought that the infidels would have been moved to generosity by so much nobility of soul; but all the effect it had upon them was, that they condemned him to a severer confinement, in which he was detained for more than three years.

On his release, he made ample reparation for his previous avarice by devoting the wealth he had accumulated to the foundation of new commanderies and other means of defence against the untiring enemy of the Christian name; but all his efforts and self-sacrifices were paralysed and rendered of little avail by the divisions that prevailed. The contest for the papacy caused a schism among the knights; and as there were too competitors for the chair of St. Peter, so there were; two grand masters, both arrogating to themselves the supreme command of the order.

It was then that Bajazet, the son of Amurath, began his extraordinary career. One province after another was overrun and ravaged by his armies; from Europe he passed to Asia, and thence back again to Europe, attacking Christian and infidel alike in the very wantonness of success. Even the frontiers of Hungary were laid waste; and having taken some prisoners of that nation, he sent them back to King Sigismund; with the following insulting message: "Tell your master that I will pay him a visit next spring; and after driving him from the land, I will pass over into Italy, and plant my standards on the Capitol of Rome."

Indeed it was his common boast that his horse should eat his oats on the high altar of St. Peter's. In 1395 the fatal battle of

Nicopolis was fought, which seemed well-nigh to promise the fulfilment of this insolent threat. Sigismund of Hungary there found himself at the head of a hundred thousand men,—the army of a new crusade which had at length been raised through the exertions of Pope Boniface IX.,[1] who proclaimed a plenary indulgence for all who should repair to the rescue of Hungary and the neighbouring kingdoms. It was composed of the forces of France, Venice, Greece, Hungary, and the Knights of St. John. Sixty thousand horse (according to some writers), "all of tried courage and enterprise," says the old chronicler, "the very flower of Christian chivalry, were there, led on by the Count de Nevers, a prince of the French blood-royal."

But the battle was lost with immense slaughter;[2] Sigismund escaping with the grand master, Philibert de Naillac, in a single galley, to Rhodes, and leaving (it is said) twenty thousand of his followers dead upon the field. Ten thousand Christian prisoners, among whom were three hundred of gentle birth, were led out on the morning after the conflict, with their hands bound behind them and halters round their necks, and butchered in cold blood before the eyes of Bajazet himself, who sat at the entrance of his tent from daybreak till four in the afternoon to enjoy the horrid spectacle, and forced his unhappy captive, the

---

1. "In his bull, he bewails the sins of Christendom, which had brought upon them the scourge which is the occasion of his invitation. He speaks of the massacres, the tortures and slavery which had been inflicted on multitudes of the faithful. 'The mind is horrified,' he says, 'at the very mention of these miseries; but it crowns our anguish to reflect, that the whole of Christendom, which if in concord might put an end to these and even greater evils, is either in open war, country with country, or if in apparent peace, is secretly wasted by mutual jealousies and animosities," Newman's *Lectures on the History of the Turks*, pp. 177-8.

2. The loss of this battle seems mainly attributable to the rash and arrogant confidence of the French *chevaliers*. The general conduct of the crusaders likewise was not such as to warrant any expectation of God's blessing on their enterprise. Not only did they, at the siege of Raco, refuse quarter to such as laid down their arms, but immediately before the first onset at Nicopolis they massacred a number of Turkish prisoners who had surrendered under promise that their lives should be spared. (Creasy's *History of the Ottoman Turks*, vol. 1. pp. 58-60.) This act of cruelty, however, has been attributed not to the veteran knights, but to some headstrong and intemperate men among the juniors who took the matter into their own hands. *Sutherland*; vol. 1. p. 809.

Count de Nevers, to stand by and witness the death-pangs of his comrades.

They were offered the Koran or the sword; and as one by one they made profession of the Christian faith, they paid the penalty of their fidelity with their lives. "It was a cruel case for them," says Froissart, "thus to suffer for the love of our Saviour, Jesus Christ; and may He receive their souls!" This victory brought Bajazet to the walls of Constantinople. His generals overran Styria and the south of Hungary; the sultan himself led his victorious armies into the north of Greece, while his lieutenants, crossing the isthmus of Corinth, subdued the whole of the Morea. Athens was taken in 1397, and the Crescent, the symbol of barbarism, shone over the ancient seat of learning and the arts. The metropolis of the East, for which the emperor gained a temporary but ignominious respite by turning one of the churches of the city into a mosque, and consenting to pay an annual tribute of 10,000 *ducats*, would doubtless have speedily fallen into the power of Bajazet but for the appearance at that moment of a rival on the scene.

Manuel Palæologus had in vain sought the assistance of the European princes; the wars in which they were engaged prevented their heeding his appeal, In his extremity he had recourse to Timour the Terrible,[3] the *khan* of Tartary, whose jealousy of

---

3. Commonly called Tamerlane, from Timourlenk, *i e.* Timour the Lame,—the name given him by his countrymen on account of the effects of a wound received in early life. His massacres were of a wholesale description. At Ispahan he had a tower constructed of 70,000 human heads; and when Baghdad revolted, he exacted no less than 90,000 for the same purpose. On his march to Delhi, the future capital of his empire, he ordered a general slaughter of his prisoners, 100,000 in number; compelling each of his captains and soldiers to kill his captives with his own hands, under penalty of being themselves put to death, and their property and wives given up to the informer. But Von Hammer relates an instance of his cruelty still more horrible. At the taking of Sebaste, 4,000 Armenian Christians had capitulated, on the condition that, though they were to be sent into slavery, their lives were to be spared. No sooner, however, had they surrendered than the tyrant, faithless to his oath ordered them to be buried alive with circumstances, of the most atrocious barbarity. They were thrown ten together into deep pits with their heads tied between their knees; planks were then laid across, and earth heaped upon them; and there they were left, in their living graves, to die a death of slow and lingering torture.

Bajazet's successes induced him readily to listen to the embassies of the Greek emperor. The result is well known: on the plains of Angora (a.d. 1402),—the same where Pompey overthrew the power of Mithridates,—the Turks and Tartars met, and after a bloody contest the triumphs of Bajazet were terminated forever, and he himself, foiling into the hands of his savage conqueror, was subjected to a captivity the ignominy of which has pained for him a compassion and sympathy to which his crimes and infamous vices were far from entitling him.

It followed as a matter of course, that the dominions of Bajazet were simply transferred into the hands of Timour; and with the single exception of the knights of Rhodes, all the princes of the East submitted to his yoke, or acceded to his alliance. Their stubborn independence brought on them a declaration of war from the Tartar despot. It seemed insufferable that one small island should presume to withhold its allegiance to a monarch whose dominions exceeded those of Alexander and of every conqueror the world had ever seen, and whose power was acknowledged by the Christian sovereigns of Anatolia, as well as in all the provinces of the East; yet Rhodes, small as it was, presented so formidable an aspect, with its masses of fortifications, that he determined on, first of all reducing the city of Smyrna, whose position in the very heart of the Asiatic provinces, seemed to bid defiance to his arms.

Timour's object was, however, scarcely so much the actual subjection of the place as the gratification of a proud ambition; and well knowing that a city which had so long resisted the power of the Turks would prove no easy conquest, he declared to William de Mina, the governor appointed by the grand master, that he would be contented if his banner were suffered to float from the citadel, without proceeding to a siege, or depriving the knights of their actual possession. But the demand was scornfully rejected: not that the Hospitallers, for one moment entertained a hope of withstanding the attack of the Tartars; unsupported as they were by any succours from Europe, and isolated in the midst of the enemy's dominions; but Smyrna was the post of honour which, entrusted to them as it had been by the Pope himself, it would have been eternal disgrace to the order either to abandon or surrender: and though the season was winter, Timour exasperated by the haughty reply of the garrison, at once commenced the siege.

In fifteen days he had thrown a mole across the harbour, which deprived the Christians of all succour from without, and brought the Mongol troops close to the seaward parts of the town; the resistance he encountered, however, was worthy of the fame of a city, of which a Persian, historian declares, that it had sustained a seven-years' siege under Bajazet, had never paid tribute to anyone, or ever been in the power of any Mussulman prince from the period of its conquest by Biandra. Attacks and sallies were daily interchanged; and whilst both parties displayed prodigies of valour, victory could be claimed by neither. The mines formed by the Tartars were of no effect; for the besieged crushed all who entered them by the enormous stones, or rather rocks, which they dashed from the summits of the walls.

At length Timour, impatient of delay, ordered a general storm; an enormous number of wooden towers were erected, in which the besiegers succeeded in approaching the fortifications; and from these they threw themselves off the ramparts, covering their manoeuvre by a shower of arrows, the density of which darkened the very air. In vain did the brave defenders struggle to force back the torrent of their enemies; they poured in from every quarter in countless numbers: nevertheless the same Persian writer, Cheresiddin Ali, assures us that the assault lasted from morning to sunset, and that the obstinacy of the defence equalled the ferocity of the attack.

> "No-one," he says, "had a moment's repose; the intrepid besieged ceased not to send forth a shower of arrows, Greek fire, and stones, without giving breathing-space for a minute; and all the while there fell an extraordinary storm of rain, as though the universe were about to be swallowed up in a second deluge; yet still, in spite of the horrors of the tempest, Timour continued to give his

orders to his generals, and to stimulate the courage of his soldiers."

As soon as the miners had effected a breach, the apertures were filled with naphtha and other combustibles, and these being fired at once, the walls fell all together with a hideous crash; and the Tartars, forcing back the defenders, entered the city, and commenced an indiscriminate slaughter of every living being it contained, sparing neither sex nor age.[4] A very few escaped by throwing themselves into the sea, and swimming to the vessels without the port; but a vast number were drowned.

Several vessels had been despatched from Rhodes with succours, but were unable to land their troops: among them, according to Cheresiddin, was the carrack, or great galley of the order:

"It was full of armed men," he says; "but when they approached the city, they saw no longer any vestiges of it,— neither town nor castle remained, for all had been razed to the ground; and the stones, furniture, and everything therein had been cast into the sea. Therefore, when they saw this, they put back their galleys; but Timour ordered that a number of Christian heads should be thrown from engines on board their vessels; and this was done so skilfully that some rolled upon their decks. Then those on board, recognising the ghastly tokens, gave up all hopes, and returned to their own country."

Such is the description of the siege left by the Mussulman historian, who, while he does honour to the courage of the defenders, is, of course, little able to appreciate the generous devotion of their death. The defence of Smyrna, first undertaken under religious obedience, had been persisted in from the same honourable motive. They had been avowedly stationed in that remotest outpost of Christendom to offer themselves, if need

---

4. Here also Timour reared a tower of human heads; but as neither garrison nor town afforded a sufficient number to raise the structure to the accustomed height, he was compelled to have a layer of mud placed between each row of heads.

were, as victims for the safety of Europe; and the destiny, far from appalling them, had only seemed glorious in the eyes of men whose vow and vocation it was to die for the Cross they bore upon their breasts. So when the black flag of Timour was hung out on the last day of the siege,—his accustomed signal of "universal destruction,"—they knew very well that the hour of sacrifice was come, and welcomed it, as the martyrs did their torments. The dawn saw them at the altar; Mass, and a last communion, and an offering of their life to God, made solemnly, yet withal with a certain joy and exultation, preceded the last struggle at the ruined ramparts.

> "They captivated their will to obedience unto death," says a modern historian of the order, "and fell for their own honour and the protection of Christendom."

Nor was the devotion of the order content with this heroic defence; it did not deem its obligation to obedience satisfied, even when Smyrna was a heap of ruins, and all its defenders destroyed. Philibert de Naillac, considering that to his order had been confided the defence of whatever was left in Asia capable of being defended, proceeded, on the departure of Timour for Persia, whither he was called by an invasion from India, to reconnoitre the coasts of Caria, with the purpose of establishing a fresh garrison in some fortress of that province. About twelve miles from the isle of Lango, in the Gulf of Ceramis, there rose an old castle on the ruins of the ancient Halicarnassus;—a body of troops had been left in it by Timour; but Naillac, leading thither a small fleet in person, surprised and cut to pieces the Tartar garrison, and erected on the site of the old fortress another of extraordinary strength and solidity, which he dedicated to St. Peter, and which became the asylum of refuge on the coast of Asia for such Christian slaves as found means to effect their escape from Turkish, or Tartarian bondage.

There is something in the description left us of this fortress that combines the character of romance with the noblest spirit of chivalry. Naillac surrounded it with the strongest fortifications that art could devise; there were walls of enormous height and thickness pierced for cannon, to keep off the approach of hostile vessels by sea; whilst on the side of the land the defences were yet stronger; ramparts and bastions stood one against another, and to gain entrance to the fortress it was necessary to pass through seven lines of these ramparts and their seven gates. Over the last gate, however, appeared a motto which breathed the true spirit of a knight of the Cross, whose trust was less in his own sword or valour than in the favour of the God of armies:

Nisi Dominus ausftdierit civitatem, frustra vigilat qui custodit eam.[5]

Standing thus proudly on the rocky peninsula of the Carian Gulf, St. Peter's of the Freed, as it was called, became in one sense another hospital of the order. A strong garrison was put into it, and a number of vessels were constantly at anchor in the harbour, ready at the first note of alarm to issue forth, and either alone or in conjunction with the galleys of Rhodes and Lango, to sweep the seas of the hordes of pirates and corsairs that infested the coasts. Many too were the Christian slaves who, escaping from the chains of the infidels, found refuge within its walls; and the inmates were never weary of inventing and practising new devices for the relief of the refugees. Among others, the knights kept a race of large and sagacious dogs, whom they trained to go out and seek for those who might have sunk exhausted on the mountains unable to reach the castle walls. The instinct of these dogs was extraordinary: we read of one Christian who, escaping from the hands of his masters, threw himself into a well when closely pursued, rather than fall again into their hands.

Here he was tracked by one of these watch-dogs, who, unable to get him out at least succeeded in saving his life. The well was dry, and the man had received no injury from his fall, but would infallibly have died of hunger but for the fidelity of the Hospitallers' dog. For many days did the noble animal bring him in his mouth all the share of food given him for his own daily support, dropping it down into the well below. At length

---

5. "Unless the Lord keep the city, he who keepeth it watcheth in vain."

it was observed that the dog was growing thinner everyday; and his continual excursions after breakfast in the same direction exciting curiosity, some of the servants of the garrison set out to watch what he was about; the truth being thus discovered, the man was saved, and the dog given his place in the history of the order, of which he had proved himself so worthy a member.

Naillac was amongst the most able of the grand masters of that period, and was recognised as the protector of all the Christian states of the East. He saved Cyprus from the horrors of civil war by a disinterested and judicious interference; and in his day, says Vertot:

> there was no corsair vessel that dared approach the Lycian coast. Every where he was acknowledged as the most powerful Christian prince of the East; he had more than, a thousand knights under his command in the convent at Rhodes; and the greater number of the isles of the Sporades were subject to him, The sea was covered with his fleets; and the Rhodian vessels, under the escort of his galleys, earned their commerce into every port.

Most of these ships and galleys were prizes taken from the Saracens, who were even constrained at length to sue for peace, and despatched an embassy to Rhodes to arrange the terms. The conditions of pacification were all in favour of the Christians; and amongst them Jerusalem was not forgotten. It was stipulated that the Holy Sepulchre should he surrounded with walls, and that six knights of the order should he allowed a residence close by, free from all tribute, and with power to receive pilgrims into their house as of yore.

If we must add to these statements the fact, that Naillac, in common with those of his knights settled at Rhodes, was on the side of the anti-popes during the great schism to which we have already adverted, our readers must not be hasty in condemning him. Those were days when the right side was hard to be distinguished amid the confusion in which, from various causes, the whole matter was involved; and if Naillac was in error, he at least bore no inconsiderable part in the efforts made by the councils of Pisa and Constance to extinguish the schism: nor were they without success; and before he died, he had the satisfaction of seeing that unity which had been restored to Christian Europe, shared also by the order of which he was the head. No greater proof can be offered that the knights of Rhodes were animated by no schismatical spirit than the fact, that in their island the union between the Greek and Latin churches, established by the Council of Florence, was ever inviolably observed. Rhodes was probably the only state in which the two rites were kept in use among a people who were yet closely bound in one communion, and who never felt the jealousies of other Eastern countries, where Greek and Latin were the watchwords of party strife.

During the fifty years that elapsed from the siege of Smyrna to the fall of Constantinople, the war with the Turks continued with unabated vigour. Their empire revived after the death of Timour; and for many years Rhodes maintained a twofold struggle with Turks and Saracens; from the latter of whom they suffered two invasions and a siege of forty days, when so gallant a repulse was given to the infidels, that, as Vertot tells us, the young nobility of Europe, and especially those of France and Spain, were filled with an enthusiasm for the glorious body that, unaided and alone, kept off the dreaded foe whose arms were everywhere else invincible; and the best blood of Christendom flowed into the order, which indeed stood in no small need of such reinforcements. Very few details of any interest, however, have been left of these achievements, and we are left to gather what the position of Rhodes was at this period from the continual circulars and briefs addressed by the popes to the monarchs of Christendom, calling on them, out always in vain, to unite in one vigorous effort against that common enemy now only kept at bay by the Knights of St. John.

It is indeed impossible to overestimate the zeal manifested by the Roman Pontiffs for the preservation of Christendom: even from writers hostile to their interests we gather an idea of their extraordinary vigilance in this matter; and doubtless but for their ceaseless exertions the progress of the infidels would have extended far beyond the boundaries of the Grecian empire. Had those exertions been seconded, as in the days of the crusades, the result might have been very different; but the princes of Europe never heartily entered into the cause; and though year after year the danger became more threatening, the appeals and entreaties of the popes were received but with apathy and indifference.

It is satisfactory during this period of the history of the order, when doubtless, though surrounded by peril, its greatness and glory were at their height, to find a distinct notice of the austere and religious spirit still preserved alive and vigorous in Rhodes. With their ports filled with a flourishing commerce, and their treasury enriched by continual captures from the infidels, the knights themselves elevated to the position of temporal princes, and courted by all the nations of Europe as the defenders of Christendom, we find them derogating in nothing from the severe simplicity of their institute. Those of the brethren who were settled: in the commanderies of Europe had indeed greatly fallen off from regular discipline; but at Rhodes, which was the real heart of the order, we read that:

> everyone lived in the exact practice of the rule and of the statutes. In the midst of their continual hostilities the knights were never dispensed from their austere forts during Lent and Advent, or from their abstinence on Wednesdays; and in the refectory and other parts of the house no one ever dared to break the silence which was observed as regularly as in a community of monks. [6]

In 1451 the Ottoman throne became vacant by the death of Amurath II, who was succeeded by a prince destined to be the deadliest enemy whom Christendom had yet beheld. This was Mahomet II., surnamed the Great, who even then, though scarcely twenty-one years of age, had acquired a fame for talent, valour, and ferocity, which made him the terror of Europe and of the world. His vast capacity was waited to so detestable a

---
6. Vertot.

character that he has been called the Mahometan Nero; in truth he was of no religion; and if, as is said, his mother had been a Christian, and he had himself been originally brought up in the true faith, and instructed in its mysteries by the Greek patriarch, it is probable that his fury against the Cross was accompanied with all that bitter and unquenchable hatred which ever marks the apostate.

On his accession to the throne his court was filled with ambassadors from all the eastern states, including that of Rhodes, to propose treaties and alliances of peace. Mahomet received them all with the utmost courtesy, and swore to establish a universal pacification; meanwhile his emissaries were actively employed in every direction preparing for the conquest of Constantinople; and scarcely had a year elapsed from his elevation to the sovereignty, when he marched upon the Greek capital, proclaiming his intentions in the war-cry which was his manifesto,

"Constantinople—and then Rhodes."

There is not certainly an episode in history of more melancholy or more absorbing interest than that which relates to the final extinction of the Christian empire in the East. The Greek emperors are for the most part so entirely unworthy of our sympathy, that we are scarcely prepared for that momentary flicker of a great and noble spirit which illuminates the fall of the last successor of Constantine. He bore his name as well as his dignity, and it is not too much to say that he bore both worthily and well. Long and zealously had he laboured to heal the calamitous schism which for ages had separated his people from the communion of the Holy See, and thus from Europe and the whole Latin world; but unhappily with but little success. Now, when the ferocious enemy of the Christian name was before the gates and almost within the walls of the city, division in all its worst forms of bigotry and fanaticism distracted and paralysed the efforts of the brave defenders.

The infatuated Greeks, at the head of whom was the Grand Duke Notaras, refused to cooperate with the Latin auxiliaries who had been despatched to aid the remnant of what was once the Greek empire in its last struggle for existence. There was the Cardinal Isidore, whom the Pope had sent in the hour of need with a small body of veteran soldiers; and there were bands from Spain and Venice, as skilled in all the arts of war as they were bold in fight; and above all, there was the celebrated Genoese, John Giustiniani, a host in himself, with his seven noble compatriots in arms, and three hundred chosen followers. But union and conceit there were none: it was as if two hostile armies were arrayed against each other, while the common enemy was battering at the fortifications and about to precipitate himself upon the devoted city.

Notaras, indeed, openly vowed he would rather see the sultan's turban in Constantinople than the cardinal's hat; and though some confessed that, if compelled to make the choice, they should prefer the yoke of those who at any rate believed in Christ and honoured His Virgin Mother to that of the dreaded and detested Turk, yet even at the last, when the enemy were pouring through the streets, and the church of St. Sophia was filled with crouching multitudes pressing round the altars in all the agony of terror and despair, Ducas declares that had an angel from heaven appeared to them and said, "Only accept the union, and I will disperse your enemies," they would have remained deaf to his voice, and chosen rather to be slaves in subjection to the Moslem than freemen in communion with the See of Rome. The wretched monks, who seemed to be possessed body and soul by the author of strife and division, kept the minds of the populace inflamed at the highest pitch; a very frenzy, as Von Hammer expresses it, seemed to have seized upon the convents, and the religious,—if the term can be applied to men who had neither faith nor the fear of God,—protested they would sooner acknowledge Mahomet than accept the creed of the Catholic Church.

The emperor was fully equal to the tremendous occasion; as able in disposing the troops and resources at his command as he was valiant in fight, he was indeed, in every sense, the hero of the siege. But with subjects so divided and so disloyal, what could the highest genius or the most generous devotion achieve? He reckoned but 9000 combatants of all kinds within his walls, which were fourteen miles in extent; while the forces that were advancing against him are said to have been 250,000 in number, without counting a fleet of 250 vessels, having on board 24,000 men. Nevertheless the last Constantine vowed never to yield except with life itself; and Mahomet, on his part, swore that the walls of Stamboul should be either his sepulchre or his throne. The siege lasted but two-and-forty days; we can only marvel that the defenders held out so long; and, though perhaps it scarcely belongs to our subject, there is something so touchingly beautiful in the account of the last struggle, that we may be excused for giving it a place in our pages.

It was the evening of the 28th of May 1453, when the cries, and shouts from the vast multitude of the besiegers warned the Christians that the final assault was in preparation for the following day. Constantine collected around him a little band of faithful followers, and addressed them in animated terms. He concluded thus:

> My heart is very full; and yet I can say nothing more. There is my crown; I received it from God, but I place it in your hands; tomorrow I shall fight to deserve it still, or to die in its defence.

His words were drowned by the sobs and tears of those who listened, but he did not seem to share their grief. Raising his voice above the murmurs and exclamations of the assembly, he said, with a cheerful and joyous air, "Comrades, it is our fairest day; there remains only to prepare for death, and then to die."

Very early in the morning he proceeded to Santa Sophia, and received the Holy Communion; and turning from the altar to the weeping crowd that filled the church, he asked them to pardon him if he had failed to make them happy, and to forgive him all he had ever done amiss. When they had answered him, more with tears than words, he went out to the gates of his palace, and mounting his horse, rode to the ramparts, and stationed himself at the breach. Everything was yet silent; but as the sun rose the combat began, and at noon all was over. For two hours the assailants made no impression on the gallant band that stood like a rampart of iron before that chasm in the wall. Wave upon wave of Moslem warriors rushed madly forward, only to dash themselves to pieces against the steady solid phalanx that confronted them. In vain did Mahomet in person rally his disheartened troops, and urge them on by promises and threats, and even blows; not a man could hold his footing on that mass of ruin.

The prize seemed almost to be torn from his very grasp; when Giustiniani, who was fighting by the emperor's side, received a mortal wound, and was carried from the walls only to die on board his galley. From that moment the tide of battle turned; a body of *Janizaries*, (see note below) headed by one of gigantic size and strength, with desperate effort threw themselves upon the barricades. They perished to a man; but the little band of heroes staggered under the fury of the assault, and ere they could recover from the shock, host upon host bore down on them; almost at the flame moment a party of Turks, who had entered well-nigh unopposed through an unguarded gate, took them in the rear. Resistance was no longer possible against such overwhelming numbers; the mighty flood swept like an inundation into the city, and carried all before it. Constantine was seen fighting in the thickest of the crowd, crying, as it is said, for death from some Christian hand. When his body was found, after the contest had ceased, it was too much covered with wounds for form or feature to be recognised; and only the jewelled sword, still grasped within his hand, and the golden eagles in his buskins, betrayed the identity of the last emperor of the East.

Note:—The *Janizaries* (*Yeni tscheri*, or "new troops") were competed entirely of the children of Christians, who had been forced, usually at a tender age, to adopt Mahometanism. They were torn from their parents, and trained to renounce the faith in which they were born and baptised, and to profess the creed of Mahomet. They were then carefully educated for a soldier's life; the discipline to which they were subjected being peculiar, and in some respects severe. They were taught to pay the most implicit obedience, and to bear without repining fatigue, pain, and hunger. At first they were made to share with the peasants the labours of the field, after which they were drafted into the companies of the *Janizaries*, but only to commence a second *noviciate*.

Sometimes they were employed in the menial duties of the palace; sometimes in the public works, the dockyards, or the imperial gardens. But liberal honours and prompt promotion were the sure rewards of docility and courage. Some attained to the highest dignities in the state; and one of them married the sister of the sultan. Cut off from all ties of country, kith, and kin, but with high pay and privileges, with ample opportunities for military advancement and for the gratification of the violent, the sensual, and the sordid passions of their animal natures amid the customary atrocities of successful warfare, this military brotherhood grew up to be the strongest and fiercest instrument of imperial ambition which remorseless fanaticism, promoted by the most subtle state-craft, ever devised upon earth, As the Turkish power extended itself in Europe, care was taken to recruit the chosen corps from children who were natives of that continent rather than among the Asiatics.

This terrible body of infantry, so long the scourge of Christendom and the terror of their own sovereigns, was during three centuries (the conquering period of the Ottoman power) recruited by an annual enrolment of 1000 Christian children; so that no less than 300,000 baptised souls were thus made the polluted and sanguinary ministers and agents of Mahometan crime and dominion. From the year 1048 in the reign of Mahomet IV., the recruits were taken from among the children of *Janizaries* and native Turks; and finally the whole corps, 20,000 in number, was annihilated in our own day by means of a barbarous massacre. *Creasy*, vol. 1. pp. 20-24,161; Newman's *Lectures*, pp. 137, 267-8,

"Never," says Vertot, "was there seen so sad or so frightful a spectacle as that which was presented at the fall of Constantinople." The Turks rushed through the streets massacring as they went along: forty thousand men were put to the sword; a yet greater number of every rank, age, and sex, were sold as slaves; and the city which once had been the centre of learning, refinement, and civilisation, became changed in a single hour into the seat of the most barbarous fanaticism. The circumstances attending the end of the unhappy Notaras are too horrible for recital.

At first Mahomet treated him with courtesy, bestowed gifts upon him, and promised to reinstate him in his honours and possessions. Deluded by these flatteries, the traitor gave up the names of all the principal dignitaries and officers of state, who were instantly proclaimed through the army, and a large reward offered for their heads. Refusing to comply, however, with a brutal order issued by the monster amidst his drunken orgies, he was immediately put to death, with all his children; their bodies thrown into the streets, and their bloody heads, by the tyrant's order, placed in a row before him on the banquet-table.

Many noble Christians, and among them all the Greeks, whose lives he had promised to spare, were butchered the same day. The Cardinal Isidore, not being recognised, was sold as a slave; but he contrived to escape on board a vessel that was lying in the harbour, and survived to write a touching narrative of all that he had witnessed and endured. As to the atrocities perpetrated on the inhabitants of the city during the first fury of the capture, and for the six months that succeeded this fatal triumph of the Ottoman arms, we may well shrink from entering on their relation; a sensation of horror thrilled through Europe at the reports which came one upon another of deeds that seemed too terrible for belief. Impieties, enormities unutterable,—all that was holiest profaned and outraged with abominations that were worthy of the loathsome malice of fiends; the pictures of the saints torn to shreds; the sacred vessels and vestments put to the vilest uses; the crucifix—the image of the Redeemer—borne in mock procession, with the cap of the *Janizary* placed derisively on its head; the fonts turned into horse-troughs; and the very altars, on which had been offered the Adorable Sacrifice, defiled with nameless brutalities.

Constantinople had fallen; Santa Sophia had become, what it still remains, a Turkish mosque; the foul creed of Mahomet had usurped the temple of the Most High; and the infidel was enthroned for centuries in the metropolis of the once Christian empire of the East. And Rhodes knew well enough that at her the next blow was to be directed. Sir John de Lastic, the reigning grand master, hastened to prepare for the worst, and summoned all his knights throughout Europe to assemble for the defence.

> "We command you," he says, "to come hither instantly, where your presence is urgently required. Not a day elapses but we hear of some new slaughter of the Christians by the grand Turk, whose inhuman cruelties are told us, not by idle rumour, but by those who have seen what they relate with their own eyes. Look, therefore, for no further letters, commands, or exhortations; but the moment you receive this message delay not to set out for Rhodes by the quickest conveyance love or money can procure."

Constantinople—and then Rhodes! such had been the war-proclamation of Mahomet II.: nor was it long before his heralds appeared to summon the knights to acknowledge his pretensions. A yearly tribute of two thousand *ducats*, or war to the last extremity: such were the haughty conditions offered by the conqueror.

The reply was such as might be expected:

> "Tell your master," answered Lastic, "that our predecessors purchased this island at the price of their blood; and that we will give our lives rather than sacrifice our independence, or that of our religion."

Nothing, doubting that such a reply would soon draw down on the order the fury of the sultan's arms, Lastic at the same time despatched ambassadors to all the European courts, though with little hopes of deriving any succours from thence. The ambassador to France was Peter D'Aubusson,—and this is the first mention of a name which is among the greatest in the chronicles of the Hospitallers of St. John. A fresh league, which the indefatigable efforts of the Pontiff, Calixtus III., had succeeded in forming against the Turks, obliged Mahomet to defer his enterprise against Rhodes, and thus gave the knights a further time to prepare.

Two men were still found on the frontiers of the Turkish empire before whom the arms of the Ottoman failed to be invincible: these were Scanderbeg the chief of Albania, and the gallant regent of Hungary, John Corvinus Hunyades. Scanderbeg, whose real name was George Castriotes, after being taken as hostage when nine years old, and brought up in the religion of Mahomet, had seized an opportunity of escaping to his native mountains, and openly professing the Christian faith. He was reckoned the greatest commander of his time; and taking advantage of the nature of the country, he succeeded in repeatedly beating large armies sent against him by the Turkish sultans with a mere handful of men.

When, after the fall of Constantinople, every other province of Greece and the Morea submitted to Mahomet, Albania still held out, and the very name of Scanderbeg struck terror into the infidels, whom he defied. For twenty years he maintained the unequal contest. At length, as he lay at Alyssio, weak and dying of fever, news was brought him that the Turks were in the neighbourhood devastating the village and country. He called for his armour, but could not rise to put it on; nevertheless his followers carried his banner before them to the scene of combat; and at the first sight of that well-known ensign, the infidels turned and fled. He lived to hear of this last success, and then expired; and the Turks, when they took Alyssio twelve years after his death, had such an opinion of his valour, that, disinterring his bones, they made amulets of than to wear in battle.

It is said his favourite horse would not suffer any other to mount him when his master was gone, but turning wild and savage, died a week after the decease of the noble chieftain. The independence of Albania expired with its prince. Yet, though delivered from one of his most formidable opponents and now master of the whole of Greece, Mahomet was still forced to delay his great expedition against the Knights of Rhodes. He did not, however, entirely spare them; but in every attack his galleys made on their islands, they met with a repulse which warned him that the subjugation of Rhodes would be a far different enterprise from the taking of Constantinople. He was compelled to fear as much as he hated this unconquerable order; he found it everywhere.

At Lesbos, led on by Zacosta, the grand master, they wellnigh succeeded in repulsing the assault of his most valiant troops, and would have saved the island, but for the detestable treachery of its Greek governor, Gattilusio. This miserable man, after giving up the brave knights to slaughter, thought, if not to gain the reward he coveted, at least to save his life by adding apostasy to perfidy. But Mahomet did not grant him long impunity; on some frivolous pretext he had him thrown into a dungeon, where, shortly after, he was strangled.

Three hundred of the garrison of Mitylene, when they saw that all was lost, had surrendered on a solemn promise that their lives should be spared; but no sooner were they in his power than the base and cruel Turk had them murdered to a man, and that by the most frightful death he could devise—they were all sawn asunder: this was now the tyrant's favourite mode of taking vengeance on his vanquished foes, being, as he conceived, the most horrible torture that human ingenuity could inflict. The severed and mangled limbs of his victims he ordered to be thrown to be devoured by dogs and birds of prey.

Negropont, then subject to the republic of Venice, was the next point of attack; and though the Venetians had shown but little friendliness to the order, whose commercial rivalry they feared, yet, says Vertot

    the grand master Orsini, believing himself bound by his profession to defend the states of every Christian prince, instantly sent armed galleys to their assistance, and at the head of a brave troop of knights, who were to endeavour to land upon the island and throw themselves into the beleaguered town, was the Commander D'Aubusson;

    who indeed was, at that time, the most distinguished chief of his illustrious body.

    Nevertheless Negropont fell, as Lesbos and Constantinople had already fallen. The Ottoman forces numbered no less than two hundred thousand men, and were supported by a powerful fleet; yet were the bold knights eager for the fight, and loudly demanded that they should be led against the bridge of boats which the enemy had constructed. But the Venetian admiral, seized as it appeared with a sudden panic, refused the enterprise, drew off his vessels, and left the defenders to their fate. Already had the besiegers made three desperate attacks upon the town, but with such loss to themselves both of men and ships, that even Mahomet was beginning to despair: now, however, their courage and hopes revived; and taking advantage of the consternation inspired by the withdrawal of the Venetian fleet, though once again repulsed in a fifth bloody assault, they carried the works and poured down upon the place. Erizzo, the intrepid governor, disputed every inch of ground with the assailants, and fought his way from street to street until he gained the citadel, where with good courage he still continued the defence; but when provisions and ammunition failed, and he beheld his little garrison daily thinned by death and exhausted by fatigue and wounds, he was compelled to sue for terms and offer to surrender on the sultan's plighted word, that his life and the lives of his companions should be safe from harm.

    Mahomet swore by his own head that the heads of Erizzo and of all who were with him should be uninjured; but, furious at the loss of thousands of his best and bravest troops, when the garrison had laid down their arms, he caused them all to be massacred, the Greeks alone excepted, with circumstances of the most barbarous cruelty. Some he had impaled, others cut in pieces, or stoned to death. Erizzo himself he doomed to be sawn in two; boasting that thus he scrupulously kept his oath to the very letter, since he had sworn to leave his head untouched. The brave Venetian had a daughter, Anne Erizzo, young and beautiful, who, to the dauntless courage of her noble race joined all the indomitable fortitude of a Christian martyr. Mahomet, a monster of sensuality as of cruelty, had her brought into his presence: the virtuous maiden scorned alike his vile solicitations and his angry threats, till seized with fury, he drew his *scimitar* and at a single blow severed her fair head from her chaste body; thus, as Vertot expresses it;

> gratifying to the full the wishes of this heroine, who, by the sacrifice of a frail life and a beauty even frailer, earned for herself an imperishable bliss.

The inhabitants were now at the mercy of the conqueror; but the very enormity of the crimes which were perpetrated in this as in every other instance forbids their being detailed.

"Words cannot express," says the same historian, "all the cruelties exercised at the taking of Negropont; the whole island was filled with carnage and horror, for the Turkish soldiers, following their sovereign's example, made a merit of their ferocities."

The rage of Mahomet when he saw the galleys of St. John in the midst of the Venetian fleet broke out into a kind of madness: the conqueror of two empires and of twelve kingdoms, as he haughtily termed himself, he felt the resistance of this single island enough to counterbalance all his success, and he sent envoys to Rhodes to declare war to blood and fire, swearing that he would exterminate the entire order, and put every member of it to the sword. But still the blow so often threatened was doomed to be delayed. Fresh leagues against the Turkish sultan gave time for fresh fortifications and armaments at Rhodes; they were conducted under the direction of D'Aubusson himself, whose capacity all recognised, so that he was the soul and animating spirit of the whole order; nothing escaped his vigilance, and to his charge everything was committed; war, finance, fortifications, all were under his superintendence, and all, whether superiors or inferiors, listened to his word as law. It is no wonder, therefore, that on the death of Orsini in 1476, D'Aubusson was chosen as his successor; and it scarcely needed the votes of the chapter to declare an election which had already been made by the unanimous voice of his brethren.

Chapter 4

Character of D'Aubusson

The course of our narrative has now brought us to the first of those remarkable sieges which constitute the chief interest in the history of the Knights of St. John. The circumstances briefly detailed in the foregoing chapter will have enabled the reader in some measure to appreciate the devotion and gallantry of their resistance, and the peril of their position when the vast armament of the Ottomans bore down on Rhodes,—that little island which lay alone amid the wreck of Christianity in the East, like the single rock which lifts its head above the raging waters of a mighty deluge. But the event itself stands out with so much prominence in the annals of Christian chivalry—it is so honourable to the illustrious society whose exploits we have undertaken to narrate, and especially to the commander whose election to the grand-mastership we have just recorded, that our story must take something of a less desultory character; and though we cannot pretend to offer a finished portrait of every great man who appeared in an order of heroes, his name at least deserves a different kind of notice.

Peter D'Aubusson was descended from one of the most illustrious houses of France; Norman in its origin, and allied to the royal Norman blood. He was a soldier from his youth, but a man of letters also; and, to use the expression of the French historian;

> the extent and facility of his mind sufficed for everything.

The popularity of his name, great as it was in his order, was even more enthusiastically felt among the populace of Rhodes. The extraordinary joy manifested by them at his election had something in it for different from the. ordinary popular rejoicings at a coronation—it was from the heart; and men no longer feared Mahomet now that D'Aubusson was at the head of the Knights of St. John. His first act was a careful inspection of the entire island in person; and on his return, he summoned all the knights once more to assemble in Rhodes, and in the chapter general of the following spring was invested with absolute power during the ensuing siege, which all now felt to be close at hand. Indeed, it was a remarkable testimony to the extraordinary capacity of this grant man, that an order so jealous for the preservation of its constitutional privileges voluntarily created him its dictator, not only in military, but also in financial and political affairs.

He held an irresponsible power, yet from no act of usurpation on his own part; nor do we ever find him taking advantage of the boundless confidence of his subjects to prolong or extend his authority; but, on the contrary, he himself restrained it, and after holding the administration of the treasury for three years and regulating its disorders, he refused to retain it longer, out gave it back into the hands of the ordinary officers of the finance. His genius was as universal as it was commanding. He was at the head of every department: he made his own gunpowder, and directed the building of his own ships; he surpassed the first engineers of his age in a practical knowledge of the science of defence, was an excellent chemist, and assiduous in his personal services in the hospital, where he showed that he thoroughly understood the treatment of the sick.

Hitherto the various summonses addressed by previous grand masters to the knights of distant provinces had produced but little result; but the name of D'Aubusson gave a magical effect to his commands. From every quarter the knights flocked in with singular promptitude, and many of the European sovereigns contributed large sums to facilitate their journey. Mahomet saw that there was at least little chance of taking Rhodes and its defenders by surprise; for which reason he tried every means of throwing the grand master off his guard. Among these were pretended treaties for truce, and the despatch of a multitude of spies and feigned embassies; and lastly, an attempt to introduce dissensions among the people of Rhodes, and win them over from the cause of the order. The sultan doubtless thought it a surpassing stroke of policy to suggest to the Rhodian Greeks, as a lure, the unlimited exercise of their religion free from all Latin domination. But the result showed that he knew little of the state with which he had to deal.

There was no jealousy of sect or party known in the religion of Rhodes; and every effort to sow dissension among the natives was met by the indignant cry, "We are all of one belief! here there is neither Greek nor Latin; for we are Christians, the servants of Jesus Christ and of His blessed Mother!" This unity of religious belief had ever been one of the chief blessings and privileges enjoyed under the rule of the order; But it was especially and vigorously protected by D'Aubusson, who, with the utmost zeal, guarded against any thing that could introduce the fatal seeds of schism or dissension; and was accustomed to say that he reigned over Christians, not Latins or Greeks, and that even the schismatics, if there were any such, should be treated with strict impartiality. The fact was, however, that, with individual exceptions, the adherents to the Greek rite in Rhodes were in communion with their Latin brethren; for the large and wise policy of the grand masters had still succeeded in preserving alive that union which, settled by the Florentine Council, had never existed elsewhere but in theory and in name.

If Rhodes was beautiful to the eye and captivating to the imagination, when first Villaret and his companions set foot upon its shores, much more so was it now, when the lapse of a hundred and seventy years had made it the centre of southern civilisation, and the riches of a long commercial prosperity had been lavished on its adornment and the cultivation of the domestic arts. All around the grand and battlemented walls of the capital there spread in sweet contrast gardens, villas, and vineyards; most verdant hills darkened with woods of pomegranates and oranges; a rich suburban district,—the glory of a city in times of peace, and its worst enemy in the perils of a siege.

All about this garden-world there sparkled streams and fountains of bright and delicious water; there was no water like that of Rhodes, nor any country to compare to its rich and beautiful soil, at least in the mind of its inhabitants.

> "It was," says one of its own citizens,[1] "the favourite, sweetest island of the sun, where the air was ever pure, and the country ever smiling."

The first act of D'Aubusson, on his investiture by the chapter with the supreme and absolute command, was one of stern but most necessary sacrifice. The suburbs were to be destroyed; the trees and gardens cut down and wasted; and even the churches razed to the ground, so as to prevent the enemy from finding shelter under the city walls. The Rhodians watched the process of destruction with tears of regret, so very dear to their hearts was the beauty of their capital; but all knew that the calamity was inevitable, and so, silencing their grief, they lent their aid to make a desert of their paradise, and spared nothing; only, says Vertot,

> before destroying the church of our Lady of Philermos, they carried the image of the Blessed Virgin thence to the principal church within the city walls; for it had been preserved from time immemorial, and was greatly revered.

All the fields were now laid waste, and the forage carried into the city; many of those beautiful crystal springs were choked up and rendered useless; in short, there was nothing left in the island which could furnish support to the enemy's troops, or which the barbarians could destroy.

Over all these details, and a thousand more besides, D'Aubusson's watchful superintendence presided; and combin-

---

1. Gulielmus Caoursinus.

ing the quick eye of a military commander with the tenderness of a paternal sovereign, he insisted on personally seeing that every individual among the citizens, as well as the knights, was properly provided and cared for; and though he demanded great sacrifices from all, there was nothing of sternness or indifference in his manner of exacting them. Rather he found the means of inspiring all around him with his own heroic and chivalric spirit. The Rhodians were not a warlike people, yet they caught fire from their sovereign's animating words and noble example. And as to the knights, how could they resist those grand and lofty appeals?

> "I summon you," he writes to the absent brethren, "in virtue of those solemn vows you have made to the God of heaven, and at the foot of His altar. It is your mother calls you,—a mother who has nursed you in her bosom, and is now in danger. Shall a single knight be found to abandon her to the rage of the barbarian? I will not think it; it would be unworthy of the nobility of your origin, and still less of the piety and valour of your profession."

He addressed the chapter in the same exalted strain:

> "Soldiers of Christ," he said, "in a war so holy as this, it is Christ Himself who is at our head; fear not, for He will never abandon those who fight but for His interests. In vain does the impious Mahomet, who recognises no God but power, threaten to exterminate us: his troops may be more numerous, but ours at least are no vile slaves like his; I look round me, and I see only men of noble and illustrious blood, brought up in virtue, and sworn to conquer or die, and whose piety and courage might alone be the pledges of a certain victory."

In fact, besides the members of the order, there were a considerable number of volunteers collected at Rhodes from all nations, particularly from France: all of them gentlemen of high birth and renown, filled with a generous enthusiasm, and a devotion to the cause of the order and to its heroic chief. Amongst them was D'Aubusson's elder brother, the Viscount de Monteuil, who received a high command; and throughout the siege no jealousy ever arose between these volunteers and the knights, but rather a generous and friendly rivalry, and a heartiness of obedience and co-operation, that could only have proceeded from the noblest spirit, inspired and kept alive by the admirable policy of the grand master. There was something very remarkable in this affectionate unity of the defenders of Rhodes, presenting so lovely a contrast to the treachery and dissensions of other sieges.

> "It was to be found," to use the words of the French author, "in the citizens equally with the knights; Greek and Latin, all were alike; and it passed even to the women and children, who vied with one another in working at the fortifications which D'Aubusson had ordered to be commenced."

The city of Rhodes stood on the declivity of a wooded hill on the border of the sea; it was surrounded by a double wall flanked by large towers, and beyond the wall was a deep and broad ditch. There were two ports; the first of which, defended by a tower called Fort St. Elmo, served for the smaller galleys, while the second, constructed for larger vessels, had two defences, known as Fort St. John and Fort St. Michael. [2] By the side of this latter port were two small gulfs, the fortifications of which were so contrived as to guard the entrance of the ports. Two miles from the city rose the hill of St. Stephen, and, on the other side, Mount Philermos,[3] celebrated for that shrine of our Lady to which allusion has been made, and which was a place of pilgrimage not only to the islanders but to all the neighbouring states.

It was on the 23rd of May 1480, that the great fleet of the in-

---

2. Such is Vertot's description. Von Hammer's account differs; but the subject is involved in some confusion.
3. Now called *Sunbullu, i. e.* "covered with hyacinths." (Von Hammer.)

fidels at length appeared in sight of Rhodes. The signal of its approach was given from the watch-tower on Mount St. Stephen, and thither the grand master repaired to survey the force destined for the conquest of the island and the destruction of the order. It was a grand and terrific sight; a hundred and sixty large vessels of war, and a very cloud of galleys, *feluccas*, and transports, having on hoard a vast body of troops as well as artillery of most formidable size.

The sea was darkened for miles by this immense armament; and the landing was soon commenced, under favour of a heavy fire from the enemy's artillery, with pomp and music, as though they had been victors coming to a conquered city. Despite the efforts of the knights, the hostile troops succeeded in entrenching themselves in the neighbourhood of Mount St. Stephen, and in landing their heavy artillery, consisting of 4000 pieces of cannon, some being of prodigious size and calibre, throwing balls of flint and marble nine palms in diameter, as D'Aubusson himself declares in his despatch to the German emperor, written after the siege.

So soon as the artillery was landed and planted,—an operation which the knights were powerless to resist,—the storm of the cannonade began. For days together the walls and towers were battered by cannon, and mortars with terrible effect; nine towers were overthrown, and whole streets demolished; but the chief attack was directed against the tower of St. Nicholas, situated on the extremity of the mole which defended the larger port. After resisting the furious bombardment for several days, during which it received the shock of no less than three hundred of these marble cannon-balls, the tower fell, and the sight was welcomed by the enemy with a kind of insane joy.

But whilst they abandoned themselves to their exultation, the besieged set to work to construct a new defence on the mole itself, and labouring night and day, contrived a fortification of singular skill in the midst of the ruins, which they garrisoned with their bravest troops. This defence, devised by the engineering skill of D'Aubusson, resisted the utmost efforts of the Turks, who were driven off, after several furious assaults, with immense loss.

It is sad to find one of the most illustrious names of Christendom at the head of the infidel army; yet it was a Palæologus[4] who, under the name of Mesih Pasha, led the Turkish force. A prince of the imperial family of Greece, and born a Christian, he had renounced his faith to purchase life at the capture of Constantinople. His talents had raised him to the rank of admiral grand *vizier* in the sultan's service; and the cause of the Cross had no deadlier enemy than this miserable renegade, who sought to secure the favour of his new master by an excess of fury against the Christian name. Other renegades were in the camp, one of whom, a German engineer, with a treachery worthy of an apostate, entered the town as a spy, and representing himself as a deserter from the Turkish camp, endeavoured to possess himself of the plan of the defences; but D'Aubusson's quick vigilance detected the stratagem; and "Master George," as he was called, found himself too closely watched to be able to escape.

The assaults on the mole of St. Nicholas continued for several days; and always on the most dangerous post might be seen the form of D'Aubusson. At once captain and soldier, he refused all solicitations to retire. "The post of honour is here," he replied to Carretto, who afterwards succeeded him, "and belongs of right to your grand master;" adding with a pleasant smile; "and, after all, if I am killed there is more to hope for you than to fear for

---

4. Von Hammer questions this fact, as resting on no authority; but, however this may be, it is remarkable how many of the ablest leaders of the Ottoman forces, and of course the most inveterate foes of the Christian name, were apostates. Their malice seemed insatiable; and many of the worst atrocities recorded in Turkish warfare were perpetrated by them. It was at the instigation of three renegades from the order that Mahomet undertook this very expedition against Rhodes; and the reader of history will not fail to notice, that in almost every renewed enterprise against Christendom, an apostate from the faith was its contriver or its conductor. "If we look," says Professor Creasy, "to the period when the Turkish power was at its height,—the period of the reign of Solyman I. and Selim II.,— we shall find that out of ten *viziers* of this epoch eight were renegades. Of the other high dignitaries of the Porte during the same period, we shall find that at least twelve of her best generals, and four of her most renowned admirals, were supplied to her by Christian countries."

me:" words which were afterwards taken as a prophecy of Carretto's future elevation. A ball having struck his helmet from his head, he quietly replaced: it with the steel-cap of a fallen soldier, without seeming to heed the danger.

Bosio has left us a striking picture of him during the progress of the defences at St. Nicholas. To complete them, it was necessary for the workmen to labour continuously for seventy hours, during which time a constant watch was kept to guard them from surprise. D'Aubusson never left the spot.

"His armour," says the historian above named, "was gilt or golden, and always kept highly polished and shining; and at the head of his chosen and valiant squadron he sat on his horse the whole night long without moving, or taking a moment's repose; and the splendour of the moon, reflected from that gilt *cuirass* rendered his figure a clear and striking object."

This long night-watch, and the spectacle of the grand master in his golden armour has been noticed by almost every historian of the order; and doubtless there must have been something unusually solemn and beautiful in his appearance, which distinguished him from the numbers around him, whose conduct was nevertheless scarcely less devoted than his own.

He had all the time courtesy and modesty of chivalry; listening to the counsel of all; before declaring his own sentiments, which never failed of being received as law; he had a smile and a patient word for all; and yet withal his prompt resolution never suffered itself, when once formed, to be changed or reconsidered. All the while, great general and brave soldier as he was, he found time and strength to be carpenter, engineer, or labourer, as occasion called.

He drew the plan of his walls and ramparts, and worked at them with, his own, hands; nor was there a sally to be made, or an attack to be repelled, but D'Aubusson was to be found, at the head of the combatants. Nor was he less the Christian, because he was so entirely a man of genius and of war; his devotion harmonised with the rest of his character in its admirable simplicity. The defence of the city was not begun till after the offering of solemn prayers in all the churches; and then the image of our Lady of Philermos was exposed, and the cause of Rhodes committed to her patronage with something; of a childlike trustful confidence; and with our Lady and D'Aubusson to protect them, the Rhodians felt secure of victory.

Foiled in his first attempts, the *pasha* now resolved on a night-attack, which was to be conducted with such secrecy and despatch, and with such ingenious contrivances to boot, as should secure both a surprise and a successful issue. A bridge was constructed to reach from the mainland which the infidels had occupied to the mole of St. Nicholas; and in the night an anchor was let fall close under the foot of the tower, and the floating point made fast to it by a strong cable; It happened, however, that a Christian sailor, one Rogers, an Englishman by birth, lying concealed near the spot, had observed the whole transaction, and no sooner had the Turks withdrawn, than, plunging intrepidly into the sea, he cut the cable, and drew up the coil upon the strand. Thus was the design, entirely frustrated; for the bridge being cast loose from its fastenings, was speedily broken to pieces by the waves.

But the *pasha* had caused a second to be constructed, which, being carried across in the stillness of the night, was made fast to the mole two hours before daybreak on the morning of the 9th of June; and while all was yet dark, the Turks began their noiseless passage over it; at the same time, a flotilla of light boats was sent to co-operate on the seaward side. So quietly was the manoeuvre effected, and such a perfect silence reigned throughout the Christian defences, that the Turkish commander flattered himself that his design was undetected. But D'Aubusson was ready for him; and while the Turks were preparing to make good their landing on the mole, behind the guns upon the wall stood his resolute cannoneers with matches burning; a steady line of muskets waited but the word to discharge their murderous hail in the faces of the foe; and from every more distant quarter whence the stormers could be reached, the guns on the ramparts had been brought to bear upon the point assailed. Suddenly, from the depth of the darkness there issued a very storm of fire, which carried death and dismay into the midst of the advancing columns. At the same moment the Rhodian fire-ships bore down upon the Turkish galleys; horrible was the confusion;—the roaring of the flames; the incessant cannonading; the fire-balls blazing and flaming; the yells of the combatants; the shrieks and groans of the maimed and the dying. On the mole, on the beaches, on the waters, the battle raged with most terrific fury.

In spite of the tremendous fire poured on them from all sides, the infidels plant their ladders at the foot, and, brandishing their scimitars, scale the bastions. The assault is all along the front; the grand master stands at the breach, and around him his gallant knights, making a rampart with their bodies. The ladders are thrown down, only to be raised again by the determined foe; massive stones and boiling oil and streams of flaming fire are launched upon them,—still they press on; and those who are below in the boats and triremes discharge volley after volley of musketry and showers of arrows from their cross-bows at the knights, or endeavour with grappling-irons, which they throw upon the ramparts, to drag them down and stab them as they fall. The advantage, however, was with the Christians; and dawn disclosed to the Turkish commander the desperate condition of his troops,—the sea and the strand strewn with corpses, and the attacking columns everywhere giving way before the steady valour of the Christians. It revealed too, to the defenders, the floating bridge thronged with Turkish succours hurrying to the assault, and enabled them to point their guns immediately upon it, and shatter it to pieces.

From near midnight to ten in the morning the attack and the defence endured with unabated fury; but at length the triumph of the knights was secured; every man who had mounted the mole was killed. In vain with menaces and wild entreaties the leaders urged their troops to sustain the contest; the rout was general and complete; the victorious knights precipitated their flying enemies from the mole, and pursued them even into the waters of the harbour. Conspicuous among the Christian combatants was Anthony Fradin, a Franciscan friar, as bold in fight as he was eloquent of speech, who, plunging shoulder-deep into the sea, with his own right hand struck off many a turbaned head. In this night-assault fell 2500 infidels, and among them their renowned commander, Ibrahim Bey, the sultan's son-in-law. The loss on the Rhodian side was also great; and twelve of the brave knights of St. John were among the slain.

But this repulse served only to rouse the fury of the *vizier* to a greater height. Since St. Nicholas had proved impregnable in its ruin, he directed his next attack against the city itself. It was so torn and shaken by the previous cannonade, that, to use the words of D'Aubusson, "it retained not the least resemblance to what it was." The principal attack, however, was made on a portion of the walls which had remained as yet uninjured, in the Jewish quarter of the town, "Eight tremendous cannon, of the largest size ever seen, ceased not night and day from scourging those groaning flanks;" never for a moment was the hideous roaring of this artillery silenced; but whilst the walls gradually crumbled to pieces, the besieged, under the direction of the grand master, busily employed themselves in erecting new ramparts behind them, "planting stakes of thick green timber, and covering them, with earth and branches of stout tough underwood and thorns,"—a work which it seemed incredible should have been accomplished in so short a time. But everyone worked with equal ardour night and day.

D'Aubusson superintended all himself and set the example to the rest by incessant labour; men and women, Christians and Jews,—all lent their aid; the very nuns coming out of their convents, and bearing provision to the workmen; and when the Turks thought they had effected the easy entrance into the place by the destruction of the wall, they were confounded to find a new and stronger rampart, risen as if by magic behind the ruins, and beyond it a wide deep ditch, which had to filled before any approach could be made. Immense loads of stone were now brought and thrown into the ditch; and meanwhile the cannonade continued its ceaseless roar, accompanied by many other frightful kinds of artillery then in use: globes of fire and flaming arrows, and the serpent-guns that sent fire-balls whirling and hissing through the air like deadly flying reptiles.

The sound of the artillery was heard from Kos, a hundred miles to the west of Rhodes, as far as Castelrosso, the same distance to the east; the bombardment never ceased for a minute, and the utmost exertions of the citizens were continually called for to extinguish the flames of the burning houses. All the sick and infirm were hidden away in underground cellars and caves to escape those crushing marble balls, which were the most destructive of all the engines of attack. But the war was underground also; and by many a subterranean ditch, most cunningly concealed, did the enemy endeavour to steal into the city, or to ruin its defences. To resist the effect of the ponderous marble balls, D'Aubusson contrived to roof in one quarter of the city so securely, that the women and children were completely sheltered; whilst under his orders, the city carpenters constructed a machine for throwing back these unwelcome visitors into the midst of the assailants; and so enormous was their weight, that, we are told, they not only crushed all on whom they fell, but often dashed into and destroyed the mines with all whom they contained. This machine the knights jestingly termed the "tribute," in allusion to that demanded by Mahomet, and which they devised this novel mode of paying.

Meanwhile the Turks had succeeded in forming a causeway of stones across one portion of the ditch, which it took them eight-and-thirty days to accomplish. Thus they completely filled up the fosse, and raised a mound level with the ramparts, by which they could have readily mounted on the walls; but when they thought their work was finished, they were not a little exasperated to see it sinking and diminishing; for the Rhodians were every night working unperceived at its foundations, and carrying away the stones noiselessly into the city. Perceiving, therefore, that they were losing time, they prepared to storm without delay, and to this end proceeded to cannonade that portion of the walls which was close to the fortifications so rapidly repaired; and such was the tempest that beat upon these new defences, that no living thing could appear on them for a moment without being swept away. In the course of one day and night three hundred of those monstrous globes of rock were hurled at the torn and shattered walls.

It was then that the true character of Master George was finally detected. He was known to be an engineer of singular skill; and the knights, under whose charge he had been, and who had not altogether shared in the grand master's suspicions, led him to the spot to ask his opinion and advice. It may easily be believed what kind of counsel they received; yet, to disguise his treachery, Master George affected the utmost ardour, and insisted on working with his own hands. In doing so, however, he betrayed himself; the quick eye of his guards remarked that he fired without aim, and, as if by some preconcerted signal, seemed to draw the enemy's fire on the weakest point. He was at once seized and interrogated, and, confessing the whole design, received the richly-merited reward of his treachery and his crimes.

The assault was now evidently close at hand; nothing remained to keep the Turks from the attempt; and it is said a few Spanish and Italian knights ventured to hint at the prudence of coming to honourable terms with the *vizier*, who, well knowing the character of his opponents' valour, had shown a disposition to treat for a surrender. D'Aubusson, calling the knights around him, addressed them coldly, as though no longer members of the order.

> "Gentlemen," he said,—a term never applied to the knights, who were always addressed as brothers,— "if any of you do not feel secure here, the port is not yet so entirely blockaded but I shall be able to find means for you to retire. If, however, you choose to remain, let me hear no more of surrender, otherwise I shall certainly cause you to be put to death,"

These words, and that he called them "gentlemen," stung them to the quick; they threw themselves at his feet, and declared they were, and would ever be, his knights and subjects.

Nevertheless it could not be denied but that the crisis was one of great peril. So incessant was the cannonading that no time was given to repair the breaches; the fosses were in many parts filled up; the walls were everywhere in ruins; and no obstacle remained to oppose the entrance of the Turks into the town save the heroic valour of the defenders. Scarcely had the sun appeared above the horizon on the morning of the 27th of July, when, at the firing of a mortar as a signal, the advanced troops of the enemy rushed forward with a tremendous shout, and with the utmost rapidity scaled the walls, bore down all before them, and planted their colours before the besieged could offer any effectual resistance. And now, without prompt relief, it was all over with Rhodes; but that relief came in the person of the grand master.

> "Perceiving," such is his own account, "a great conflict at hand, we raised and planted firmly the banner representing our dear Lord Jesus Christ, and beside it that of our order directly facing the enemy; and then ensued a battle of two hours."

Crying, "Come, my brothers, let us fight for the faith and for Rhodes, or be buried under the ruins," he hastened to the spot, surrounded by a chosen band of comrades. Already 2000 Turks had occupied the ramparts, and behind them 4000 more were advancing and preparing to mount to the assault. But, nothing daunted, D'Aubusson, seizing a ladder, planted it with his own hands against the wall in spite of a shower of stones, and was the first [5] to mount, pike in hand, followed by the rest of his party. Owing to the character of the ground, and the fact that the Turks had already formed a position on the top of the ramparts, they were now themselves the besieged, and the assault was from

---

5. D'Aubusson, in his despatch, omits all personal mention of himself, and merely says, "We of the relief party ascended from Jew street," &c.

the garrison. The valour displayed on both sides was of the most signal description.

The Turks, says the historian,

"were as lions rushing upon their prey;"

the Christians,

"like the Machabees, fighting for their religion and their liberties."

The fury of the infidels was well-nigh irresistible; many of the knights were crushed under the weight of the heavy stones which were dashed down upon their heads as they strove to mount the platform which the enemy had occupied. Twice was D'Aubusson himself struck down, and thrown from the ramparts; but, covered with wounds, he returned to the charge without heeding his danger, and at length, by sheer force, the infidels were driven from their position; and the mass of the Christians throwing themselves on their ranks, a desperate struggle commenced. The grand master slew many of the boldest with his own hands; and some 800 or more were tumbled from the walls into the city, where they were instantly slain.

But their losses were quickly supplied by reinforcements from the vast multitude that covered the field below, so thickly that the eye could not discern the ground on which they stood. Now a body of *Janizaries*, urged on by the hope of a large reward, charged furiously on the knights, and fought their way to where the grand master stood, his armour flashing in the blaze of the musketry, and the short spear he carried red with Turkish blood. One while he seemed completely surrounded and overpowered by these desperate men; but though wounded in several places, and bleeding profusely, still he held his ground, and laid many of his assailants dead at his feet.

His gallant comrades, fearing for his safety, and reckless of their own lives so that they could save that of their beloved commander, threw themselves with renewed energy upon the dense mass of their assailants; and such was the fury of their assault, that:

> "at length," to resume D'Aubusson's own description, "the Turks, hard pressed, broken, wearied out, terrified, and covered with wounds, turned and fled, and so hastily that they hindered one another, and did but increase their own destruction. There fell in that conflict 3500 of them, as we learned by the corpses which we afterwards burnt for fear of infection, The panic was contagions, spreading from one rank to another, till at length the whole Moslem army was in flight."

It was indeed a complete and unexpected victory. In vain did the *vizier* attempt to rally his vast masses, now thrown into all the confusion of a hasty rout. The Christian troops, precipitating themselves from the walls, pursued the fugitives over the plain; and Mesih Pasha himself was compelled to fly with the rest.

> "In these battles," continues D'Aubusson, "we have lost many of our knights, fighting bravely in the thickest of the enemy's squares. We ourselves, and our companions-in-arms, have had many wounds; but after placing a strong garrison on the ramparts, we returned home to give thanks to God: for surely it was not without Divine assistance that we were saved from butchery; and doubtless the Almighty God sent us that succour from heaven, lest His poor Christian people should be infected with the filth of Mahometanism."

The infidels plainly had reckoned on nothing short of certain victory; their women had already prepared ropes for the prisoners, and wooden stakes for their torture; for it had been ordered that every living being above ten years of age should be slain or impaled alive, and the children sold as slaves. Their cruelty, however, was doomed for once to disappointment: the *vizier* saw plainly enough, that, after so complete a defeat, there was nothing further to be done but to embark and make the best of his way back to safe quarters, which they did with incredible speed;

so that within a few days there was nothing left of their vast armament but the corpses that strewed the battle-field as thick as the forest-leaves in autumn. During the three months of siege the Turks had 9000 killed and 15,000 wounded.

It is a pious tradition, that at the moment of the last terrible assault, as the defenders, reduced to extremity, unfurled the banners of Christ, our Lady and St. John, and cried aloud to heaven for help, the Moslems were stupefied by the sudden apparition oh the battlements of a lady of dazzling and extraordinary beauty, who extended a shield over the devoted city. By her side stood one whom the Rhodians recognised as St. John Baptist, their patron saint; and the heavenly vision struck such terror into the hearts of the assailants that they instantly turned and fled. This account was at the time universally believed by the Rhodians; and the relief of the island has always been reckoned as one among the many victories of Mary.

The Turkish historian, Afendy, however, has a different tale, which has been adopted try certain modern writers, that but for the cupidity of Mesih Pasha the forts and the island must have fallen; that at the moment when the Ottoman standard was planted on the walls, he ordered proclamation to be made that pillage was forbidden, and that the rich plunder of Rhodes belonged to the sultan; that so great in consequence was the disgust and indignation of the soldiery, that the storming columns halted in mid-career; the battalions outside the town refused to mount the breach; the Christians seized the moment when the ranks were wavering to precipitate themselves upon the besiegers, and the retreat commenced.

One would wish to have something more than the bare word of this writer in support of an account so strongly at variance with Turkish custom, and with the character and real interests of the *pasha*; but even if it be true, it derogates nothing from the ability or the heroism of the defence; neither, be it added, did the fact, if fact it were, diminish at the time the importance of the event or the magnitude of the result. The outpost of Christendom was saved; Rhodes was rescued for nearly half a century;

and when it fell, it was into the hands of a conqueror who knew how to appreciate the courage of a vanquished foe, and, infidel as he was, to keep faith with Christians.

D'Aubusson was carried to his palace covered with wounds, and for three days his life was despaired of. It was in his bed that he received from the hands of his knights the Moslem standard, and gave orders for a public thanksgiving to be rendered to the God of armies. During those three days the palace doors were crowded by anxious citizens of all ranks; and it is said their joy was less when they watched the last sail of the Turkish fleet disappear below the horizon, than when the surgeon announced to the populace that the danger was past, and, as it was thought, not without tokens of a miraculous cure.

So soon as he could walk, D'Aubusson proceeded to the great church of St. John to offer his own thanksgivings; and, as a perpetual monument of the deliverance of the city by the intervention of the Blessed Virgin, he ordered the erection of three churches in her honour and that of the patrons of the city. These churches were endowed for prayers and masses to be offered in perpetuity for the souls of those who had fallen in battle; and one was for the Greek rite: but the expression, *devout Catholics,* which is used by Bosio, shows us that the Greeks to whom he here alluded were in communion with the See of Rome, and not schismatics, as some later writers have supposed.

Nor was his care of the living less large and generous than for the dead.

> "All, down to the meanest soldier, had a share of his notice," says Vertot; "and to comfort the poor peasants and the inhabitants of the country which had been devastated by the enemy, he distributed among them corn and provisions for their support till next harvest, and took off for several years the taxes they had hitherto paid."

The same day that Mesih Pasha was driven from the walls of Rhodes, the Turks, under Ahmed Keduk, first set foot on the tempting shores of Italy, making a successful descent on the

Apulian coast, and marched at once to invest Otranto. When grand *vizier*, he had, in 1475, conquered the Crimea, and signalised his victories by the perpetration of all those outrages which have given to Turkish warfare an infamous celebrity even in the annals of blood and crime. The taking of Kafia, which belonged to the Genoese, and was a pace of great wealth and importance, was marked by a deed of the blackest perfidy. The town held out but three days; on the fourth, through the machinations of one Squerciafico, it surrendered at discretion.

The booty was immense; 40,000 of the inhabitants were sent to Constantinople, and 1500 young Geneose nobles were compelled to enter the corps of *Janizaries*. Eight days after the capture, Ahmed Keduk gave a grand banquet to the principal Armenian citizens, who, in concert with the Genoese traitor, had delivered up the town into his hands. At the end of the entertainment their host bade them *adieu* with all the politeness possible; but a different leave-taking awaited them outside. The door of the banqueting chamber opened on a narrow flight of steps, at the bottom of which was stationed a Turk, *scimitar* in hand, who, as each guest emerged, severed his head from his body. Treachery never fails to inspire contempt even in those in whose service it is practised; and the Ottoman seldom forgave such acts of baseless, although coupled, as was not unfrequently the case, with the crime of apostasy. Squerciafico himself was spaced only to be reserved for a like fate at Constantinople.

Otranto speedily fell. The inhabitants defended themselves with great courage, but the town was unprepared, and it was carried by assault after only a fortnights resistance. Of the 22,000 who formed the population, 12,000 were slaughtered without mercy; such as it was supposed might furnish a heavy ransom were reduced to slavery; the rest were subjected to treatment, compared with which slavery and death in any form would have been a welcome boon: wives and daughters brutally outraged before their husbands' and parents' faces; infants torn from their mothers' bosoms, and dashed against the walls.

The commandant, the archbishop, and his clergy, were singled out for the most horrible, of all deaths, and sawn asunder. Need it be added, that they who revelled in cruelties so truly diabolical, spared not the altars of God, or the images of the saints, or aught that was holy and venerable? All the, awful woes predicted by the Jewish prophets seemed to have come upon the world, and with such particularity and completeness, that it was difficult to see how any fuller accomplishment were possible. It was as if the mystery of iniquity were revealed, and the days of Antichrist had begun.

Despite this triumphant success on the shares of Italy, and the prospects of long-meditated conquest time opened before him, the failure before Rhodes rankled like a poisoned arrow in the heart of Mahomet. When the news, of the defeat of his armament reached the sultan, his fury was unbounded, nay, it may be said to have amounted to madness. None dared present themselves before him, and the *vizier* was thought to have had a fortunate escape, when he received no greater chastisement at the tyrant's hands than disgrace and exile.

After the first outburst of rage was over, Mahomet prepared for vengeance. Declaring that his troops were only invincible under his own command, he assembled a force of 300,000 men, whom he led into Asia Minor, designing from thence to fall upon Rhodes, and crush the audacious islanders to the dust. But his hours were numbered; he died at Nicomedia after a brief and sudden sickness, which is said to have been his first; in the frenzy of his rage pouring forth wild and passionate expressions to the last, and shrieking in the very agonies of his death-struggle the words, "Rhodes, Rhodes, Rhodes!" They carried his body to Constantinople, and buried it in the mosque he had founded, and the inscription he had himself dictated on his deathbed was placed over his tomb:

I intended to conquer Rhodes and to subdue Italy.

CHAPTER 5

Bajazet and Djem

The repulse of the infidels from the walls of Rhodes raised the order and its grand master to even a higher reputation than they had yet enjoyed. The name of D'Aubusson and his gallant knights rang through Europe, and excited an enthusiasm of admiration; and singular incidents followed on the death of Mahomet II. Which served to extend the esteem and influence of the order even among the infidels themselves.

Mahomet left two sons, Bajazet and Djem;[1] the first a mild and pacific prince, the other generous and warlike, and no mean scholar for his age and nation. Hardly was Bajazet on the throne, when he made proposals of peace to Rhodes. D'Aubusson, unwilling to accede thereto on his own authority, sent, like a dutiful son of the Church, to consult the Holy See. But ere an answer came, a strange thing happened. A struggle for the imperial power between the partisans of the rival princes ended in the defeat and flight of Djem; and as the fate of a fallen prince, whose arms had been turned against his successful competitor, could be small matter of doubt, according to the ordinary policy of the Ottoman court, Djem, now a friendless fugitive, knew that his life was not worth an hour's purchase should he fall into his brother's hands.

Whither should he go, or where apply for refuge? His decision was a singular one: something perhaps in his own frank and generous nature had endeared the name of D'Aubusson to his

---
1. Written also Zain or Zizim.

imagination; certain it is that he felt a warm and enthusiastic admiration for the heroic order which had defied his father's invincible arms, and it was to the hospitality and magnanimity of the Knights of St. John that he resolved to trust his fortunes.

Before his messengers could reach the capital of Rhodes, the position of the unfortunate prince became still more desperate. Alone on the coast of Lycia,—for he had sent his followers away, bidding them seek their own safety,—a party of fifty Mamelukes suddenly appeared from behind a rock and attempted to seize him. Throwing himself from his saddle, he leapt into the sea and struck out to a poor fishing-boat that he knew to own a Christian for its master; for, after the fashion of the times, it bore at its prow a rude wooden cross, without which no fisherman of that day would have thought of venturing to sea.

The Mamelukes, urging their steeds into the water, were close behind him,—a price was on his head living or dead; but as they almost touched their prize, the strong arm of the rowers lifted him over the side, and a few strokes of the oar sufficed to place the boat and its crew beyond the reach of the pursuers. Djem knew that his only safety was now to remain among the Christians; and hastily writing the following lines, he attached the letter to an arrow, and shot it among the Mamelukes on the shore.

> King Djem to King Bajazet his inhuman brother [2]
> God and the Prophet are witness of the unhappy necessity that drives me to take refuge among the Christians. Not content with depriving me of my just rights to the empire, you pursue me from country to country, and to save my life you force me to seek refuge among the Knights of Rhodes, the bitter enemies of our house. If our father could have foreseen such a profanation of the Ottoman name, he would have strangled you with his own hands; but Heaven will not fail to avenge your cruelty, and I trust yet to live to be witness of your punishment.

---

2. Von Hammer considers this letter apocryphal.

Djem was received at Rhodes with the courtesy due to his rank, and with all pomp and ceremony. A horse richly caparisoned was prepared for him, and so mounted he passed through the streets thronged with spectators, and strewn for the occasion with sprigs of myrtle and odoriferous flowers, which, as they were pressed by his horse's hoofs, emitted a delicious fragrance. Splendid hangings everywhere met his eye, and has ear was regaled with strains of martial music. The grand master himself came forth to greet him, mounted also on a noble steed, and followed by a brilliant train. It was a strange and might have been an embarrassing meeting: on the one side, the head of that great military order, whose very vocation it was to do battle with the infidel; and on the other, the brother of the reigning sultan, nay himself, in pretension, the very commander of the forces of Islam; and that too within those walls which had so lately and so successfully defied the Moslem arms.

But it would seem that in the whole matter the order acted but in accordance with their grand duty of hospitality. To be the asylum of the destitute and oppressed was so natural to them, that their gates opened to receive the fugitive who claimed their protection, almost without a question of his faith; for a Hospitaller to have refused to receive a guest would have been a disgrace upon the name; and moreover the rules of chivalry exacted the most scrupulous courtesy to enemies. The question, therefore, of Djem's reception was soon settled; and the treatment he received during his forty days' residence there was noble and princely, as the unfortunate fugitive himself acknowledged in the manifesto he drew up before leaving them, to place himself under the protection of the French king. For, indeed, he felt Rhodes itself was too near his brother's court; secret assassins could easily be found to reach him there; and so, with D'Aubusson's consent, he departed, falling at his feet and embracing them as he bade his generous entertainer farewell, and vowing, were he ever restored to his rights, to observe an inviolable friendship with the Order of St. John.

In France he met with but a cold reception, and retired to a priory of the order; being supported partly by an appanage which the grand master obtained from Bajazet for him by dint of skilful treaty, and partly by the private liberality of D'Aubusson himself. So munificent, indeed, was the grand master's bounty, that the chapter general declared, after an examination of the accounts, that he ought to be reimbursed out of the treasury of the order the large sums he had expended on the prince.[3]

This singular episode in the history of the order has been represented by some as an artful stroke of policy on the part of the grand master; though, indeed, it would be difficult to see what he could gain by the open protection of Bajazet's rival at the very moment when terms of peace were being negotiated with that monarch, As for any violation of safe conduct, it does not appear how far such stipulation, if stipulation there were, extended; and Taaffe is of opinion that anyhow it was faithfully observed in according him a safe and honour? Able reception at Rhodes, and freedom to depart when he pleased. It seems incontestable, indeed, that in the terms of pacification afterwards made with Bajazet, the strict guardianship of Djem, so as to prevent his making farther attempts against his brother's crown, formed one of the conditions; but it does not seem unfitting or in any way unworthy of D'Aubusson's reputation, that, whilst protecting the life of the fugitive prince, he should also prevent him from forming new plots against the sultan, whose claims to the sovereignty as elder brother could scarcely be disputed.

Our own history tells us how difficult a trust is the guardianship of a fallen and a hostile prince: in the end it must ever take the form of imprisonment; but that he was treated harshly or "like a prisoner," the author we have quoted above declares to be "ridiculously untrue." Reasons there were every way why he should be detained in honourable ward, were it only to keep a curb on Bajazet, and to save Christendom and the world from

---

[3]. This is Taaffe's defence of D'Aubusson and of the order against the charge of "making money" by Djem's captivity, as is asserted by Ottoman historians. That prince's expenditure, he says, was very great, owing to the state in which he lived, and the constant coming and going of ambassadors to and from Constantinople and other courts. The knights also maintained at their own cost Djem's only son Amurath, who became a Christian! and his family.

a renewal of the horrible atrocities of Turkish warfare. Besides, Djem's partisans were known to be the most virulent of all the infidels in their hatred of Christians in general, and of the knights in particular; and had he been allowed to put himself at their head, the greatest evils might have resulted to religion and civilisation.

The unhappy prince is supposed to have died of poison in Italy, whither by his own desire he had been removed from France. But the affair, even on the confession of those who are strong as to the fact, is involved in perhaps inextricable mystery; and indeed the whole history of those times, and of the papal court in particular, has been so overlaid with falsehood, that it is impossible, with all the existing materials before us, and after a careful and impartial collation of conflicting authorities, to arrive at any satisfactory conclusion.

But anyhow they who most blame the grand master and the order for allowing the Turkish prince to pass out of their safe keeping, never so much as hint at their participation in his death. On the contrary, they say that the first step taken for carrying out the design against his life was the removal of his faithful Hospitallers. They describe the horror and indignation felt at Rhodes when the unhappy news arrived; and declare that it was as a death-blow to the grand master, who felt that such a catastrophe was a blot on the honour of Christian hospitality, and deeply lamented the loss of one whom in their short intimacy he had learnt to regard with interest and even with affection.

However, were any exculpation of D'Aubusson send his order required, it may be found in Djem's own letter to the grand master, written shortly before his death, wherein he deplores his separation from the Knights, and assures them of his eternal gratitude; declaring, by the way, that, except that he was deprived of his usual guard of knights, which vexed him much and caused him infinite grief, he was "honourably and sufficiently well treated." [4]

D'Aubusson's was a proud position during the three-and-

---

4. Taaffe gives the letter at length. D'Aubusson's accusers of course deny its genuineness.

twenty years that his government lasted after the siege of Rhodes. The pope presented him with a cardinal's hat; all nations were proud of him; the emperor refused to declare war against the sultan without his assent; and the English king, sending him a present of guns and Irish horses, says courteously in his letter,

> The guns are for the defence of Rhodes, but the horses for the use of him whom I love and reverence as my father.

When, towards the close of his life, a new Christian league was formed against the infidel, including the emperor, the republic of Venice, and the kings of France, Castile, Portugal, and Hungary, with most of the Italian princes, a general consent was given to the papal decree which named him *generalissimo* of the Christian armies. But the result of this great league was like most of those which preceded it. War between the European sovereigns themselves soon broke it up, and each power made peace with the Moslem on his own terms; so that the order was, as usual, left alone and unsupported to carry on the war.

When the last sail of the French fleet disappeared from Lesbos, the rendezvous of the Christian allies, D'Aubusson gave way to a sadness not unusual to him, as to many a great mind besides, which, with its eye fixed on its own lofty and noble views, ever meets with littleness and disgusts in the world around. He felt there was a stain on the honour of Christendom, and the chill of that disappointment is said never to have left him.

Still he would not have abandoned all attempts to restrain the Ottoman power; and seeing the siege of Lesbos to be impracticable, he would nevertheless have made some strong and imposing demonstrations against Constantinople, more, however, to maintain a continual and vigilant reconnoissance than to provoke actual hostilities; and for this purpose he directed himself to England. But in London also he met with "ice that would not melt, seas and mountains that brought forth nothing " He was then in his seventy-eighth year, and seeing there were no hopes, as things then stood, of effecting anything for the Christian cause, he returned to Rhodes, and spent the last two years of his life in regulating the affairs of his people and of his order. The last edicts which bore his authority were full of a religious spirit: they were directed against blasphemy and public swearing, against luxury in dress, and other abuses. The great captain never forgot that he was also a religious; and none ever enforced religious discipline among his subjects with more effectual severity.

His last hour was worthy of his name, (gathering his knights around his bed, he bade them adhere to their rule; and after many holy words spoken with a calm and sweet serenity, he closed his eyes, and expired without a struggle. No prince or grand master was ever so lamented. In the funeral procession (to adopt Taaffe's description), first went every religious corporation in Rhodes; next came the Greek *patriarch* and all his clergy; then the Latin clergy of the order; a little before the bier two hundred of the principal Rhodians clothed in black, and bearing lighted torches in their hands; and following them, the knights, carrying their colours drooping, so as to sweep the ground; the bier with the corpse borne on the shoulders of the priors, and the grand crosses of the order; after which marched the long troop of mourners, two hundred and fifty in number; and loud was the weeping from the windows, streets, terraces, and roofs, and the wailing, and lamentations of the whole populace.

Over his tomb was broken his truncheon of command, together with his spurs; and so were concluded all the doleful formalities with singular testimonies of heart-felt grief. Never was son or parent more truly mourned than was D'Aubusson by his knights and Rhodian subjects. They saw in him the honour of chivalry, the father of the poor, the saviour of Rhodes, the sword and buckler of Christendom; and his death was the signal for hostilities which, during his life, had never been pursued by Bajazet, who, strange to say, really loved and honoured the famous grand master as much as he doubtless feared him as an adversary.

Bajazet had nothing of the ferocity or wax-like genius of his race. The civil war in which he found himself engaged on first coming to the throne had obliged him to recall Ahmed Keduk from Otranto, which was compelled after an obstinate defence to capitulate to the Duke of Calabria. The infidels thus dispossessed of the only place they held in Italy were happily never able to recover their footing on its shores. His reign was chiefly signalised by great improvements in the Turkish navy, and increasing power at sea. He carried on frequent wars with the Venetians and Hungarians, and took the cities of Lepanto, Coron, and Modon. The carnage at the last-named place was immense; the inhabitants being put to the sword without regard to sex or age; nearly all the nobles perished; and the bishop, Andrew Falconi, was slain while in the act of exhorting the people to fight for their faith and liberties. The conquerors set fire to the town after its capture, and the conflagration lasted five whole days. In resisting the encroachments of the Mameluke sultans of Egypt Bajazet was less successful; the result of the contest being in his adversary's favour, who, at the peace that was concluded between them, retained three strong places which he had seized and occupied.

On the whole, therefore, the Ottoman power may be considered to have remained stationary during his reign; and had he been followed by princes of no more energy, or no better success in war, the decline of the Turkish empire might have dated from his accession, or at any rate would have been anticipated many years. But the dynasty of the sultans boasts a worthy representative in his son and successor Selim. Seizing the reins of government, he commenced his rule by becoming the murderer of his brothers and nephews, if not of his father, and made great preparations for a second invasion of Rhodes.

On one occasion, indeed, his fleet, as it returned from Alexandria, menaced the island, but withdrew after making hostile demonstrations. His death, eight years after his accession, prevented the execution of the design; but a glance at his conquests during that short period may show how the circle of the Ottoman power was gathering closer and closer round the devoted island: Egypt, Syria, and Arabia, were now added to the Turkish dominions, which thus became nearly double in extent; and the crescent ruled over every country of the East, save the yet unconquered soil where waved the banner of the Knights of the Cross. Selim may be regarded as the very impersonation of the worst qualities of Mahometanism in general, and of the Turkish character in particular.

One instance of his fanaticism may suffice. He had resolved on extirpating the very profession of Christianity from his dominions; and to this end actually ordered the conversion of all the churches into mosques, and the reception of the Koran by all his Greek subjects, under pain of death. From this sanguinary determination he was diverted only by the strong remonstrances of the Greek *patriarch*, whose efforts were seconded by those of the grand *vizier* and chief *mufti*. He reminded him of the solemn pledges given by Mahomet on the capture of Constantinople, and appealed to the very Koran itself against such wholesale slaughter and direct infraction of treaties.

Selim yielded thus far that he consented to tolerate the practice of the Christian religion; but he would no longer allow some of the finest buildings of the city to be devoted to its worship; these he gave up to the Mussulmans, and directed structures of wood to be erected in their stead. Thus was completed the degradation of the once Christian metropolis of the East; and, except that their religious assemblies were not forbidden, and their priests were not proscribed, and the saying of Mass was not made a capital offence, and there was no ruinous fine for non-attendance at the Moslem service, the Greek subjects of the Porte were reduced to the same condition as were the Catholics of England in the reign of Elizabeth.

The death of Selim (September 22, 1520) raised to the throne of the Ottoman empire its greatest monarch, in the person of Solyman the Magnificent, whose name is so familiar to the students of that period of history which we might denominate "the age of Charles V." He succeeded to the vast power left him by his father at the same time that Charles was elected to the Imperial dignity: their strength was well matched, and it may be said that, by a kind of instinct, they felt themselves rivals from the moment of their accession. But the policy and character of Solyman differed widely from those of the princes who had preceded him in the government of the East. The influence of European civilisation was gradually making itself felt; and the Turks, learning something of refinement from the nations whom they subjugated, were beginning to exhibit some modification in that savage barbarism which had hitherto alone distinguished them, Solyman's government of his empire was conducted on principles of justice and equity,—virtues unknown under rulers whose only laws had been the *scimitar* or the bowstring; and the increased intelligence of the Turkish administration, while it in no wise softened the merciless character of its hostilities, added in no small degree to its power, and consequently to the danger of its Christian adversaries. Among various notes and memoranda left by the Emperor Selim, pointing out with remarkable sagacity the steps necessary to be taken for assuring the safety of his enormous dominions, the possession of two places was named as essential for the preservation of the empire:—they were Belgrade and Rhodes, both which had successfully defied the arms of Mahomet. Solyman determined on both enterprises; and preparations for the siege of Belgrade were commenced in the very year of his accession.

This bulwark of Christendom was compelled to capitulate on the 29th of August 1521. The Hungarians made a most gallant defence and resisted twenty desperate assaults; but to the overwhelming numbers of the beleaguering army and the incessant fire of the Turkish batteries were added the disaffection and treachery of allies and mercenaries. Schism again came to the aid of the infidels; and Belgrade, like Constantinople, fell into the power of the Turks. According to established custom Solyman took formal possession of the place in the name of the false prophet by "saying prayers" in the cathedral, which thus became a mosque, and was then, to use the expression appropriated to such profanations, "purged from idolatry" by the destruction of the altars and the removal of every Christian ornament and symbol. Having thus completed his first great conquest, and established a Turkish stronghold on the Hungarian frontier, the youthful sultan marched back in triumph to Constantinople.

The result meanwhile was watched at Rhodes with anxious interest; for all very well knew, should Belgrade fall, where the next blow would be aimed. Fabricius Carretto was then grand master; the same to whom D'Aubusson was thought to have predicted his election during the storming of St. Nicholas; a man of literary and refined habits, learned in all the learning of the age, which it must be remembered was the age of the Medici and of the revival of letters, skilled in all dead and living languages, a gallant warrior, and at the same time; a pacific and popular prince; the brother in arms of D'Aubusson, and the friend and correspondent of Leo X. He died in the month of January 1521; and with the daily expectation of a second siege, the choice of his successor was a matter of interest not merely to Rhodes, but to Christendom.

The votes fell on one worthy in every way to rank among the galaxy of illustrious princes, who adorned the opening of the sixteenth century: Philip Villiers de L'Isle Adam must be added to the list which already included Francis, Charles, Leo, and the Sultan Solyman. He was at Paris when the news of his election reached him, but instantly set out for Rhodes, arriving there, after happily escaping from a fire which broke out in his vessel, a violent tempest, and the corsair Curtogli,[5] who lay in wait for him off Cape St. Angelo, and through whose fleet the dauntless grand master passed under cover of the night. His arrival in Rhodes was joyfully welcomed. There had been no declaration of war on Solyman's part; yet it was scarcely needed, for Belgrade had fallen, and the intelligence was conveyed to L'Isle Adam in a letter from Solyman himself, the friendly terms of which threw but a transparent veil over the threats they were intended to convey.

The correspondence between the sultan and the grand master may fairly be looked upon as a curiosity in the history of

---

5. Subsequently appointed by Solyman grand admiral of the Turkish fleet.

diplomacy, and as such we subjoin the letters.

> Solyman Sultan, by the grace of God King of Kings, Sovereign of Sovereigns, most high Emperor of Byzantium and Trebizond, most powerful King of Persia, Arabia, Syria, and Egypt, Supreme Lord of Europe and Asia, Prince of Mecca and Aleppo, Possessor of Jerusalem, and Ruler of the Universal Sea, to Philip Villiers de L'Isle Adam, Grand Master of Rhodes, wishes health.
> We congratulate you on your new dignity, and on your arrival in your states, desiring that you may reign there happily with yet greater glory than your predecessors have done. It only rests with you to snare in our good graces. Accept our friendship, therefore; and, as a friend, be not the last to congratulate us on the conquests we have just achieved in Hungary, where we have made ourselves masters of the important city of Belgrade, having caused all such as dared to resist us to rail under our redoubtable sword. Farewell.

> Brother Philip Villiers de L'Isle Adam, Grand Master of Rhodes, to Solyman, Sultan of the Turks.
> I have well understood the purport of your letter, delivered to me by your ambassador. Your proposals of peace are as agreeable to me as they are disagreeable to Curtogli. That corsair omitted no efforts to surprise me on my passage from France; but not having succeeded in his project, and being unable to resolve on quitting these seas without causing us some damage, he has tried to carry off two of our merchant vessels on the coast of Lycia; but the galleys of the order have compelled him to fly. Farewell.

This letter was despatched by a Greek merchant, the grand master not judging it expedient to trust one of his knights in the hands of the wily sultan. But anxious to entrap a representative of the order whose presence at his court might be turned to good account, Solyman, in his second letter, pretended never to have received the reply to his first; it was intimated by his emissaries that it had not been delivered on account of the meanness of the messenger, who all the while had been seized, and tortured, to extract from him all the information he could give. Solyman meantime writes as follows:

> They assure us that the letter which our magnificence wrote to you has reached you, causing you more astonishment than pleasure. Rest assured that I do not mean to content myself with the taking of Belgrade, but that I shortly propose to myself a yet more important enterprise, of which you will soon have warning; for, indeed, you and your knights always keep a place in my memory.

This was a little more intelligible in its irony, and the grand master's answer was in the same tone.

> I am truly glad that you remember me and my order. You speak to me of your conquests in Hungary, and of your design of undertaking fresh ones, whose success you trust will be similar. I would have you consider that, of all the projects which men form, none are more uncertain than those which depend on the fate of arms. *Adieu.*

Shortly after this, a brigantine of the order was captured close to Rhodes, and the war may be said to have begun. Meanwhile there were not wanting traitors in Rhodes, who busily furnished the sultan with every information he required; one being a Jewish physician, who even received baptism for the purpose of blinding the Rhodians to his true character; another, yet more dangerous and powerful, being found unhappily in the ranks of the order, in the person of Andrew Damaral, chancellor, and grand prior of Castile. Old differences with L'Isle Adam, and a bitter jealousy of his elevation to power, contributed to induce this man to betray his trust; and it is said the final loss of the island was the result of his duplicity, as he had given a false report of the quantity of powder in the place; so that no sufficient supplies were laid in before the siege, when the vigilance of L'Isle Adam was employed in furnishing every other magazine.

Great preparations were indeed made: the ramparts were strengthened, the storehouses of forage and general provisions were replenished; fresh artillery was imported from Europe; and embassies numberless, and uniformly without result, were despatched to the Christian sovereigns to implore a timely succour. But all was in vain; Charles V. and Francis I. were just then playing their tournament for the world's applause; and in the rivalry of a miserable ambition were deaf to the call of duty. So Rhodes was left to take care of herself, the only ally she gained being the celebrated engineer, Gabriel Martinengo, who at great personal sacrifices joined the order, and was found of inestimable service during the siege.

There was a grand review and inspection of the knights and regular troops held before the grand master; a splendid and inspiriting sight. Each language drawn up before its inn—the knights in full armour, their scarlet surcoats, worn only in time of war, displaying the cross on every side; their numbers about six hundred, with some 6000 troops under their command; a handful of men soon to be matched with the swarms of an Ottoman armament. Each language was reviewed by a knight of its own division, every one touching his cross, and swearing that his arms and armour were his own. England was nobly represented, and her knights bore a distinguished part in the conflict that ensued; nor indeed can we avoid the observation, that so long as the English language existed in the order, its pre-eminent valour is noticed by all historians, and, as is well known, the important office of *Turcopolier*, or leader of the cavalry, belonged of right to the English nation.

Again we have occasion to notice and to admire the religious unity displayed at a time when jealousies between rival rites might so easily have sown seeds of dangerous dissensions. The two *patriarchs*, Greek and Latin, united in communion, knew no rivalry save that of enthusiasm in the common cause; and the spirit of the people was greatly animated and sustained by the eloquence of a Greek monk. The Greek archbishop harangued the *populace* in the streets: he was a noble old man, wise and gentle, but full of ardour; and he stood opposite an image of our Lady, holding the crucifix aloft, while he addressed his audience in strains of glowing fervour, and called on them to have trust in God and His dear Mother, and to dwell on those lofty thoughts of religion which are stronger than tower or bastion for defence; and to be firm and constant in faith and loyalty, and yield as true a service to their present grand master as they had yielded to the glorious D'Aubusson. The traditions of Rhodes, and its ancient glory, were not forgotten; and such words had the effect on the people which might have been expected: the Rhodians were like one man in their fearless vigorous resolve to suffer all things before surrender or disgrace.

It is touching to read how every historian of the order, before entering on the sad history of its downfall at Rhodes, gives, as it were, one last lingering glance over the lovely island, never again to be what it had now been for more than two hundred years. That lofty capital, with the tipper town, crested with the battlemented palace of the grand master, surrounded by the dwellings of his knights; those picturesque streets, with all the curious carvings and ornaments of early ages, the knightly escutcheons on the walls and the arched doorways, which still remain; [6] the city, round in its form, but presenting from the sea the appearance of a graceful and brilliant crescent; the forts still guarded as before, but greatly strengthened in their defences, within whose

---

6. "Such was the esteem with which the valour of the knights had inspired the Turks, that they refrained from defacing their armorial bearings and inscriptions on the buildings. For more than 300 years the Ottomans have treated the memory of their brave foemen with the same respect; and the escutcheons of the Knights of St. John, who fought against Sultan Solyman for Rhodes, still decorate the long-captured city."
"The street of the knights is uninjured," writes Marshal Marmont, "and the door of each house is still ornamented with the escutcheon of the last inhabitant. The buildings have been spared, but are unoccupied; and we could almost fancy ourselves surrounded by the shades of departed heroes. The arms of France, the noble *fleurs-de-lis*, are seen in all directions. I observed those of the Clermont Tennerres, and of other ancient and illustrious families." (*Creasy*, vol. 1. p. 263.)
"The Turks," says Taaffe, "never destroyed so much of Rhodes as the French during their first days at Malta, pulling down all the statues of renowned heroes, and chiselling out the coats-of-arms everywhere, even over the palace." Vol. 4. p. 217.

bosom the cool clear waters bathed the very foot of the houses, and mirrored in their bright expanse the picture of that pile of palaces, which, half in shade and half in sunshine, gave back the rays of the son from their marble walls with the brilliancy of gold.

How lovely it all was! and the forty years which had elapsed since the last invasion had sufficed to restore to their pristine beauty the gardens and richly cultivated country that girdled it from the land; so that if you ascended the high steeple of St. John's church, (still standing as a mosque,) you might have gazed over the fairest landscape painter's eye could desire to rest upon, and might have caught the rich scent of the roses on those peaceful fields, and watched the waving of the corn, and the rustling leaves of vines and orange-trees,—all soon to be laid waste, and trampled down in mire and blood.

It was June; the very noontide of summer beauty lay upon the sloping hills of Rhodes; and many an eye, as it gazed for the last time on the lovely scene, was blinded with the tears of a prophetic feeling which told that the halcyon days of Rhodian glory were gone forever.

The suburbs were destroyed as before; and this time with so vigorous a good will as to draw forth particular notice and commendation from the eye-witnesses. Villas, farm-houses, and cottages demolished; trees cut down; corn uprooted, though the harvest was already ripening in that sunny land; nothing was left that could afford shelter, or food, or materials of war to the invader. The country people came pouring into the city, bringing with them provisions, animals, furniture, instruments of agriculture, all in strange confusion:

> the women, with their hair dishevelled, scratching their cheeks,[7] as is the custom of the place, weeping sore, and supplicating their Lord and God, with their tiny children lifting up their clasped hands to heaven, and praying Him to have compassion on them.

---

7. Fontanus, cited by Taaffe.

The citizens were armed and organised, and the sailors and harbour-men enrolled and charged with the defence of the port; the peasants set to work as pioneers; and the slaves compelled to labour in digging trenches and repairing and strengthening the fortifications. Lastly, our Lady of Philermos was brought in in solemn procession, and deposited in the church of St. Mark, clergy and people assisting in crowds; for now, as before, the defence of Rhodes was solemnly committed to her patronage.

Nor was it long before open declaration of war was made, couched in the following terms:

To the Grand Master and his Knights, and to all the Inhabitants of Rhodes, warning:
"The piracies which you continue to exercise against my faithful subjects, and the insult you audaciously oner to my imperial majesty, oblige me to command you instantly to render up your island and fortress into my hands. If this you do forthwith, I swear by the God who made heaven and earth,—by the hundred and twenty-four thousand prophets,—by the four sacred books which fell from heaven,—and by our great prophet Mahomet,—that you shall have free liberty to depart from the island, and the inhabitants to remain therein without hurt or damage. But if you yield not instant obedience to my orders, you shall all pass under the edge of my invincible sword; and the towers, the bastions, and the walls of Rhodes shall be reduced to the level of the grass that grows at their feet.

To this peremptory summons of the sultan it was resolved in council of the knights that the only answer accorded him should issue from the cannon's mouth. Rhodes now knew that the hour of peril was at hand; the inhabitants of the neighbouring islands belonging to the order, many of them expert in war, were summoned in, and set to garrison the various forts under command of chosen knights; but ere the enemy appeared, and when every preparation had been made, each man being assigned his post and duty with a particularity the details of which might only fatigue the reader, the grand master ordered that all should make ready for action by fasts and prayer,—he himself setting the example; for whenever the cares of business and government left him a moment free, he was to be seen at the foot of the altar. The knights and citizens trusted as much in his prayers as in his valour, and were used to say that Heaven itself was interested in the cause of so holy a prince.

All through the siege he wore the same sweet gracious look; a smile ever ready upon his lips; nothing of hurry or passion in his manner, but the tranquillity that became him as a religious, well fitted with the gallant bearing of the knight. You might see him kneel down at times in his armour, just putting aside his helmet, to pray on the spot where he stood. He ate with the common soldiers, and sometimes went on guard at night like a private sentinel; and this from that true poverty of spirit for which he was remarkable, and which made men revere him as a saint at the same time that they followed him as a captain. Indeed, it was whispered that something of a supernatural, superhuman character attached to him; and they scarce knew whether to wonder most at his gifts of valour or of prayer.

It was early on the morning of the 26th of June 1522, when the sentinel on the top of St. Stephen's Hill espied the Turkish fleet advancing on the eastern side, and at the distance of about a mile. Tidings were instantly sent to the grand master, who received them as though it were a matter of which he was already well informed. It was within the *octave* of the feast of St. John; and the custom was in Rhodes to make a daily procession during that time, which the grand master would not permit to be interrupted this year, nor even on this day. Despite, therefore, the excitement and consternation that prevailed, all was conducted as though the city were in profoundest peace. The *populace* assembled in St. John's church; and after High Mass, the procession was made round the church as heretofore, only with something of unusual solemnity and care. Then the grand master came before the altar, and, going up the steps, reverently opened the tabernacle door, and took out the Most Holy Sacrament in the

Ostensorium;—first genuflecting, and remaining for a moment in prayer, he took it in his hands, and turning, exhibited it to the people; after which he prayed for them all,—for Rhodes, and for its church and children, that God would turn away the danger, and give His servants the blessings of peace.

So, replacing the Blessed Sacrament in the tabernacle, he left the altar, and causing the church doors to be shut, gave out the orders for everyone to proceed to his post.

As he himself returned to his palace after this touching ceremony, word was brought him that the enemy's fleet was close to land; he heard the news with his usual tranquillity, and only ordered the city gates to be closed. An hour afterwards the palace gates were thrown open, and there rode out a brilliant and gallant train. Many knights in armour and scarlet surcoats, the three standards floating over their heads, each borne by chosen men, to whom they had been solemnly delivered in charge; and one, whereon the white crass was quartered with the arms of the grand master, was carried by a young Englishman, who found an early death at the very beginning of the siege. L'Isle Adam, in golden armour, was at their head; and as the procession came along, and the trumpets sounded with a loud triumphant flourish, such a thrill of glad and glorious enthusiasm stirred through the crowd as banished fear; and they rushed to window and terraced roof to watch the coming of the Turkish fleet, and almost to welcome its advance.

What a magnificent spectacle! In the streets below that gorgeous chivalric procession, the finest steeds and the brightest armour, and the gallantest hearts of Christendom! Suddenly, and as though by some preconcerted signal, on every rampart and battlemented wall, from the inns of the various languages and all the posts of separate command, there wave a thousand flags. Each nation has its own proud ensign and its own representative among the Knights of Rhodes. There you may see the golden lilies of France floating not far from the royal lions of England; there is the plain cross of Savoy, first borne in honour of the order; there are the white flag of Portugal, and the time-honoured banners of Castile and Auvergne; and you know that beneath the silken folds of each are posted brave and gallant hearts, who will add fresh honour to their old renown.

Look out over the port to the tower of St. Nicholas, the key of Rhodes; twenty Provençal knights are there, claiming, as Provence ever would, the post of danger and of glory. The rest of the French you may distinguish drawn up with admirable regularity from the tower of France to the Ambrosian gate; and thence to the gate of St. George stand the Germans—you may tell them by the imperial standard. Spain and England stand together; the banner of the *Turcopolier*, Sir John Buck, waves out over their ranks; only nineteen English are there, but every man a hero, and ready for a hero's death. The grand master will head them himself; for it is thought the English bastion will bear the hardest brunt; but his ordinary post of command when not in action will be opposite the church of our Lady of Victories.

It stands below you,—and from the platform in front you may reach each post in a few moments,—a stately and a noble building; but Rhodes has many such, though none to equal St John's, whose delicate tapering steeple, "buried in air, and looking to the sky,—the deep blue sky" of Rhodes,— catches the eye when you are miles off at sea, and seems to place the glittering cross that crests its summit half way 'twixt earth and heaven. If you watch, you may see the four chief grand crosses, and their companies of relief, as they are termed, going the rounds of the ramparts. There is an hourly inspection of the defences day and night; and when the grand crosses are not there, six hundred men take it by turns to make the circuit, under two French and two Spanish knights, with rather summary directions how to treat malefactors or traitors. Very little of trial by jury, but a brief court-martial and a running noose.

Préjan de Bidoux has the charge of the batteries; he is the governor of Cos: but after beating off thirty Turkish galleys from his own island, he sent off straight to Rhodes, to beg the grand master's leave to come and join in the defence; and so soon as the joyful permission was granted, he threw himself into a small vessel, and was in the port before the Turks could stop him, though it is thought his brigantine must have pushed through the very midst of their fleet.

Lastly, those venerable unwarlike forms, bearded and saint-like, at whose approach knights and sentinels and glittering ranks kneel down as for a father's blessing, are not the least among the defenders of Rhodes. Leonard Balestein is the Latin metropolitan, reckoned the most eloquent preacher of his day; Clement, the Greek archbishop, you have already heard of; and they love one another as brothers; so that, as they go from post to post, they are seldom to be met apart.

All this you may see as you look down upon the city. But glance over the ocean, and another spectacle awaits you. The blue line of the Levant, sparkling in the summer sunshine, and kissed into life and motion by a northern breeze; and on its heaving bright expanse 300 Turkish sail, gathered from every coast that owns the Ottoman rule,—from Egypt, Syria, and every part of Asia,—and having on board, in addition to the regular crews, 8000 chosen soldiers and 2000 pioneers; whilst 100,000 men under Solyman himself are advancing along the western coast of Asia Minor.[8] Alas for Rhodes and her 6000 defenders! We may well be pardoned this glance at her as she stands in the last tour of her beauty and display. The 26th of June sees her indeed magnificent to the eye, and in all the pomp and pride of chivalry and warlike show; but soon that gay and martial music will be exchanged for the thunder of artillery, and those battlemented bannered walls will be crumbling to the dust.

We must, however, commence a fresh chapter before entering on the story of the last siege of Rhodes.

---

8. In the end there seem to have been 200,000 Turks, including pioneers, collected in Rhodes.

CHAPTER 6

Ill Success of Turkish Troops

The Turkish forces now before the capital of Rhodes were commanded by Mustapha Pasha, whose counsel had in the first instance urged on the sultan to undertake the enterprise, and to whom its conduct had been entrusted. The troops were landed on the 28th of July 1522, but siege-operations did not commence until the 1st of August, In the expectation of finding an abundance of provisions in the fertile island, scarcely airy had been brought by the fleet.

The first thing, therefore, perceived on the disembarkment of the troops was the fact that the army stood in no small danger of starvation. Instead of the abundance they had expected to meet with, they found on all sides a desert, without crops, inhabitants, or forage; for to such a state had the wise precautions of the grand master reduced the whole country round. The wells were choked and rendered nauseous and poisonous; and Mustapha soon found that to keep the field for many days together, he would require something more than the garlic, dried fruits, fish, and salt meat, which, as his physician Ramadan tells us, were all the provisions he had deemed it necessary to bring

His principal hopes of success had been placed in the operations of his miners: but at the commencement the frequent sorties of the Knights, and their ruinous fire, prevented the Turks from gaining any advantage; and what with continual conflicts in which they were always the losers, the prospect of starvation, and no hopes of booty, the soldiers of the besieging army showed symptoms of discontent which soon broke out into open mutiny. Peri Pasha, the second in command, and appointed by the sultan to furnish him with exact intelligence of all that passed, lost no time in acquainting him with the gloomy aspect of affairs; adding, that perhaps the "gentle omnipotence" of his presence might restore the courage of his troops. The celerity with which Solyman acted on this advice rivalled, says Bosio, the intrepid marches of Caesar.

Embarking with a few followers in two small open boats, he appeared at Rhodes before his approach could have been suspected, and declared to the army, who received him with all military honours, that he was only come to punish their rebellion and decimate his cowardly battalions. The interference of Peri Pasha, perhaps prearranged, turned him from this design; and the troops, recalled to their duty by his presence, sought to regain their reputation for valour and discipline by entering on the siege with an ardour hitherto unparalleled. If we are to judge by the language employed by Ramadan in his history of the expedition, the Turkish soldiery were stimulated to the conquest of the island by descriptions addressed to their vilest passions,—descriptions which, by throwing a veil of voluptuousness and romance over the most detestable enormities, were calculated to stifle every feeling of humanity in their breasts, and to make them regard the worst crimes they could perpetrate as the legitimate rewards of bravery and daring. But what else could be expected of a creed so foul and revolting? With a Mahometan heaven as the hoped-for reward, sensuality the most licentious must be a virtue and a merit in the eyes of the "true believer."

The loss sustained by the garrison in their sorties, though slight in comparison with that of their opponents, was judged by the grand master too great to make the continuance of this mode of conflict prudent or advisable. A hundred or a thousand men were little for the enemy to lose, whilst the fall of a single knight was felt as a disaster by the Christians. Keeping close, therefore, within their ramparts, they left the infidels at liberty to. erect their batteries and make all their dispositions undisturbed, save by the artillery from the walls. The high steeple of St. John's served as an observatory from whence every movement of the hostile forces could easily be discerned. From its summit the whole camp and city might be viewed, spread out as on a map; and the Turks were well aware of the use made of the building by the Christian engineers.

Very early, therefore, it became the mark for their artillery, and almost the first cannonade directed against it brought it to the ground. The Turks had with them twelve monstrous guns, two of which discharged, as on the former occasion, balls eleven or twelve palms in diameter.[1] And now began the same furious and incessant firing which had been endured at the previous siege; day and night might be heard that long continuous roar, responded to by a fire as hot and destructive on the part of the garrison. Mines, too, underneath burrowed the ground in every direction; and it is said that Martinengo, the engineer of the order, broke into no less than fifty-five of these in the progress of his operations.

The walls of Rhodes were of prodigious height; "as high," says the Arabian physician before named, "as Sultan Mahmoud's minarets, and broad as the streets of Constantinople." To command these, therefore, the Turks undertook a truly wonderful work, being nothing less than the construction of two vast mounds or hills, artificially composed of earth and stones brought together with immense labour, which rose ten or twelve feet above the battlements, and gave extraordinary effect to the batteries which were planted on their summits. The laborious engineering works undertaken by both parties during the siege were indeed of an herculean character; and though such operations are for the most part of little interest to the general reader, yet they become invested with an almost romantic character from the scale on which we find them here conducted. In the attack on St. Nicholas, for instance, the *pasha*, remembering the fail-

---

1. Some of these enormous balls are still found from time to time in front of the walls and within the fortress; proof positive of the truth of the assertion made by historians. The Turks also used shells for the first time in this siege. (Von Hammer.)

ure of his predecessor at the former siege, dressed his batteries, and worked them by night only, every morning dismantling the guns and burying them in the sand.

He flattered himself he had succeeded, when he saw the western rampart fall in ruins; but all the while his labour had been rivalled and surpassed by his indefatigable opponents, who had built and armed a new fortress within the old one; so that, as the outer ruin fell, like a curtain drawn aside, it but displayed a new wall, which stood behind bristling with cannon, and rendering necessary the recommencement of the whole attack.

We shall not, however, call on our readers to accompany us through the course of these operations; but passing over three months of weary battery and bloodshed, ask him to enter St. John's church on an afternoon in the first week of September, where he will find a crowd of all ranks (but women mostly, for the men are at the walls,) praying silently, while the choir is just about to begin vespers. Kneeling in his wonted place is Villiers de L'Isle Adam; he is ever there when not engaged in active conflict; and just now there is a lull in the cannonading, as though the enemy were perplexed at the obstinate resistance, and were planning a fresh method of attack. His noble venerable countenance is sad, though not discouraged: how should it be otherwise? His little force is now reduced to scarcely 3000 men besides the knights; of them 300 alone are left.

The powder is failing; rumours of treachery everywhere abroad, and no news of succour yet from Europe. A courier has been sent to Rome, and bears the news that the struggle is desperate; women fighting because there are not men enough to work the batteries, and no provisions left but bread and water. He wears his *cuirass*,—for indeed he never lays it aside, but even in church is always ready for a hasty summons; just now, however, there seems a little respite; that long and deafening roar is still, and you may hear the sweet voiced of the choir as they intone the versicles:

Deus, in adjutorium meum intende: Domine, ad adjuvandum me festina.

But the rest is drowned in a sudden interruption. First a strange and hideous rumbling underground: the city trembles as from an earthquake; then a shock, and a loud explosion, shrieks of dying and wounded, and cries of combat; a wild disordered confusion of all noises, and the hill of stones and rocks upon the roofs, give notice of some great disaster. So indeed it was; for the greater part of the English bastion had been blown into the, air by an enormous mine; and the Turks, taking advantage of the confusion, were preparing for the assault.

"I accept the omen," cried the grand master, as he repeated the words which the choir had just sung; then turning to the knights who surrounded him, "Come, dear brothers," he said, "we must exchange the sacrifice of praise for that of our lives" and seizing a lance from an attendant, he hurried to the spot.

Not all the bastion was destroyed; but the part still standing was already in possession of the Turks, when the grand master and his intrepid followers appeared upon the scene. Not a dozen in number, they throw themselves on the enemy; everything is swept before them; the heavy blows from the stalwart arms hew in pieces all that opposes them; the banners just planted on the walls are torn down and thrown into the ditch, and their defenders flung after them as easily as though they were no greater weight than their own turbans.

In vain Mustapha heads his beaten soldiers sword in hand, and slays the foremost in retreat; in vain batteries play upon the smoking ruins, and column after column of fresh troops endeavour to regain the post occupied by such a handful of opponents, nothing can resist the Christian knights; and soon from the walls and every quarter that overlooks the scene there pour down on the besiegers' heads stones and fire-pots and other horrible war-missiles of the time—streams of flaming pitch and brimstone, that burn and blind them as they press forward to the breach, and deadly volleys of artillery which lay rank after rank upon the field. It was an hour's combat; but at length the thick masses of the enemy were forced to retreat. Never had the besiegers received so terrible a repulse; and Solyman, as he walked over the ground viewing the myriads of his slain, was filled with a very passion of anguish when he marked amongst them the form of his favourite officer, the young chief of the Ottoman artillery.

Five days passed without any fresh attack. The *Janizaries* were murmuring at the prolonged struggle, which they deemed but a hopeless sacrifice of their blood, when Peri Pasha resolved on leading a new assault in person, directed this time against the Italian bastion. Extraordinary preparations were made on the part of the Turks: their troops, divided into seven bodies, were led on by chosen chiefs, and over each waved a standard solemnly committed to the charge of men chosen from the bravest and most ferocious of the veteran soldiers. Everything was done to impress the troops with a sense of the importance of their enterprise, and to inspire them with a confidence of victory. They approached the walls in profound silence, unperceived by their adversaries, and then raising a loud yell dashed up the breach, and made their way to the inner fortification.

The guards were few in number, and were soon cut to pieces; the night too was dark, and favoured the design of the assailants; and the garrison, wearied out with constant watching, were scarcely able to rouse themselves for the defence. Everything seemed gained; and Peri Pasha, followed by his seven standard-bearers, was in the act of directing all his strength upon the remnant of the besieged, who, though wounded and grievously thinned in numbers, still held their ground with an obstinate resolution,—when the Turkish line wavered as by some sudden panic; their arms, raised high to strike, fell powerless to their sides; and hesitating and scared, they shrank back upon those behind, as a gigantic and powerful form stepped between the ranks of the combatants, and seemed to clear the ground before him by the very majesty of his presence.

The flash of the fire-arms and the gleaming torch-light fell upon his face, and a shout of triumph rose from the Christian soldiers as they recognised the person of their grand master, who, with a few of his chosen knights, seemed to multiply himself, says the French historian, so as to be at every post of danger. Fontanus, an eyewitness, declares that at his very appearance, without the striking of a blow, the Turks drew back in fear; while turning to his followers, he exclaimed "Come, comrades, drive back these fellows from the breach; we must not fear men who are beaten every day."

His words were received with a cheer of victory, as they dashed upon the Turks with an impetuous shock: then you might have seen the grand master drive back the enemy with his single arm, [2] and as they threw themselves pell-mell from breach and rampart, the handful of defenders were left masters of the field.

This was the 13th of September. Another four days passed without the assault being renewed; when Mustapha, whose former failures had earned him a disgrace, gave orders for a fresh attack on the ruined bastion of England, determining to carry it at all costs, or die in the entrenchments, rather than again appear before Solyman after a new defeat. Achmet Pasha at the same time was to storm the quarters of Spain and Auvergne; and the besieged, thus divided in their strength, would, it was hoped, be unable to resist.

The battalions of the Turks, five in number, were met on the summit of the ruined ramparts by the English knights, with the *Turcopolier*, Sir John Buck, at their head. He was the first to fall; but in spite of their leader's death, the English gained the day, and held their shattered ruin by main courage and strength of arm for yet another month. After this repulse, the infidels began to think of abandoning the enterprise as hopeless; for they were wont to say one to another, that the knights could never be beaten in the presence of their chief; and as for "the cursed L'Isle Adam, he was everywhere at once."

Whilst they were hesitating and taking counsel, and whilst Solyman was endeavouring to infuse new spirit into their failing hearts, the treason of the Jewish physician was discovered, and met with its merited reward; and rightly interpreting the

---

2. "*Le grand maistre repoussa l'ennemi enpersonne, la teste baissée, et la pique en main.*" (Goussancourt.)

various movements in the enemy's camp to betoken the approach of some new and prodigious effort, the Christians spent the interval in preparations for meeting an assault general, which was indeed the plan on which Solyman had determined. For, as he said;

> whilst we attack these *giaours* at one place only at a time, we make war for their amusement; rather must they be assailed on all sides at once,—overwhelmed, inundated by our countless numbers, and, if not exterminated from the earth under our sabres, compelled to sue for mercy at our hands."

The 24th of September was the day indicated for this great attack, which was to be made at once on all four quarters of the city. From noon till midnight of the day before, heralds continued traversing the infidel camp crying, "Tomorrow is the assault; the stones and the land are the sultan's; the lives and the goods of the citizens are the prize of the conquerors." The grand master, after making the best disposal in his power of his little company, addressed them and the inhabitants in a few simple words. But there was little time for exhortation or farewell; for at break of day the wild trumpets from the *Janizaries*' band gave the signal for the advance; and those who stood at their posts on the walls could plainly see the sultan's throne erected on an adjacent hill which commanded a view of the whole field, so that his troops well knew that they fought under their sovereign's eye.

On they come under cover of a shower of arrows and the fire of their side batteries; they reach the walls, and are received by hissing streams of boiling oil, and fireballs that fill the air with a thick and noisome smoke; the bastions of England, Provence, Spain, and Italy are the quarters of attack, but the bloodiest fight is on that of England, and thither the grand master hastens, his presence in itself being like a very host of succour. The scaling-ladders are thrown down, and the ditch below is choked with the prostrate Turks; the cannon are pointed on their dense masses, which they rend and tear with a terrible carnage; charge after charge is made by the maddened infidels, but the English will not yield; priests, monks, even children join in the defence, and tiny hands may be seen hurling stones and sticks upon the advancing stormers with an audacity which nothing will appal.

All about the town the women may be seen running from bastion to bastion, carrying water to the wounded, whom they even bear off upon their shoulders. At one time forty Turkish standards are waving on the ramparts; but in a moment they are torn down, and the Cross is planted in their room. The assault is repulsed from England, and the cry is now, "Spain! Spain!"

Glancing in the direction of the Spanish bastion, L'Isle Adam sees the green flag and the crescent of the infidels on the topmost summit of the walls. In a moment he is on the spot: "Auvergne to the rescue!" rings from the ranks of the French, as the grand master stands among his countrymen, and with his own hands points the cannon of that bastion down upon the breach of Spain. The Turks dare not advance to secure their victory; and in another moment the commander De Bourbon, at the head of the French chivalry, is on the platform, and his knights are seen tearing down the colours, and clearing the ground at the point of their swords. But the *aga* of the *Janizaries* who leads on that spot is not to be so easily repulsed; he rallies his men, and charges through the thick of the fire with mad impetuosity, when he is met by L'Isle Adam and his guards, and a conflict ensues, so long and desperate that far out to sea the blue waters are dyed with streams of blood, and the breach of Spain becomes a heap of dead and dying.

Six hours it lasted, and then a reinforcement from St. Nicholas decided the day in favour of the Cross. Solyman himself was compelled to give the signal for retreat; and the masses of his troops fell back broken and disordered, leaving 20,000 corpses on those unconquerable walls. The grand master, without laying aside his armour, or taking rest or food, directed his steps to the church to give thanks to God for a victory so costly and yet so surpassing in its glory; and Rhodes, after that day of carnage, had another week of rest So immense had been the slaughter during this conflict, that we are told the cessation of hostilities arose from both parties being compelled to withdraw from the walls, where the stench of the bodies was unendurable. Solyman, enraged at his repeated discomfitures, condemned both his unfortunate generals to death; and it was only at the earnest entreaties of the other pashas, who threw themselves in tears at his feet, that he was induced to spare their lives. Mustapha was sent as governor into Egypt, and Achmet Pasha was placed at the head of the army.[3] But for assurances of his spies and the traitors within the walls that Rhodes was at its last gasp, it seems certain that he would have abandoned the enterprise altogether. But a council of war being held, it was determined to renew the assault on the eighth day.

Accordingly the whole line of walls was stormed for three days successively; the English bastion, still the post of danger and of glory, though now a mere charred and ruined fragment, being this time held by a picked body of French, for every English knight was dead. In one of these battles Martinengo fell desperately wounded,—a great loss to the Christians, whose movements had been mainly directed by his skill; but the grand master thenceforth took his place, and for thirty-four days, we are assured, he never left the bastion of Spain, where the chief struggle was maintained, taking no rest save on a mattress they laid for him at the foot of a battery;

> acting sometimes as a soldier, and sometimes as an engineer, but always as a general,

And exposing his life with a fearlessness that made his preservation something like a perpetual miracle. It was at this period of the siege that the treachery of Damaral being suspected, he was tried and condemned. Some have doubted his guilt, and represented that his misconduct consisted in nothing worse than

---

3. Mustapha was recalled the next year at the earnest representations of his wife, the sultan's sister, and restored to the imperial favour. The end of Achmet was, that, being deprived of his office of grand *vizier* and sent to Egypt, he excited the Mamelukes to revolt, and was defeated and killed. He had even entered into correspondence with L'Isle Adam, and made proposals for restoring Rhodes to the order.

a coldness and slackness in his duties, proceeding from jealousy of the grand master; however that might be, it is certain that he met with a traitor's death.

We shall not ask our reader to accompany us through the history of the last month of uninterrupted fighting. During that extraordinary struggle, Rhodes presented the spectacle of a city entirely unwalled, with neither gates nor ramparts left, garrisoned by about 2000 wounded and exhausted men, yet keeping at bay the entire Turkish force at the point of their swords. In vain did Solyman in his addresses to his soldiers assure them that there was nothing to keep them out of the city; it lay open on all sides, and thirty men might ride abreast into its breaches: the artillery no longer played on the ramparts, but on the houses themselves. Yet still, whilst the remnant of the Christian garrison stood before their ruins, every effort of the infidels was in vain; and as often as they advanced within hearing, they were received with jests and defiances, taunted for their cowardice, and incited with bitter mockery to come up into the city, and take it if they could. Hardly were there left men enough to make the line of defence complete; the women stood sometimes by their sides, praying and encouraging their sons and husbands to fight on to the last for liberty and faith. And thus things continued until the beginning of the month of December.

There can be no doubt that, had succours arrived from Europe, the place would have been saved; for the Turks, who are said to have lost by war and disease no fewer than 90,000 men, were well-nigh in despair, particularly as the weather had become stormy, and threatened the destruction of their fleet. But there was no help from Christendom for its brave defenders: compliments in plenty, and fine words to the ambassadors who were despatched to represent the threatened danger; but whilst the sovereigns of France and Spain were courteous enough to say that Rhodes was the spectacle of the universe, they were too busy in a war of foolish rivalry to send a single galley to its aid. The knights scattered through the various countries of Europe made every effort to reinforce their comrades; but the tempests that raged during many weeks prevented them from arriving in time. The French knights were forced into the ports of Sardinia; a Spanish flotilla which had made its way to the harbour of Rhodes was beaten off by the Turks, and obliged to retire; and lastly, a few English knights, under the gallant veteran Sir Thomas Newport, persisting in the attempt to keep at sea, their vessel foundered in the storm, and every soul on board was drowned.

It was now that Solyman, desirous of getting possession of the city on any terms, and perhaps not unwilling to obtain a reputation for clemency, had recourse to negotiations; and a certain Genoese who was found in the camp was despatched to represent to the besieged the misery which a prolonged resistance would infallibly bring on the unoffending inhabitants when the city should at length be taken, whereas a timely surrender would prevent all the horrors of a storm. L'Isle Adam, however, rejected all overtures with the enemy, as contrary to the statutes of his order, and declared his own firm resolve to be buried under the ruins of Rhodes sooner than consent to yield his trust into the hands of the infidel. Emissaries from the Turkish camp appeared again and again before the walls; the grand master ordered them to be fired upon; the citizens, weary of the contest, threatened to treat for terms on their own account; still he was inflexible.

But he was unsupported: not but that his knights were as ready as himself to die, sword in hand fighting against the infidels; but they could not resist the crowd of weeping citizens who stood about the council-door begging them to save their wives and children by a timely compliance with honourable terms; and their voices prevailed; for at length, after long hesitation, L'Isle Adam was forced to yield; and doubtless the concession cost him more than all the suffering and disaster of the last six months of bloodshed. He consented to take advantage of the first overtures that were made to treat for a surrender. The opportunity soon came: on the 10th of December the sultan caused a flag of truce to be hoisted on a neighbouring church outside the walls, and despatched two of his officers with a letter offering to allow the knights and citizens a free embarkation, carrying goods and chattels with them, in case of capitulation; otherwise an indiscriminate massacre of all, without distinction of age or sex, and that instantly; to which was attached his signature in letters of gold.

The grand master in return sent two envoys, who begged a three days' armistice for deliberation; this Solyman refused, and hostilities were renewed. The infidels were again repulsed with great slaughter; but the townspeople, terrified at the peril that impended, came in a body and entreated L'Isle Adam to renew negotiations. He consented; but to gain time, he sent Achmet Pasha the treaty by which Bajazet had, in the most solemn form, guaranteed to the order the free possession of Rhodes. Achmet no sooner cast his eyes on the parchment than, in a fit of rage, he tore it in pieces and trod the fragments under foot; and not content with this, he drove the envoys from his presence, and sent an insulting message to the grand master by the prisoners taken the same day, whose fingers, ears, and nose he inhumanly cut off.

At length, however, as no prospect of relief appeared, and all hope of prolonging the defence was gone, L'Isle Adam consented to the terms proposed by Solyman, and the treaty was signed. Terms so honourable to the Christians had never yet been granted: the exercise of the Christian religion was to be free; the churches unprofaned; the children were not to be seized and brought up in the faith of Mahomet; the knights and inhabitants were to be afforded a safe passage out of the port; and the Turks bound themselves even to supply vessels for this purpose should they be required. Moreover, the holy relics and the sacred vases of the church of St. John were to be given up to the Christians, as well as the cannon with which to arm their galleys; the Ottoman army retiring from the walk during the evacuation of the place, and leaving only a guard of 4000 *Janizaries*.

Two days after the signing of the treaty, L'Isle Adam visited the sultan in his tent, and being admitted to his presence, after being kept waiting for many hours in a pitiless storm of snow, was received with an almost involuntary respect. For indeed there was a majesty in the very look of the grand master which none was ever known to resist; and although Solyman was not prepared to evince much courtesy to his fallen adversary, yet we are told, after the two had gazed at one another for a few moments in silence, the haughtiness of the Ottoman sovereign was forced to yield, and giving his hand to the grand master to kiss, he even attempted to console him under his misfortunes, offering him the highest rank within his power to bestow, if he would embrace the Moslem faith and join his service; to which L'Isle Adam's reply may be imagined.

Unhappily the fair terms of Solyman's treaty were but little regarded. A fresh band of *Janizaries* landing in the island on Christmas Eve, broke into the city, and, armed only with clubs, pillaged the houses of the principal inhabitants, and committed every manner of atrocity. The church of St. John was the principal object of their fury: they defaced the *frescoes* on the walls, dashed the images to pieces, overturned the altars, flung out ornaments, relics, everything; dragged the crucifix through the mud, and in their search for hidden treasure broke open and demolished the very tombs of the grand masters. This done, they mounted to the top of the tower, "called the faithful to prayer," and that same hour turned the sacred building into a mosque.

From the church they proceeded to the great hospital, where, as we learn from an eye-witness, they beat the sick in their beds with such violence that many died, and among them one of the knights of the order, who was flung from the corridor and killed. The Christians they met with in the streets they fell upon with their clubs, murdering some on the spot; they robbed the townspeople who were carrying their goods down to the ships, compelling them to carry their own property on their backs, like beasts of burden, to the camp; women and young girls, some mere children, they made the victims of their brutality.

The fault, however, is not to be attributed to Solyman, who hastened to put a stop to these excesses; and entering the city in person, proceeded to return the visit of the grand master in his own palace. Whatever his motive, none can deny that in his transactions with the knights Solyman observed a moderation which was worthy of his title of "Magnificent:" not, perhaps, so loyal and sincere a generosity as that which has often been seen displayed by Christian chivalry, yet presenting a most striking contrast to the ferocious barbarism of his predecessors; and it is said, that during the final interview between him and L'Isle Adam, he was so touched with the resigned and tranquil deportment of the venerable hero, that, turning as he left the palace to one of his generals, he observed, "It is not without regret that I force this brave Christian to leave his home in his old age."[4]

The Turks entered Rhodes on the morning of Christmas Day. At that same hour Pope Adrian was offering the Holy Sacrifice on the high altar of St. Peter's: suddenly a stone detached itself from a projecting cornice and fell at his feet, as though to warn the Universal Pastor that one of the outworks of Christendom was lost to the Church.

---

[4]. Fontanus declares that the sultan gave the grand master his right hand, and even raised the imperial diadem a little from his head in saluting him; a ceremony never used by Ottoman sovereigns even towards Mahometan kings. "It is but justice to say," adds Boisgelin, "that his troops, belonging to a nation of all others most adverse to the arts, would have thought the splendour of their victory tarnished had they possessed themselves of the arms and escutcheons of the knights, which (as was mentioned in a previous note) they permitted to remain uninjured." The archives and the relics were also faithfully preserved, and given up to the Knights, who carried with them at the same time their beloved image of our Lady of Philermos.

CHAPTER 7

Departure From Rhodes

It was the Feast of our Lord's Circumcision, 1523. Fifty vessels, crowded with a mixed multitude of citizens and soldiers, were standing out to sea, having among them the grand *carrack* of the order of St. John and the scanty remnant of the Knights of Rhodes. Alas, that title was now lost forever! they were literally without a home, heating about on those stormy waters, as Villiers and his five followers had done 200 years before when flying from the walls of Acre. L'Isle Adam never showed himself greater than in misfortune. During the hurry and confusion of embarkation under the eyes of his enemies, he had maintained the same tranquil dignity he had ever displayed; remembering everything and the needs of every one; not forgetting to send to all the knights of the dependent islands and fortresses, including St. Peter's of the Freed, bidding them join him in Candia.

Few knights, indeed, were to be found on board those fifty vessels; the exact number that survived the siege is not given, but it must have been very small. Most of them, sick and wounded, were received into the *carrack*, where L'Isle Adam commanded in person; the remainder of the fleet was chiefly occupied by the Rhodians, who preferred to abide by the fortunes of an order whose wise and gentle government had rendered it so dear, rather than trust to the generosity of the infidels. Yet, though their choice was freely and promptly made, it was a sad one. Many gazed on the shores of their darling island till the low dark line sank beneath the horizon, abandoning themselves to a transport of grief. But the danger of their present situation served in some degree as a relief, by calling on them for efforts to preserve the crazy badly-fitted vessels from shipwreck.

The storm continued unabated; and on reaching Candia several of the galleys were driven on the coast, and many valuable lives were lost. However, after numerous disasters, the whole mustered at the rendezvous appointed at the town of Setia; the knights from the distant stations before named also joined them; and a general review was made of the whole body, which, including men, women, and children, amounted to about 5000 in number, of whom not 1000 were members of the order.

But their condition was truly deplorable; sick and wounded, half-naked, and wholly without support, these Rhodians, whose loyal devotion caused the grand master no small embarrassment, gathered about him like helpless children, and seemed to appeal to his protection and tenderness as infants to a mother. At Rhodes, six months before, they had been among the noblest and wealthiest of its population; now they were a crowd of beggars, dependent on the charity of their sovereign for a daily alms. Yet their deep and touching affection for his person showed itself as enthusiastically as ever; and as he appeared among them, and went through the shivering and weeping ranks, he too, who had never shown one touch of weakness, even in the anguish of his last humiliation, could not endure the sight, but burst into a passionate flood of tears.

Yet even the most stoical heart might well have softened at trials such as these; and the self-control of L'Isle Adam in the midst of suffering sprang not from stoicism, but from the firm and chastened temper of one who joined the soldier's heroism to the impassible tranquillity of a monk. Nature must needs assert her claims; and her voice so cried within his heart in that sad hour, that all his fortitude gave way. He seemed to see again the bloody ramparts of the city, whereon had fallen comrades and brothers-in-arms, so long and truly tried; these Rhodian followers too, so simple and affectionate in their truthfulness, cast utterly into ruin, and leaning on him for bare support; his order, it might be, tottering to its fall; the world before him, and not a port or harbour he could call his own, whither he might guide his people. All this was knocking at his heart, with the remembrance too of Rhodes and its glories, and the disgrace and ruin of the Christian cause; the Cross overthrown, as it seemed, forever in the East; and the recovery of Jerusalem, that cherished hope of the children of St. John, become a mint and airy dream.

Even their position in Candia was of doubtful security; for the island was the property of the Venetian republic, whose generosity to a fallen rival was scarcely to be trusted. Happily, however, the governor at that time was the noble Paul Giustiniani, of a family whose name alone was ever sufficient security for greatness of soul and devotion in the Christian cause. He delighted in showing a singular respect to the grand master in his misfortunes, and came to meet him with demonstrations of extraordinary honour. Trusting to his friendship, L'Isle Adam remained in Candia until his vessels could refit; and meanwhile held a chapter general, and sent word of his coming to Messina, where the greater part of the knights absent in Europe had assembled from different quarters, and were preparing to embark for Rhodes when the news reached them that all was over.

The intelligence was received in Europe like a thunderclap, and, too late, filled all the sovereigns with shame and self-reproach. "Nothing has been well lost but Rhodes," was the exclamation of Charles V.;— one of those sayings which have become historic, and which yet was a valueless and empty flattery from the man whose word, a month before, might have sufficed to save the island. Another addition to the numbers assembled at Setia soon arrived in the persons of Leonard Balestein and all the Latin clergy of Rhodes, who, contrary to treaty, had been summarily turned out by Solyman so soon as the knights had departed, with the brief explanation that he would have no Latins in his states. Solyman's generosity, in fact, was of a limited kind; he coveted a name for magnanimity in the eyes of the European sovereigns, and was ready therefore to purchase his reputation for "magnificence" by some sacrifices; but it could not conquer the innate selfishness of the Moslem character, or, as it would seem, its ferocity; for among the tidings brought by Leonard was that of the seizure of Amurath,[1] the son of Djem, who, having embraced Christianity, had lived at Rhodes with the knights after his father's death; but now, falling into the hands of the jealous despot, was, with his two sons, strangled in the presence of the whole Turkish army, and his wife and daughters sent to the Imperial harem at Constantinople.

On the first day of Lent the Christian fleet left the hospitable shores of Candia, directing its course still westward, with the purpose of taking up its temporary quarters in the harbour of Messina. The naval skill of England was even then universally allowed, and the conduct of the fleet was committed to Sir William Weston, now Turcopolier of the order. The *carrack* and ships of war made straight for Sicily: but the grand master did not accompany them; like a tender father, he had taken as his charge the care of his poor sick Rhodians, and a long and disastrous voyage he had, not reaching Messina until the first week in May. Fontanus describes his landing.

He had been long and anxiously expected by his knights, who hurried to the shore to greet him. It was a sad but touching spectacle to see the miserable, shattered vessels, without anchors, rudders, and with torn sails and broken masts. Around their sovereign stood a ragged and sickly crowd; it was a marvel that they had made the voyage at all: but you might see where their confidence had been placed, and who had been their guide; for a flag, torn and weather-beaten, was floating over the deck, whereon you might discern the half-effaced figure of the Mother of Sorrows, holding her dead Son in her arms, with the motto,

Afflictis spes unica rebus,[2]

and this was the ensign of the fleet.

---

1. He had hoped to escape from the island in disguise, in the company of the Knights; but had been detected by the sultan's spies.
2. "In adversity our only hope."

Seven hundred knights stood on the shore, and with them mingled the nobles of Sicily and the ambassadors from foreign courts; but at the sight of such distress, and of their beloved grand master, who had chosen, like a good shepherd, to abide with the weakest of his flock, there arose front the illustrious body nothing but a wail of weeping; and this was the welcome of L'Isle Adam on the soil of Sicily. As he landed, the viceroy advanced to receive him; and then came the meeting with his knights— those who had been absent from Rhodes, and now could offer only their sympathy and their tears. The populace too pressed about his person, and, kneeling, kissed his feet and dress. Everyone was bare-headed; and perhaps there has rarely been witnessed so touching a demonstration of honour to fallen greatness.

The first care of the grand master, when lodged in the palace prepared for him, was to turn it into a hospital for his sick. True and worthy Hospitaller, he retained unchanged and unsullied the spirit of his religious vocation, and served as humbly and as untiringly as though he were a novice in the famous Xenodochia. If or were his knights unworthy of so admirable a chief.

> "It was a moving spectacle," says Vertot, "to see these men, so formidable in war, now animated only with ft spirit of charity; devoting themselves to the meanest services, carrying the broth to the sick, making their beds, and, as it seemed, concerned with nothing but their consolation and relief."[3]

Next came a stern investigation into the conduct of the absent knights. There was enough strength in the forces assembled at Messina to have succoured Rhodes; but, after a severe court-martial, the fact was proved beyond a doubt, that they had done what men could do to join their comrades, and had failed; many having perished in the attempt, like the brave old English

---

3. *Les Chevaliers, selon leur ancienne instruction, pansoient et setvoient les malades, mesme le grand maistre: oe qui fit admirer toute la ville de Messine, et les autres villes où les Chevaliers ont demeurés."* (Goussancourt)

bailiff Sir Thomas Newport, and others whose fate was similar. In short, the honour of the order was declared to be unstained; and when the tribunal returned a verdict that no man had been found guilty, L'Isle Adam exclaimed, in a burst of thankful joy;

> May God be praised forever! who in this hour of misfortune has proved to me that the loss of Rhodes could not be attributed to the negligence of my order.

So soon as this affair was completed, the grand master prepared to set out for Rome, to confer with the Pope as to the steps advisable to take for the preservation of the order. After being detained a month on the Neapolitan coast, in consequence of pestilence breaking out among his followers, he and his colony cast anchor in the port of Città Vecchia. At Rome he was received with extraordinary honours; the cardinals coming forth in their own persons to meet him, together with a large and brilliant cortège of barons and princes, all the various dignitaries of the Church and magistrates of the city, besides the papal guards, and a numerous squadron of cavalry; and so in grand procession, amidst the shouts of the *populace* and salvoes of artillery from the Castle of St. Angelo, he passed through the streets, and was conducted to the Vatican, where he was hospitably entertained.

Within a few weeks after the arrival of L'Isle Adam, Pope Adrian VI. expired, and, by a singular chance, was succeeded by Cardinal Julius de Medicis, nephew to Leo X., and himself a member of the order of St. John, who had exchanged the military for the ecclesiastical profession, and now assumed the title of Clement VII. It was natural, and to be expected, that some advantage should accrue to the wanderers from the elevation to supreme power of one of their own brethren; and accordingly one of the first acts of the new pontiff was to assign the city of Viterbo for their temporary residence, granting them permission at the same time to keep their fleet in the harbour of Città Vecchia until such time as they should be able to find some more fitting settlement.

On the 25th of January 1524, therefore, L'Isle Adam set out

for Viterbo, "the most delicious city of the Pope's dominions, and most magnificent after Rome," as Fontanus calls it. The knights proceeded first, the Rhodians next,—for in all the wanderings of this second Æneas, as he may well be termed, his Rhodians were never forgotten; nor did they forget their devotion to our Lady of Philermos, but carried her on their shoulders, and would have carried her to the end of the world, if their nomadic life had lasted for another century. It was just a year since the fall of Rhodes; want and suffering had sadly ravaged the ranks of the little colony; the Rhodians died in great numbers from the pestilence, and the knights were reduced to such poverty, that L'Isle Adam was forced to grant them a dispensation to work at menial crafts in order to support themselves and their unfortunate dependants. Yet Bosio tells us, that in these trying extremities there was no instance of any abandoning their rule; and L'Isle Adam, amidst all his sorrows, at least had the consolation—and there could be none greater—of ruling over subjects faithful to their plighted vows.

So soon as he had seen his followers in some degree settled, the indefatigable chief set out upon fresh journeys to every court of Europe, to negotiate, if it were possible, for some permanent and independent residence. His activity and perseverance were extraordinary. Spain, France, and even England, he visited by turns; nor was it without necessity; for some of the princes of Europe, Henry VIII. among the number, after suffering the order to be driven from Rhodes before their eyes, were now occupying themselves with the design of seizing upon its possessions, as though it were extinct. L'Isle Adam, however, very soon made Portugal and England understand that, fallen as was the order, it was not quite come to that; and the "defender of the faith" was, it is said, so moved by the eloquence and heroic bearing of the venerable old man, that, instead of plundering him at that time, he received him with royal magnificence, and presented him with a jewelled basin and ewer, still preserved in Boisgelin's time in the treasury of the order.

Not to weary the reader with negotiations, which were indeed most wearisome and vexatious to endure, the chapter-general at length, after many prorogations, met at Viterbo in the month of February 1527, to consider the final answer to be given to the proposals of the emperor. They were not too generous; Charles, indeed, was not a man from whom great acts of generosity were to be expected; and on the present occasion he certainly endeavoured to drive as profitable a bargain with the order as he could. The islands of Malta and Gozo were offered to their acceptance,—subject, however, to the emperor, and with the most unfair and harsh condition of their undertaking to garrison and defend for him the town of Tripoli on the coast of Africa—a second Smyrna. Commissioners were appointed to report on the nature of the territory thus offered; and there is an amusing *naïveté* in the account, which Boisgelin, usually so simple and unpretending in his style, gives us of the result. It was, he says, to this effect:

> That the island of Malta was nothing but a rock of soft sandstone, about six or seven leagues long and four broad; that the surface was scarcely covered with three feet of soil—very stony, and quite unfit for growing corn; that, with the exception of a few springs, there was no running water, nor even wells; that wood was so scarce as to be sold by the pound, so that the chief fuel was dried dung, or wild thistle; that the greater part of the houses of the capital were uninhabited—the circumference of the town not being more than 1303 paces, that the miserable walls surrounding it were open thirty paces in breadth; that the shore was full of rocks; the port defended by a small and ruinous castle, whose artillery consisted of one cannon and a few mortars; and that, owing to the barrenness of the soil and the frequent descents of the corsairs, the twelve thousand inhabitants were poor and wretched;—in a word, that a residence in Malta appeared extremely disagreeable, indeed almost insupportable, particularly in summer.

So much for the island. As to the fortress of Tripoli, there was but one opinion; without fortifications, and situated on a foundation of sand, which rendered their erection impossible—subject to inundations—surrounded by the territories of the king of Tunis, and with a soil that produced nothing but dates, the commissioners declared that its occupation could only expose the knights placed there to certain death.

All this was very different from the glories of Acre and the richness of beautiful Rhodes;[4] yet there was no choice. Already they had been forced to leave Viterbo,[5] in consequence of the breaking out of plague, and to recommence their wanderings, to Corneto first, where we again find notice of their charity to the sufferers, and the exact discipline preserved among them; thence to Nice, where a temporary resting-place was prepared for them by the Duke of Savoy; so that they who had hitherto offered hospitality to Christendom were now forced to beg it at the doors of the European princes. There had been some intention of endeavouring to reconquer Rhodes, and an attempt had been made to seize on Modon in the Morea; but all these designs proved abortive; and at length, having agreed to accept the emperor's offer, the deed of donation of Malta, Gozo, and Tripoli, received the imperial signature; the condition of feudal subjection to himself being withdrawn as interfering with the neutrality which the order was bound to observe between Christian princes, and the payment of a falcon yearly to the Sicilian government substituted in its stead.

Tripoli, however, must be garrisoned; on that point Charles was inexorable, and accordingly two galleys conducted thither

---

4. Lord Carlisle, in his *Diary in Turkish and Greek Waters,* speaking of the present relative condition of Rhodes and Malta, says, "I have qualified myself for adjudging that, in most respects, the tables are now turned between the two islands; and they certainly afford a very decisive criterion of the results of Turkish and Christian dominion."

5. A few weeks before their removal, in the spring of 1527, the Imperialists, who were marching to the sack of Rome under the Constable Bourbon, spared Viterbo, out of respect, it is said, for the grand master; although they plundered the neighbouring town, ill treated the inhabitants, burned down the churches, and committed excesses rivalling in atrocity those of the Turks themselves.

the ill fated knights chosen for that duty; whilst a timely present from England of nineteen superb pieces of artillery and 1023 cannon-balls, enabled them to furnish something to its defence. Nothing now remained to be done but to take possession of the new territory, which was speedily done (October 26th, 1530); and thus, in the eighth year after their departure from Rhodes, the knights again saw themselves established in an independent sovereignty, and, once more changing their title, became thenceforth known through Europe as the Knights of Malta.

There was little of exultation in the sentiments with which they entered on their new dominions. The sterile soil, the burning climate, and the squalid population, recalled sad thoughts of Rhodes, with its abundant harvests and odoriferous orange-groves, its fleets and armaments and prosperous commerce, and the palaces of its wealthy nobles. But L'Isle Adam had a greatness of soul that rose superior to circumstances, and at once set about constructing habitations for his knights and laying the foundation of a hospital—not forgetting, at the same time, to provide for his poor Rhodians, and to concert measures for the amelioration of the condition of the inhabitants themselves. The last days of L'Isle Adam were, however, clouded with fresh sorrows; he lived to see the breaking out of that great religious revolution which was to change the face of Europe. In the proscriptions and martyrdoms that took place in England, we have the names of four knights of the order [6], who gave their

---

6. Some account of these English martyrs may not be here out of place. The first knight who suffered death in England for the faith was Adrian Fortescue, beheaded on the 8th of July 1539 After him followed two others, Ingley and Adrian Forrest, "who," says Goussancourt, "being called on to recognise the king as head of the Church and to approve of his ordinances, chose, rather, courageously to suffer death than to live in delicacy, having made ship-wreck of the faith. Thus they gave their lives as gloriously at home as they could ever have done in combat."
Henry offered Sir William Weston, Lord Prior of England (the priors sat in parliament on an equality with the first barons of the realm), a pension of 1000*l.* a year; but that knight was so overwhelmed with grief at the suppression of his order that he never received a penny, but soon after died, and was buried in the chancel of the old church of St. James, Clerkenwell. Marmaduke Bohun, whom Goussancourt calls "the blessed," was beheaded under Queen Elizabeth in 1585. Many others died in prison, in the same reign, from the horrible sufferings endured in their confinement; among whom we find the names of Sir Thomas Mytton and Sir Edward Waldegrave.

lives for the faith, many others perishing in prison; while scarcely a month passed without bringing fresh refugees to Malta, where the paternal tenderness of the grand master supplied them with the means of support. But the extinction of the language of England, and the gloomy cloud that hung over the Church, laid the last weight on that burden which had long been pressing down the heroic soul of L'Isle Adam to the dust. He died in the arms of his knights, on the 21st of August 1534; and over his tomb they engraved these words:

Hic jacet Virtus victrix Fortunæ.[7]

The effects resulting from the expulsion of the knights from Rhodes, and their temporary suspension from all active operation against the infidels, were soon felt throughout Europe. Solyman, secure from their attacks, was free to turn his attention to the northern frontier of his empire, where the recent fall of Belgrade, and the distractions of the kingdom of Hungary, seemed to hold out promise of an easy conquest.

Louis of Hungary, a prince wholly unequal to the government of his factious and ambitious nobles, rashly gave battle to the superior forces of the sultan on the fatal field of Mohacs, where he fell, with the flower of his troops, on the 28th of August 1526. The battle lasted only two hours, yet in that short space of time there perished with their young monarch 4000 knights (comprising the greater portion of the Hungarian nobility), eight bishops, and 20,000 common soldiers. In true Tartar fashion, a pyramid of 2000 human heads was raised before the imperial tent; and, ere he resumed his march, Solyman the Magnificent had 4000 prisoners massacred in cold blood! As he advanced he ravaged the whole country with his troops, burning towns and cities, and slaughtering the inhabitants even on surrender; so that it is calculated that Hungary lost no less than 200,000 of her people in this terrible invasion; and when he withdrew his army, laden with immense booty, he dragged with him into slavery, and to all the horrors which slavery among the

---

7. "Here lies Virtue victorious over Fortune."

Turks involves, 100,000 captives.

The death of Louis increased the disorder of affairs by raising the question of a disputed succession. The crown had indeed been previously settled on the representative of the house of Austria; but Zapolya, the ambitious *wayvode* of Transylvania, seized the occasion to proclaim himself king, on the plea that none but an Hungarian could reign in Hungary. Finding himself unable, however, to resist the power of the Archduke Ferdinand and his party among the magnates, he had recourse to the unworthy policy of calling in the Ottomans to his aid. The year 1529, accordingly, saw the terrible hordes of the Turkish invaders again let loose on the frontiers of the kingdom. Before them marched a wild irregular force of 30,000 men, whom the Germans denominated "the sackmen," and whose atrocities, under their leader Michael Oglou, were of the most appalling character. Hungary was soon overrun; and within five months from the day when they crossed its frontier, the vast army of the Turks, amounting to more than 300,000 men, appeared under the walls of Vienna (September 27th, 1529).

Never had the dreaded standards of the infidels been known to advance so far into the heart of Christendom since the day when the Moors had received their decisive overthrow on the field of Tours. But there seemed little chance of such a triumph to the Christian cause in the present case; for Vienna, with ruinous and inadequate defences, and a garrison of no more than 20,000 men, could scarcely look to offer more than a brief resistance to such an overwhelming force. By the first prisoners who were taken by his skirmishers Solyman had sent back a message to the following effect:

> That should the city venture to resist, he would not retreat till he had reduced it; and then he would spare neither old nor young, nor the child in the mother's womb; and would so utterly destroy the city that men should not know where it stood. He would not rest his head till Vienna and the whole of Christendom were under his subjection; and it was his settled purpose within three days, namely, on the

feast of St. Michael, to break his fast in Vienna.

Nor to the terrified inhabitants did this seem any idle threat; for, as they gazed from the walls, they could behold nothing but a forest of tents stretching as far as the eye could reach; and the reports which had been brought in by fugitives from the country told of horrors which fulfilled to the letter, and even surpassed in savage atrocity, all that menace could express or imagination depict. One by one all their communications from without were cut off, and the mines and batteries of their assailants began their fatal work.

The siege may be said to have formally opened on the 29th of September; but in spite of their superior numbers, every effort of the Turks to render themselves masters of the city was unsuccessful. On three different days they assaulted the walls, which had been reduced to ruins by the explosions of their mines, but each time they were repulsed with loss; and the superstition of the Turkish troops came in aid of the heroic defence of the garrison to bring about the abandonment of the enterprise. The law of Islam commanded three attacks on an enemy, and no more; when, therefore, the third assault failed, the soldiers, yielding to the fatalism of their nation, declared their unwillingness to prosecute the attempt any further. A last desperate assault was indeed made on the 14th of October, but with the same result that had attended those which had preceded it; and Solyman, yielding to necessity, gave orders for a retreat.

An hour before midnight the army began to move, and marked its departure by one of those frightful deeds of cruelty so frequent in the annals of Turkish warfare. The *Janizaries* set fire to the huts they had constructed, and to all the forage and plunder they had collected but were unable to carry away. At the same time they commenced a general massacre of the Christian prisoners, of whom vast numbers had been brought into the camp by the "runners and burners" during the three weeks of the siege, reserving only the fairest youth of both sexes, whom they tied together by ropes and hurried away into an infamous captivity. The old men and women, and the little children, they threw into the midst of the burning piles, while such as were of an age to bear arms they cut to pieces or impaled. The shrieks of the unhappy beings were heard distinctly by those who thronged the city walls; they could even see by the light of the flames the work of butchery that was going forward, and the writhing forms of their fellow-countrymen, and thus had terrible and sensible proof of the despair of the ferocious enemy and of the horrors which awaited them had that enemy been victorious.

The morning showed the Ottoman army in full retreat; and a general discharge of artillery announced to the inhabitants of Vienna the realisation of hopes which they had hardly ventured to entertain. Once more the bells of the churches gave forth their joyous peals; a *Te Deum* was sung in St. Stephen's, and High Mass celebrated in thanksgiving to the Most Holy Trinity.

Solyman's forces retired across the Turkish frontier, and spite of the rapid success which had attended his march through Hungary, the expedition failed in its main object; for the establishment of Zapolya as tributary king of Hungary, or rather of that portion of the country which he held in occupation (a dignity he retained till his death in 1540[8]), was but a poor result for the campaign which had been undertaken with the boastful design of erecting the victorious trophies of the Crescent on the very banks of the Rhine. It is amusing to read the arrogant terms in which the sultan announces to his faithful subjects the results of the campaign, and with cool effrontery would have them believe that, in his magnanimity, he had forborne to push his conquests further than justice or the interests of the empire

---

8. It was arranged by a secret treaty between Ferdinand and Zapolya that the latter should retain the crown till his death, when the whole of the kingdom should revert to Austria, Zapolya's son retaining only his hereditary dignity of countship of Zips. But at Zapolya's death his widow asserted the rights of her son as king of Hungary, and called in the sultan to her aid. Solyman turned the country into a Turkish province, professing all the time to be merely holding it until the child had attained his majority. War with Austria continued for many years, until, in 1547, a truce for five years was concluded, which left the sultan in possession of nearly the whole of Hungary and Transylvania, and which bound Ferdinand to the humiliating condition of paying a tribute of 30,000 *ducats* a-year. Hostilities were resumed on the very day the armistice expired.

demanded, and had disdained to crush the foe he had humbled and chastised.

One of his bulletins thus concludes:

> An unbeliever came out from the fortress (Vienna), and brought intelligence of the submission of the princes and of the people, on whose behalf he prayed for grace and pardon. The *padishah* received his prayer with favour, and granted them pardon. Inasmuch as the German lands were unconnected with the Ottoman realm, that hence it was hard to occupy the frontier places and conduct their affairs, the faithful would not trouble themselves to clear out the fortress, or purify, improve, and put it into repair; but a reward of 1000 *aspers* was dealt out to each of the *Janizaries*, and security being established, the horses' heads were turned towards the throne of Solomon.[9]

But in spite of these endeavours to conceal the truth even from himself, Solyman never forgot the repulse he had sustained; and it is said that he imprecated a curse upon any of his successors who should renew the attempt.

Nevertheless we shall hereafter see the Ottomans encamped for a second time before the city of Vienna, and shall have to relate the story of its glorious deliverance, which forms one of the most striking features in the history of the struggle between the Crescent and the Cross.

---

9. Von Hammer, as cited in *Two Sieges of Vienna* (Murray).

CHAPTER 8

Exploits of Knights in Africa

It was but natural that the gratitude of the order towards the emperor, to whom it owed its present independence, should be eagerly manifested on the occasion of his enterprise against Barbary; and accordingly, during the twenty years that succeeded the death of L'Isle Adam, we find the Knights of Malta foremost in every engagement with the corsairs of Algiers and Tunis, and earning a reputation on the coasts of Africa not unworthy of their ancient fame. The northern provinces of Africa had gradually fallen into the power of the Moorish pirates, under their celebrated chief Barbarossa;[1] and their constant descents from thence on the coasts of Spain and Italy rendered a declaration of war from the emperor not merely just but actually necessary.

The sieges of Goletta and Tunis opened the campaign; and at both places the valour of the knights contributed in no small degree to the success of the Christian arms. At Tunis the scarlet banner of St. John was seen first in the assault, first also to be planted on the bastion, surrounded by its knights, whose white crosses rendered them conspicuous to the whole army. Their

---

1. Khaireddin, better known in Europe by his surname of Barbarossa, was a native of Mitylene, and with his brothers practised piracy in the reigns of Bajazet and Selim, the latter of whom he formally recognised as his sovereign. He seized the strong city of Algiers, desolated the coasts of Naples, and captured Tunis. Solyman took him into his service, and conferred upon him the highest naval dignity, making him his admiral, or *kapitan pasha*. In the great battle off Previsa, September 28th, 1538, he defeated the combined fleets of the Pope (Paul III.), the emperor, and the republic of Venice.

soldierly appearance, when they presented themselves before the emperor, drew an expression of admiration from his lips: "These are your brethren," he said, turning to the Prince of Portugal, a member of the order; "had we more of them, we might be sure of victory." Indeed, the victory, so far as Tunis was concerned, might certainly be attributed to them; if, as we are told, the flight of Barbarossa was occasioned by an incident within the fortress, thus related by Vertot.

There was among the slaves confined at Tunis a certain Knight of St. John, by name Paul Simconi, the same who, when only eighteen years of age, defended the Isle of Lero against the infidels with surpassing courage. On the approach of the imperial army, Simconi determined on a bold stroke for liberty. Gaining over his jailers, he contrived to break his own chains and those of his fellow-prisoners, and, proceeding to the armoury of the castle, they all armed themselves with whatever came first to hand, and falling on the Turkish garrison cut them to pieces, and made themselves masters of the fortress. Barbarossa, hearing the tumult, hastened to the castle gates, but was received with a fire of musketry; and discovering what had happened, exclaimed, "All is lost now these dogs are masters of the place!" and immediately took to flight. When Charles entered the city,[2] therefore, he was met by Simconi, accompanied by 6000 Christians, all of whom he had contrived to deliver from their chains; and as he embraced the gallant Hospitaller he exclaimed, "Brave knight, blessed for ever fee your generous valour, which has assisted my conquests, and added to the glory of your order!"

In these battles on the coast of Barbary, the grand *carrack* of the order held a distinguished place. So very wonderful a production of naval skill cannot be passed without a word of notice,

---

2. At the taking of Tunis (July 21st, 1535) the Imperialists and liberated slaves committed such frightful excesses that Vertot says, it seemed as if Christians tried to rival and even to surpass the worst barbarians in cruelty and licentiousness. The details he gives are of the most revolting description. Tunis was retaken by the corsair Ouloudj Ali, in 1570, with the exception of the citadel, which was still held by the Spaniards. Don John of Austria retook it; but at the end of eighteen months it again fell into the power of the Turks, in whose possession it has since remained.

and may be given as a piece of the romance of ship-building. It was not the same which had been brought from Rhodes, but a new one built at Nice after the accidental burning of its predecessor. It had two things in particular to be admired: first, that it was built with such precautions against infection in time of pestilence, that even while the plague raged at Nice, and the air was so pestilential that the birds dropped dead as they flew over the city, there was not a sick man known on board; next, the construction of this extraordinary vessel was such that nothing could sink it. It was sheathed in metal, and perfectly cannon-proof; but in spite of its size and weight, swift as a *felucca*. Its dimensions are not given; we only know that it could take in provisions of water and stores for a six-months' voyage; that its oven baked two thousand loaves at a time; that it had eight decks, an armoury for five hundred men, magnificent suites of rooms, and delicious artificial gardens, where large pots of orange, lemon, and cypress trees created a cool and fragrant shade. After this, it must be allowed that England must silence her boasts about "the Royal Harry."

In fact, the naval skill and power of the order was fast on the increase: their reputation for boldness in navigation we may gather from the words of Charles the Fifth during a storm off the Gulf of Spezia, where he narrowly escaped shipwreck. Through the murky atmosphere some galleys were observed riding out the hurricane, and even attempting to continue their voyage in despite of the elements.

"Whose are those vessels?" asked Doria in surprise; "are they madmen, who keep at sea in such weather?"

"No," replied the emperor, who overheard him; "they are only Hospitallers:—no galleys but theirs can brave a storm like this."

In the end Barbarossa fled to Constantinople to implore the succour of Solyman; and the knights, in hourly expectation of a visit *en passant* from their old enemies, applied themselves to prepare for their reception. As to Tripoli, it was equally incapable of defence or fortification, yet still Charles turned a deaf ear to all representations addressed to him on the subject; it was to be held anyhow, and by the knights alone. And held it was for one-and-twenty years; during which time, in spite of its ruinous condition, the knights not only stoutly defended "the ill-conditioned place," as it is termed by Boisgelin, but made from thence such continual aggressions on the infidels, that Tripoli and its garrison became the terror of all the corsairs of Barbary, and more than once they were driven disgracefully from its shattered walls.

During the expedition against Algiers (1541), the knights showed their usual valour. So many offered themselves as volunteers, that, had all been accepted, Malta would have been left without defenders; so that Homedez, the grand master at that time, was obliged to limit their numbers to four hundred. At Majorca they joined the emperor, who insisted on immediately setting out for Barbary in spite of the stormy season, for it was towards the end of September. Andrew Doria, the veteran commander of the fleet, ventured on a remonstrance.

"My liege," he said, "be persuaded to abandon this enterprise, for *pardieu*! if we go, we shall all perish."

"And are not twenty-two years of empire enough for me, and seventy-two years of life for you?" replied Charles. "By St. James! if we do perish, we may both die content."

Spite of the prognostics of shipwreck, the army disembarked safely before Algiers. It consisted of twenty thousand foot and six thousand horse, Germans, Italians, and Spaniards—each nation forming a separate body. The knights held a conspicuous place and fought dismounted:

> "Their surcoats of crimson velvet" (says the author of a narrative sent to the pope), "over which glittered their white crosses, making them an object of remark; while they bore themselves with a proud and martial air which struck terror among the barbarians who approached them."

A severe storm of hail, accompanied with piercing cold, produced such an effect on the imperial troops, that they were almost unable to resist a night attack directed against them by the

Moorish garrison, and the first conflict was a severe one.

The gallantry displayed by the Hospitallers on this occasion is illustrated by many anecdotes. Among others who distinguished themselves was a young French knight, Nicholas de Villegagnon, who, being wounded severely by a Moorish horseman, sprang behind his adversary on the crupper of his steed, and, plunging his dagger into his heart, spurred the animal through the ranks of the Moors, and so reached his own fine in safety. A rally was made round the banner of St. John, and the struggle was maintained with spirit, when Ferdinand Gonzaga, one of the imperial generals, rode up to the spot.

"Sir Hospitaller," he cried, addressing the grand bailiff of the order, "it is not enough to beat these dogs,—chase them back to Algiers, and enter the city with them; your knights are used to take towns without guns."

His words roused the enthusiastic chivalry of those to whom they were addressed; and dashing upon the Moors with wild impetuosity, they drove them before their horses like a flock of sheep until they reached the city gates, which the governor closed in the very face of his own soldiers, lest the Christians should enter with them. Nevertheless Ponce de Savignac, the standard-bearer of the order, rode up fearlessly and drove his poniard into the doors, and galloped away before his audacity was perceived. He fell, however, in the combat of the ensuing day, directed exclusively on the Maltese quarter; for, as the knights a second time pursued their enemies to the gates of Algiers, he was struck by a poisoned arrow. Feeling himself wounded, he called a soldier to support him. "Help me to bear up the standard," he cried; and leaning on the shoulder of his comrade, he had the courage and resolution to stand there, with the banner in his grasp, until he fell dead upon the ground.

The losses sustained in these conflicts were by no means the worst disasters that befell the Christian army. A terrible tempest nearly destroyed their fleet; and as galley after galley was driven upon the rocks, the troops were sad spectators of the slaughter of their crews by the inhuman Arabs. The number of vessels destroyed in this tempest was something incredible. The crew of one of the Maltese galleys, *The Bustard,* believing it impossible to save her, endeavoured to run her on the rocks, that they might abandon her; but Azevedo, the commander, obstinately refused his consent. In vain they represented that she was old and unfit for service; and that the lives of the men were of more value than a few worm-eaten timbers.

"I know nothing of all that," he replied, "but only that this galley has been entrusted to my care by the order; and, by the arm of St. John! I will slay the first man who talks of leaving his post;—you will save her, or die upon her decks." Inspired by his resolution, they did save her, and brought her safe back to Malta.

The army meanwhile, without tents, provisions, or hospital equipage, was soon reduced to extremity; and the siege was raised.

The successor of Barbarossa in the chieftainship of the Moorish corsairs was the celebrated Dragut (or Torghoud). Brought up from childhood in the service of the Ottomans, he had attained the highest reputation for skill and ferocity among all the brigands of the African coast. He had recently possessed himself of the strong city of Mehdijé,[3] situated between Tunis and Tripoli; and his neighbourhood to the two towns in possession of the Christians rendered an attack on this fortress absolutely necessary. The Imperial fleet was led by Doria; and 140 knights, under the bailiff De la Sangle, joined the expedition with 400 troops (1530).

The siege was long and bloody; but it is scarcely so much to the military operations before the walls of Mehdijé that we desire to direct the reader's attention, as to a far more beautiful and impressive spectacle which was then displayed. La Sangle may be taken as a fair and worthy example of the spirit of his institute;—wise in council, dauntless in battle, but in all characters most religious and humane. The prolonged siege soon

---

3. European historians *(e.g.* Vertot) have confounded this place with the town of Africa, or Afrikiya. (Von Hammer.)

produced the usual sufferings among the invading army; and pestilence made even greater ravages among the troops than the arms of the enemy. The brave old Hospitaller, however, only felt the emergency to be a call upon the best exertions of himself and his knights.

"Our first duty, gentlemen," he said to his comrades, "is hospitality, for to that we are bound by our vows; let, therefore, every Hospitaller give his tent to the hospital of the order, and serve, as becomes him, in the infirmary." The proposal was received with enthusiasm; a land of canvas hospital was improvised out of the tents of the knights; all the sick were received into it, and served tenderly and unweariedly by these brave and noble men: and never, surely, did their deeds of prowess gain them half the title to our praise, and to the recompense of eternal fame, which was earned by their heroic charity in the hospital of Mehdijé.

Dragut was a formidable adversary, and kept his opponents well employed; every day witnessed some sortie and bloody conflict, in which the Christians suffered considerable loss. During the second assault on the town the knights claimed the post of honour; the great banner was carried at their head by the commander De Giou, and as the attack was made on the side of the sea, they advanced to the assault through the water, which rose as high as their shoulders; for, impatient at the stoppages of the boats against the sandbanks, they threw themselves sword in hand into the sea, and thus gained the foot of the ramparts under the fire of the garrison. In a few moments the banner of St. John waved from the summit of the walls; but its brave defender fell dead at the same instant. Copier, another commander, instantly seized it ere it fell; and through the whole of the combat that followed, in the very thick of the firing, he stood calm and unmoved, holding it aloft above his head.

The Imperial troops, however, despairing of carrying the place, were about to give way, when Gimeran, a commander of the order, discovered a narrow entrance, through which he forced his way at the head of the knights into the heart of the city. This decided the day, and the place was immediately taken and sacked: the principal mosque, however, was blessed and converted into a church; and there the knights and officers who had fallen in the bloody contest were interred. When the town was afterwards abandoned, the remains of these heroes were removed to Sicily, and placed in a magnificent mausoleum in the Cathedral of Montreal.

Dragut, in despair at the loss of Mehdijé, repaired to the court of Solyman, and represented that the cause of the Crescent would be ruined and forever disgraced if the Knights of St. John were not speedily exterminated. The sultan, who readily entered into his views, and was continually irritated by hearing of fresh victories achieved by an order he had thought to crush forever, empowered Dragut to assemble all the corsairs of Africa, in order that, being united to the Turkish fleet, they might proceed to the work of "extermination" by carrying fire and sword to Tripoli and Malta, the two chief nests of the "dogs of *giaours*."

At the first rumour of an attack on Malta, the knights hastened to assemble for its defence, without waiting for a summons. Among those first to arrive in the island was the commander Nicholas de Villegagnon—the same whose prowess before Algiers we have already noticed. He was one of the most popular men of his order; the more so, perhaps, that Homedez, the grand master at that time, showed a cold and avaricious disposition which raised him many enemies, and rendered the display of reckless and romantic chivalry, such as that of Villegagnon, doubly welcome among the younger knights. Malta was in a most destitute state; and Homedez, as is said, from motives of self-interest, resisted all the representations that were made to him as to the necessity of securing its defences.

"It was a needless expense," he said; "these rumours of Turkish armaments were premature and ridiculous; and if you attended to them, you might attend to nothing else."

Nevertheless, on the morning of the 16th of July 1551, three days after he had expressed himself to this effect, he beheld from the windows of his palace the arrival of the whole Ottoman fleet, sailing before a favourable wind, and about, as it seemed, to cast anchor before the principal fort of the island. That of the old city, or *borgo*, was defended only by a small fort, now without a garrison; for all the forces on the island had been called in to guard the fortifications of St. Angelo, then the residence of the order. The terrified inhabitants of the city hastened to despatch messengers to Homedez imploring succour: but the grand master refused; he had need, he said, of all his forces to defend St. Angelo.

"At least," returned the envoy in despair, "let us have Villegagnon with us"—a singular compliment to the bravery of that knight; nor did he decline the post, although, as he represented, the defence of the old city required at least the presence of a hundred men.

"I expect courage and obedience, not reasoning, from a knight," replied Homedez. "You can have six companions; if they are not enough, and you are afraid of the business, someone else may be found to undertake it."

Villegagnon keenly felt the taunt, and instantly rose to depart. "I will show you, sir," he replied, "that fear, at least, has never made me shrink from danger."

He set out at once, accompanied by six French knights; finding some horses grazing outside, they threw themselves on their backs without saddles or bridles, and reached the town. Gliding unperceived to the bottom of the walls, they made signals to the inhabitants, who lowered a rope; and thus all seven with their guide entered the fort under the eye of the enemy.

Meanwhile the Turkish fleet had been making the circuit of the island, considering the best point of attack. As they appeared before the fortified heights of St. Angelo, Sinam, the Ottoman general, called Dragut to his side. "Is that the castle you have represented so weak and defenceless?" he exclaimed; "why, no eagle could choose a better eyrie."

"Truly, *signior*," added a veteran corsair, who stood by his side, "it were hard to steal the eagle's eggs. Dost thou see yon rampart, where the scarlet banner floats? When I was a slave in the *giaours'* galleys, some twenty years ago, my shoulders helped to carry up the stones that built it; and you may take my word for it, ere you cast it to the ground, summer shall go and winter come, for its foundation is the rock itself."

"Enough," replied Sinam, "we land at the town below; and ere we batter the kennel of these dogs about their ears, we will teach the islanders how to show hospitality to the sultan's troops."

Accordingly the troops landed on the lower part of the island, and prepared to invest the old city, when a shout from the walls was heard, accompanied with discharges of musketry and repeated cries of joy;—it was the welcome which the citizens were giving to Villegagnon and his comrades.

"It is the Spanish fleet!" exclaimed one;

"The galleys from Naples!" cried another;

"The garrison of St. Angelo are coming down!" cried a third: and within an hour Sinam's troops had re-embarked. After a descent on Gozo, in which they succeeded in carrying off six thousand of the inhabitants into slavery, the fleet directed its course to Tripoli; but it must be allowed that this was but a pitiful commencement of the war of "extermination."

The garrison of Tripoli consisted chiefly of some fresh levies of Spanish and Calabrian troops; and the mutiny of these men, unaccustomed to face the enemy, brought about the speedy fall of the place; for Vallier, the marshal of the order, who held the command, perceiving the impossibility of resistance, felt himself justified in agreeing to terms of capitulation; a determination, however, which disgraced him in the eyes of his order, and on his arrival at Malta with his knights he was condemned to imprisonment.

It was in the August of 1557 that the death of La Sangle, successor to Homedez in the grand mastership, necessitated a new election, and placed John Parisot de la Valette at the head of an order in whose history he was destined to play so distinguished a part. Convinced that another attack on the island was meditated at no distant period, the first care of La Valette was to put his island in something like a state of defence; and with the generous purpose of sharing the dangers of his people, he removed his residence from St. Angelo to the *borgo*, from whence he was better able to direct the progress of the works. The final determination of Solyman to renew his attack on Malta was occasioned by the loss of a valuable galleon, laden with goods for the ladies of the *seraglio*, which was captured by the knights under the brave Romegas after a sharp engagement of five hours. This the sultan regarded as a sort of personal insult; and vowing vengeance against the order, he declared that, cost what it might, Malta should be destroyed.

Accordingly the Algerine fleet of corsairs, under Dragut, was speedily summoned to join his forces and prepare for the contest. His design was no secret; and La Valette employed the interval in assembling troops and provisions, and assigning to each of his followers their posts and duties in the coming siege. Like his predecessors D'Aubusson and L'Isle Adam, he had nothing but the valour of the order on which to depend. The pope contributed a sum of 10,000 crowns; but allies he had none, save the brave viceroy of Sicily, Garcias de Toledo, who visited him personally in the month of April, and promised to be back with succours before the end of June; France was distracted with Huguenot wars; Germany had enough to do to preserve her own frontiers; England, under Elizabeth, was ready to help the Turk himself against the Church; and Spain alone showed any disposition to assist the knights, though as yet the caution and deliberation of Philip II. had come to no decision on the subject.

La Valette, however, was equal to a great emergency; he had filled every office in the order, and thoroughly understood his position—nay, it seemed the peculiar destiny of his order to be the forlorn-hope of Europe, and to enter the arena with the infidels under circumstances which gave its combatants the valour of desperate men. Seven hundred knights, besides serving-brothers [4] and 8500 paid soldiers, formed his army of defence.

---

4. Taaffe puts the number at 474 knights and 67 servants-at-arms, giving Bosio as his authority; but it does not appear that Bosio considered his list to be complete. His division according to countries is as follows: (continued on next page)

Among these we find but one Englishman, to represent a nation formerly the foremost in the list; yet, sad as is the contrast, it is pleasant to record his name—he was Sir Oliver Starkey. Possibly there might have been others; but their names have escaped the record of the historian; and, considering the times, it may be matter of surprise that even one could yet be found.

Before entering on the story of the last great siege sustained by the order of St. John, it may be well to offer some description of the city and its defences, which will better enable the reader to understand the position of the contending parties.

A narrow tongue of land, running out into the sea on the north-east coast of Malta, separated two large and commodious ports: the Great Harbour, now Port Valetta, to the east; and Port Musiette to the west. As yet it was not built upon; except that Strozzi, prior of Capua, had raised at its extremity a strong castle, which bore the name of Fort St. Elmo. This fortress commanded both harbours, but was itself liable to be cut off Irani communication with, the mainland in time of siege. Within the larger port were two promontories: the outermost of ,which was occupied by the little town, or *borgo*, and was defended by

	Knights	Servants at Arms
Provence	61	15
Auvergne	25	14
France	57	24
Italy	164	5
England	1	0
Germany	13	1
Castile	68	6
Arragon	85	2
	474	67

Prescott says that "the whole force which La Valette could muster in defence of the island amounted to about 9000 men. This included 700 knights, of whom about 600 had already arrived. The remainder were on their way, and joined him at a later period of the siege. Between 8000 and 4000 were Maltese, irregularly trained, but who had already gained some experience of war in their contests with the Barbary coasts. The rest of the army, with the exception of 500 galley-slaves and the personal followers of the knights, was made up of levies from Spain and Italy." *History of the Reign of Philip II.,* book 4. chap. 3.

These volumes, which have appeared since the present sketch was written, contain a detailed and very animated description of this memorable siege.

the castle of St. Angelo; the innermost was called La Sangle, after the grand master who first fortified it, and had also at its extremity a fort named St. Michael, round which a straggling population had gathered. Between these two promontories the galleys were moored; and the mouth of the port was closed by an iron chain.

In distributing the various posts of defence the same order was observed as at Rhodes. Each language had its own place assigned to it. To France was given the charge of the *borgo*; to Italy the promontory of La Sangle; while fifty Spanish knights held the castle of St. Angelo; and sixty more, under Deguarras, bailiff of Negropont, were sent to reinforce the garrison of St. Elmo, commanded by an aged knight named De Broglie. From the *borgo* to St Angelo were to be drawn up the knights of Arragon and Navarre, and on the other side those of Castile, Provence, and Germany; while the platform at the foot of the castle was guarded by a Spanish knight, with some of the crews of the galleys, whose business was to work nine pieces of ordnance, and to defend the mouth of the port and the great chain—a very marvellous production, so thick that nothing had ever been seen to equal its enormous dimensions, and fastened by the anchor that had belonged to the great carrack of the order.

When La Valette had formed these dispositions of his forces, he caused the same scene to be enacted which had formerly been displayed at Rhodes—a general review of all the troops, each before his own inn; their arms and numbers were examined, and their skill tested by shooting at a mark. His own appearance among them, as he passed from line to line, was received with shouts of enthusiasm; and truly his bearing was one well calculated to rouse the ardour of his followers. He had that same air of tranquil serene intrepidity which distinguished L'Isle Adam, and which bore with it the assurance of success, because it breathed a higher trust than mere confidence in human skill or valour. His eye was perhaps a little stern; but if so, you forgot its sternness as you gazed at that sweet and placid mouth, whose delicate lines declared the presence of a refined and cultivated mind, and the tenderness which at times accords so well with a brave and dauntless spirit.

Every heart beat with a noble pride as the grand master approached the assembled troops, and checking his horse, addressed them in the following terms:

> Comrades, a cloud of barbarians is about to burst upon our coast; they are the enemies of Jesus; and in the coming contest it is to be decided whether the Gospel or the Koran shall triumph. At such a moment God calls on us for those lives which we have devoted to His service. Happy they who shall first offer Him this sacrifice! But, to render ourselves worthy of such a grace, let us renew our vows at the foot of His altar; and seek in the Blood of Christ, poured out to us in His sacraments, that true indifference to death which will render our arms invincible.

As he closed his address he moved towards the great church of St. John's, where the Blessed Sacrament was exposed for adoration, and whither he was followed by all the knights. Every one confessed, and approached the holy table;

> There was not an unshriven man among them. The remainder of the day was spent, as became men preparing for death, in reconciling differences and taking a brotherly farewell; and before nightfall everyone was at his post.

CHAPTER 9

Arrival of the Turkish Fleet

It was the 18th of May 1565, a little before sunrise when the guns of St Angelo gave the signal of the enemy's approach. As the sun rose over the western ocean it displayed the magnificent spectacle of the whole Turkish fleet, consisting of 181 vessels, besides a number of transports, bearing on towards the coast. They had 30,000 men on board, the flower of the Ottoman army; 4500 being *Janizaries*, under the command of Mustapha Pasha and the celebrated corsair [1] Admiral Piali [2] Dragut and Ouloudjali were to follow speedily with the forces of Tripoli and Alexandria. Solyman is said to have spent five years in the equipment of this force; far less numerous than that formerly despatched against Rhodes, but furnished with such vast and formidable resources of all kinds, in stores, artillery, and machines of war, that it was thought its equal had never before been brought together.

The defenders of Malta had ample time to survey the force prepared for their attack; for, as though to display their strength, the Turkish vessels made the entire circuit of the island several times, being watched by the gallant Copier, marshal of the order, who, at the head of a small body of horse and about 600 foot,

---

1. This Turkish corsair (commonly called Ochiali) made himself famous in the succeeding reign. We shall meet with him again in the battle of Lepanto.
2. Piali was by birth a Groatian. On the 14th of May 1560 he had defeated and almost annihilated the combined Christian fleet commanded by the Genoese Doria, the favourite admiral of Charles V. The battle took place off the island of Djerbé.

159

was charged with the duty of reconnoitring the enemy's movements, and harassing them during their disembarkation. Late in the day the vessels dropped anchor opposite Citta Vecchia, the intention being to deceive the marshal, for in reality there was no thought at landing in that direction; and finally the whole army disembarked at Marsa Sirocco, a bay in the vicinity of the *borgo*, and proceeded to fortify their position so as to secure themselves from the sorties of the Christians.

The first few days were spent in spirited engagements between the skirmishing-parties on both sides, which La Valette allowed in order that his men might get accustomed to the appearance and method of fighting of the Turks; but the impetuosity of the knights was so great, that it required all the authority of the mud master to get the city gates closed; and he saw the necessity of keeping his men within their enclosure if he did not wish to bring on a general engagement, which, with such unequal forces, would, he well knew, be madness. The 20th of May fell on a Sunday? many Masses had been said, and a solemn procession made in all the churches; the evening of the same day the Turkish artillery opened on the town, being principally directed against Fort St. Elmo, which was indeed the key of the Christian position. La Valette, regardless of the entreaties of his attendants not to expose ins person, ascended the bastion of Provence, from whence he could command a view of the whole scene.

It was indeed a splendid spectacle. Thirty thousand men drawn up in the form of a vast crescent, and seeming to cover the whole face of the country: the bright burning sun lit; up their gilded armour and gay attire, their standards and many-coloured tents and flags, of which there was an infinite number of every hue; so that, to use the expression of an historian,

they looked like a multitude of flowers on a luxuriant meadow,

while from their ranks arose a soft and exquisite music from all kinds of martial instruments. Sometimes you might see a cloud of skirmishers separate from the dark mass of troops; for the marshal and Deguarras hovered on their flanks, and kept up a continual and harassing attack. Nevertheless both parties felt that this kind of desultory conflict was but waste of time, and La Valette knew as well as did the Turkish chiefs themselves that the attack would soon commence in real earnest on St. Elmo. Nor was he deceived; on the 24th the cannonade against that fort commenced both from sea and land; and once more those marble balls, which had done such terrible execution on the walls of Rhodes, were heard thundering against the bastions with terrible effect. La Valette well knew the importance of the post and its danger, and did what he could to relieve it by daily reinforcements sent in boats by night, which returned with the wounded.

One day, as he stood watching the fire of the Turks from his usual post on the Provence bastion, La Cerda, a Spanish knight, appeared before him with a message from the garrison.

"So please you," exclaimed the envoy, "the bailiff of Negropont bids me say, that if the fort be not speedily succoured, it must fall; it cannot hold out another week under the fire of the eighty-pounders."

La Valette looked at him surprised. "What great loss has befallen you, sir," he said, "that makes you cry thus for help?"

"My lord," replied La Cerda, "it is no time for delay: the castle is like a sick man, whose strength is exhausted, and can only be kept up by constant nourishment and care."

"I will be its physician," said the grand master haughtily; "I will bring with me these who, if they cannot cure you of your fears may at least save the fortress by their valour."

In fact, he would have himself accompanied the reinforcements he despatched but for the interference of his council; for, as he was wont to say, he dreaded but one thing, and that was the possibility of a feeble defence. At length he consented that fifty of the order, with two companies of soldiers, should return with La Cerda to the post of danger. This reinforcement was placed under the command of the bold Medrano, and ere it departed to the fort was further increased by several knights from Sicily, who volunteered to share the fortunes of their brethren.

The great battery of the Turks, finished on the last day of May, was a curious structure; built at Constantinople in separate pieces of timber, so as to be put together on the spot, and now erected before the devoted fortress, whose garrison consisted of no more than 400 men. It was of enormous size, and decorated with fourteen standards of different colours: removed at first only 180 yards from the castle walls; afterwards another battery was added, which discharged thirty heavy pieces of artillery at the distance of but thirty yards, It was a very tempest of fire; and that the walls could stand at all under such an assault is matter of surprise. The outer ravelin was stormed on St. Elmo's day, the 3rd of June; and the scene was anxiously watched from the *borgo*. From the other quarters of the town every incident of the fight could be distinctly discerned; and the Christians were compelled to be spectators of their comrades' danger, while they were powerless to succour them; for St. Elmo was surrounded on all sides by its besiegers, and its communication with the old city entirely cut off.

Is all lost then? The parapets are crowded with turbaned heads; the ravelin is not only in the possession of the infidels, but is levelled to the ground; its defenders retreat to the main body of the fortress. But the Turks press hard upon their ranks; and as both parties, mingling together in a hand-to-hand fight, enter the court between the outworks and the citadel; the confused sound of yells and cries of every description announces to the excited beholders that a combat of no ordinary kind is raging in that narrow space. What can it mean? Will they storm the citadel itself before the batteries have formed a breach? There it is again; you may almost catch the taunting words of the combatants, as they confront each other face to face. But the Turks have surely got the worst; for there, in that pent-up court, there comes down upon them from the ramparts overhead such a storm of stones and wild-fire and boiling-oil, such volleys of musketry and the annihilating fire of cannon, which at that short range play on their thick masses with horrible effect, that they are forced to fall back on the ravelin.

It was but to prepare, however, for a fresh attack; for, mad as the design may seem, the Turks had resolved on storming St. Elmo that very day, without waiting for the aid of breach or mine. The cry of "Scaling-ladders for the walls!" may now be heard; and scarcely are they brought but you may see the wild tumultuous rush with which they throw themselves on the ramparts, only to be hurled headlong on the rocks below. But the madness of savages has seized their ranks; they care nothing for the risk of death,—nothing for the crushing stones and torrents of burning pitch poured upon their defenceless heads; they scream curses and blasphemies at their adversaries, and you may catch their cries of rage and defeated malice, while there rises from that narrow neck of land a thick offensive smoke, through which glare lurid flames as in the crater of a volcano; and the dense cloud hangs over the water, gradually concealing everything from view, so that at length you can but guess what kind of work is going on at that beleaguered fortress by the sounds that issue from the spot.

What meanwhile has been the situation of the garrison? Almost a desperate one: and yet they are the victors of the day. A hundred men, and twenty knights besides, have fallen in their ranks: but the bodies of three thousand of their enemies are lying on the rocks beneath; and, spite of all their frantic efforts, they have been compelled to retire defeated from the walls. And how have those hundred and twenty died? Do we find in their defence the same savage brute ferocity as was exhibited in the onslaught of their assailants? Surely, if so, such butchery were scarcely worthy of a record from a Christian pen. But it was not so; they combated to death, yet died as became the champions of the heroes they were.

"Save yourself, comrade," cried the French Knight Bridier de la Gordamp; "and count me as a dead man, for the ball is very near my heart."

"By the fair fame of Auvergne, I will not leave you till I bear you to a place of safety," said his companion; and, lifting him in his arms, he carried him through the fire to a sheltered nook.

"Now go, dear brother," said the wounded knight, "I can but die; and down there yonder they are fighting for the faith."

The other left him, as he desired; but when the fight was over, he searched in vain for his comrade, alive or dead. "Where is Bridier?" he said to the knights around him, "he had not strength to make his way within; I surely thought he had spoken his last word by our side."

At length a track of blood upon the steps that led to the chapel within the fortress attracted their attention; they entered and approached the altar, and found the dead man, with his hands clasped as if in prayer, lying at its foot; he had felt the hand of death, and, summoning all his strength, had crawled away to die in quiet, and in the presence of his Lord.

"He had ever led," says Goussancourt, "a most religious life."

Much of the same spirit is shown in other anecdotes, and a certain sweet and noble chivalry breathes through the conduct of the knights, which singularly contrasts with the mad barbarism of their assailants: it is as though, through the bursts, of a wild and terrible hurricane, we caught the rich tones of some lofty martial strain.

The attack lasted from daybreak till noon; and at nightfall La Valette succeeded in bringing off the wounded, and throwing a small reinforcement into the place, in spite of the fire of the *Janizary* musketry. The bailiff and the commander Broglio, both badly wounded, would not accept the permission granted them to retire, but, together with many others of the garrison, preferred to remain and die at their posts. They might be seen, regardless of their sufferings, in the thickest of the fire, carrying earth to strengthen the ramparts, or administering help to the wounded; and, when unable to render more active service, you might see them drag themselves beside the artillery-men, and help them in the working of the guns.

Meanwhile La Valette had made frequent representations to

the viceroy Toledo that his promised succours were badly needed; but they still delayed: only a small galley arrived from Sicily, bringing the gallant knight Miranda, who instantly volunteered to join the garrison at St. Elmo. His presence in the fortress had as astonishing effect,—for he was a man equally renowned for piety, courage, and military skill,—and his presence gave new life to the defence. Nevertheless it became every day more desperate: the ramparts were in ruins, the garrison worn out with constant fatigue; for, after days spent in conflict, their nights were employed in burying their dead and the torn and mangled limbs of those dismembered by the cannonade. Scarcely could you tell them to be men, so disfigured were they by the smoke and the wildfire that blazed around them; their faces braised and burnt, and not one unwounded man among them. It was now the 6th of June; and while the guns of those terrible batteries still stormed against the ruins of St. Elmo, the Turks, after many fruitless efforts, succeeded at length in almost cutting off all communication between the fortress and the town.

A wall was erected on the ravelin, which seemed to enclose the castle and entirely to shut it in from the mainland; and in this extremity it was determined to despatch a messenger to La Valette to inform him that St. Elmo was no longer tenable. Medrano, who was charged with the delivery of the intelligence, succeeded in making his way to the *borgo*. A majority of the council were for abandoning a position which it was impossible to hold; but La Valette, although he felt bitterly the hard necessity of refusing to recall the devoted troops, maintained that every day St. Elmo held out was worth a week to the safety of the island, for the *borgo* could not be attacked till the castle fell; and the council came round to his opinion.

> "It is a sacrifice," wrote the grand master; "but to such sacrifice of our life for Christendom our vows and profession bind us. The succour from Sicily is daily expected; and till it come, the decision of the council is, that St. Elmo must not be abandoned, but that its defenders must abide in it until death."

It was a hard sentence; for the castle was rocking to its foundations, and the noise of the miners underneath could be distinctly heard; nevertheless Miranda and the elder knights, with the heroic old bailiff, received it with a shout of enthusiasm. But the younger brethren, to the number of fifty, protested that, rather than wait tamely to be butchered like sheep in a pen, they would sally out upon the foe, and perish to a man in one desperate encounter. This resolution they signified in a letter to the grand master. His reply was stern and peremptory. He bade them remember they were bound by their vows to fight and die, not in such manner as they willed, but as he their commander directed. That he might not appear, however, to slight their protestation, he sent three commissioners to report on the state of the defences.

Two out of the number sided with the remonstrants; the third, an Italian knight named Castriot, not only declared the place still tenable, but boldly offered himself to undertake its defence; and this he repeated to the grand master on his return. Volunteers presented themselves on all sides, and in such crowds that La Valette's only embarrassment was what selection to make. The complainants were told that their prayer was granted; they should be relieved that very evening, and within the walls of their convent might feel themselves, at least for the present, in safety. Stung to the quick by this sarcastic reply, the young knights humbly sued for forgiveness and for permission still to die at their posts. La Valette was at first inflexible, but yielded at length to the entreaties of the penitent brethren, and the new levies were dismissed. The hired troops also had betrayed their discontent. However, they too were at length shamed into resolution; for when they found that their departure was not opposed, and that hundreds in the ranks of their comrades on shore were eager to take their places, they declared that they would not be the first to retire, but would stay and die with their commanders.

With extreme difficulty a fresh reinforcement of fifteen knights was now thrown into the fortress, who were received with such cheers and demonstrations of rejoicing, that the Turks, led to believe some powerful succour had arrived, were only driven to renew their fire more heavily than before, Dragut had arrived (June 2nd) with thirteen galleys, containing each 100 men, and ten *galliots*, having on board 810 soldiers. With the guns of his ships he constructed a battery on the point of land which still bears his name, and firing across Port Musiette, swept the western flank of St. Elmo with terrible effect; and then from land and sea, both day and night, the enemy's artillery continued to bombard the defences of the fort, as well as of the castle of St. Angelo. At length a yawning chasm in the walls showed that a practicable breach was effected; and Dragut fixed the 16th of June for the assault general on St. Elmo.

Let our readers, therefore, transport themselves to the heights above the city, and watch the scene beneath. The whole Moslem fleet gathered like a forest round the mouth of the harbour,— for the attack is to be by sea as well as by land; the trenches filled with Turkish troops,—all, however, preserving a profound and singular silence; and 8000 horsemen before the bridge which faces the great front of the castle, where Mustapha Pasha commands in person, his presence being indicated by the great standard given into his hands before leaving Constantinople by the sultan himself. As to the garrison, they are well prepared for the attack; and, thanks to La Valette's constant succours, their numbers are again complete; yet they are but 400 men.

A knight stands to every three soldiers around the walls; heaps of stones are arranged at regular distances, with instruments of war not known in our day, and of the most terrible description; large hoops, which, dipped in certain combustible preparations and set on fire, are cast among the masses of the enemy, and surround some two or three with a circle of certain death; pots of wildfire, which break when hurled on the heads of the storming-party, and scatter their burning contents far and wide; and other inventions of a similar kind, then in common use, which gave a peculiar honour to the sieges of the time. The wounded have their duties assigned to them, namely, to bring food and wine to those on the walls, and to drag away the dead or dying from beneath the feet of their comrades. In short, Christians and Moslems are ready and impatient, and only wait the signal of attack.

It was given by the planting of the sultan's standard on the bridge; and the yell that burst from the Turkish line warned the garrison that their assailants were at hand. Thirty of their chosen men, bound by fearful oaths to enter the fortress together or die in the attempt, stormed the weakest bulwark, and would have infallibly succeeded but for the quick eye of La Valette, who watched all from the castle of St. Angelo, and directed two guns to bear upon the spot, which swept twenty of them away, and the remainder were compelled to retire. Still the attack on the other quarters was unabated in its fury. Mad with drink and with a wild religious fanaticism, the half-savage bodies of the Moslem troops threw themselves on the ladders, but never reached the top. Down came the fiery hoops and the stones and hissing wildfire, and swept them away by twenties at a time.

All up and down the walls there seemed to flare and blaze those streams of liquid fire; and in the dense ranks of the assailants, those on whom it fell were unable to escape. Even when fresh stormers struggled to the parapets they met a wall of pikes they could not pierce; hand to hand the foemen grappled amid the showers of arrows and volleys of musketry that poured in from the trenches; but the strong arms of His Christian knights thrust off their enemies, and again the ladders were emptied and the walls left free. Then Dragut and Mustapha advanced, and choosing two of the most ferocious of their men, committed to each a splendid standard, and bade them plant them on the walls. In a moment the gilded banners are glittering on the ramparts; but in another they are torn away, and their bearers are hurled lifeless into the ditch. After a terrific conflict of six hours the infidels abandoned the attempt, leaving more than 9000 of their companions dead under the walls.

It was now that Dragut met his doom. As he stood outside the trenches, mating dispositions with Mustapha for screening off the fire of St. Angelo, a ball from that fort splintered a rock close beside him, and a fragment of the stone struck him on the head. He fell on the instant speechless and bathed in his own blood; and the *pasha*, to hide the catastrophe from the soldiers, threw his cloak over him, and had him carried to his tent, where he lived only long enough to learn the ultimate fate of St. Elmo.

Again, then, the victory is with the Christians; there is a service of thanksgiving in the great church of St. John's, and a call for fresh volunteers; for out of the four hundred who held St Elmo that morning not a hundred are left alive. Seventeen of the knights had fallen, and among them the brave Medrano, who, in the act of tearing a Turkish standard from the rampart, was himself struck down by a bullet from an *arquebuse*.

Before nightfall, the reinforcement, led by thirty knights, is safe within the walls, ready, when the morning comes, to renew the combat with undiminished valour. It is said that La Valette himself marvelled at the ardour of his brethren: they contended for the glorious post of sacrifice as though for martyrdom; and such perhaps it was,—for their death was not for conquest or ambition, but for the safety of the Christian world.

The Turks now resolved to cut off all communication between the fortress, and St. Angelo and the town, by continuing the line of entrenchments to the Great Harbour, where a battery of heavy guns could command the landing-place. While the works were in progress the garrison were kept in a state of perpetual alarm: all through the day an incessant fire was directed against the already ruined ramparts, and at night continual attacks, real or feigned, allowed the exhausted defenders no interval of repose.

On the 18th of the month the investment was complete, and the little garrison knew that their hour was come. It was with unspeakable anguish that La Valette had watched that impassable barrier closing each day around the devoted band, unable to offer any succour to his brethren, or even to embarrass or retard the enemy's work. The 20th was the Feast of Corpus Christi, and never perhaps was it celebrated under circumstances of greater solemnity, or such as were more calculated to inspire devotion. The Blessed Sacrament was born in procession the whole circuit of the town, care only being taken to avoid such points as were most exposed to the enemy's artillery. At its head walked the grand master, and after him came the knights, clad in their dark robes with the white cross upon their breasts. The entire population accompanied them to the great church, where, prostrate on the pavement, they adored the Most Holy enthroned above the altar, and besought Him to have pity on them in their extremity, to grant to their brethren at St. Elmo the aid which no human power could give, and not to allow His worshippers to fail into the hands of the enemies of the faith.

All through the 21st the cannonading continued with increased severity, until the tottering walls of the castle were in many places levelled to the surface of the rock on which they stood; and on the next day the second assault was made: the whole army of the infidels against four hundred men. Thrice the enemy renewed that terrible charge, and thrice they were withstood. The defenders seemed to be possessed of a supernatural strength and a presence that was ubiquitous; and once again the shout—a feeble shout indeed—of "Victory! victory!" which reached the *borgo*, told the Christians that their comrades had gained the day.

But a messenger from the fort; diving under water, and with wonderful dexterity escaping through the Turkish boats, brought a letter which told La Valette that two-thirds of their numbers were fallen, and the rest, wounded and exhausted, could scarcely lift their swords. Fresh succours were instantly despatched, but for the first time found it impossible to approach; for eighty of the Turkish galleys lying off the harbour darted forward to intercept them on their way, and so rapid were their movements, that, seeing they would infallibly be surrounded if they attempted to force a passage, the volunteers were forced reluctantly to retire. The garrison had watched them from the wall, and now learnt too surely that there was nothing more to hope. Daybreak would bring the last assault, and they could but die; but how should the night be passed? Surely as became the Hospitallers of the Cross. They dressed each other's wounds, and each man comforted his fellow with noble and religious words; Miranda and the bailiff devoted themselves to the soldiers; and all confessed and communicated; then, embracing one another like brethren in Christ, they went to the walls, and those who could not stand were carried thither in a chair, and sat at the breach grasping their swords in both hands, and waiting for the enemy.

The morning broke at last; it was the vigil of St. John. The Turks came on with shouts of certain victory, which were proudly answered by the cheers of the garrison. For four long hours they withstood charge after charge from their assailants with heroic firmness; those who could not rise on their feet still kept up a fire of musketry, until their ammunition was so exhausted that they were forced to collect the grains of powder out of the pockets of their fallen brethren. At the end of that time only sixty men were left alive; but these maintained the defence with such undaunted courage, that at eleven o'clock the infidels discontinued the assault, and gave them a brief respite while they prepared to renew the combat with redoubled fury.

As the besieged were enjoying the short breathing-space the signal was heard for the recommencement of the attack; the Turks poured in on every side, and in fact there was nothing to keep them out,—the walls were gone, and the guns silent now for want of powder,—only a few brave men too weak to stand, with broken limbs and ghastly bleeding wounds, yet with their last breath, wielding their pikes and two-handed swords, they confronted the invaders, and seemed to defy them to do their worst.

"In, followers of Islam!" shouted the *pasha*; "the dogs can do you no harm!" and with yells of fiendish malice the wild troops of the Spahis and Dahis burst into the fortress. The gallant old bailiff D'Egueras was the first to meet them lance in hand, and the first to fall from a blow that severed his head from his body, and laid his white hairs on the bloody ground. Francis Lanfreducci, before he died, struggled to the spot where a beacon was prepared to give notice to the *borgo* that all hope was gone; he fired it, and at the same moment expired from his wounds. The fight was soon over for want of combatants, yet one was left alive—Paul of Novara, who, summoning his last energies, charged boldly at the whole front of his enemies and drove them bodily from the breach; then, overpowered by numbers, he fell with his face to the foe, and the bloody scene was over. Five Maltese soldiers alone escaped by casting themselves into the water and swimming to the shore. Nine knights also, it is said, who were posted near the end of the fosse, were taken prisoners by the corsairs. These were the sole survivors of the massacre; for the Turks gave no quarter, Mustapha having offered a prize for every Christian head, and this in pursuance, as is said, of orders from the sultan. Twelve others at the point of death were found, like Bridier de Gordamp, lying before the chapel-altar, and being seized, were hung up by the feet, and then crucified.

The *pasha* himself now entered the fort, and struck by the insignificance of the place, rightly judged that the conquest of the *borgo* would be no easy task. "What, he exclaimed, "will be the resistance of the parent when the child has cost us eight thousand of our bravest men?" To intimidate the knights, therefore, he had recourse to horrible barbarities. The heads of four of the principal brethren, among them those of Miranda and the brave old bailiff, he caused to be fixed aloft upon a pole with their faces towards the town; then ordering search to be made among the heaps of dead that covered the ramparts, he selected the bodies of the knights, some of whom still breathed, and first gashing their breasts crosswise and tearing out their hearts, he cut off their heads and feet, and nailed their mangled trunks upon wooden crosses;[3] then, throwing over each their scarlet surcoats, he cast them into the sea, trusting that the waves would bear them to the foot of the castle of St. Angelo, where they might meet the eyes of the grand master and his knights.

---

3. Goussancourt gives the names of thirteen as having been found still alive by the Turks. One—Lawrence de Bonlieu—before being fastened to the cross, was first flayed!

The awning tide brought them to the shore; the sight drew tears from the eyes of La Valette, and those torn and mangled bodies, being lifted reverently and tenderly, were kissed and honoured as the relics of glorious martyrs. Happy were they in their comrades' eyes, thus bearing the cross, and bound to it to the last.

"Grieve not for the fall of St. Elmo," said La Valette to his council, "but rather give God thanks that the noble few who held it could keep their post, so long. If now they have been forced to yield, yet has their death been glorious, and their end, which the infidels deemed disgrace, fit funeral for Hospitallers of the Cross."

Yet, spite of his words, the anguish of the grand master was not to be concealed; and he changed his residence, so as no longer to see from the windows of his palace the fort which recalled the slaughter of his comrades; and his countenance, though it lost nothing of its lofty serenity, was lined and worn by suffering strongly mastered and suppressed.

From this time La Valette gave no quarter, as, notwithstanding the contrary inhuman practice of the Turks, he had hitherto done. So far, at least, he was justified by the laws of war; but not satisfied with this, he was carried on to the committal of an act which,—whatever might be the usage of those days, and whatever excuse may be framed for it from the consideration of the ferocious barbarity of the adversary he had to deal with, and the maddening horror inspired by the sight of the mangled remains of his brethren, bearing on them the marks of the torments they had undergone,—cannot but be regarded as a stain on the pure glory of this Christian knight.

He gave instant orders for the execution of the prisoners; and that the brutal foe might learn the sudden vengeance which their cold-blooded cruelty had brought down upon their comrades, he caused their gory heads to be fired into the Turkish camp. Doubtless he hoped to strike terror into the infidels, and to teach them the danger to themselves of converting warfare into butchery. But such fierce reprisals seldom produce any salutary effect, while the recital gives a painful jar to the feelings with which we love to regard these heroic champions of the Cross.

The loss of the Christians in the defence of St. Elmo is differently estimated; but the common account puts it at 1300 men, of whom 130 were knights.[4] When we reflect that a handful of warriors withstood for the space of a month the whole strength of the Ottoman army, and consider the deliberate nature of their sacrifice in an enterprise where victory was never once contemplated, but in which they sought only to secure the safety of the island by a prolonged resistance, we shall not hesitate to place their devotion at least on a level with that of the three hundred heroes of Thermopylæ,—far above it, if we remember that in their case patriotic ardour was rendered holy by religious zeal:

"The profession of our oath," said the grand master in his letter, "is to sacrifice our lives for Christendom."

---

4. Prescott says that the number of Christians who fell amounted to about 1500, of whom 128 were members of the order, The loss of the infidels he estimates at 8000.

Chapter 10

St John's Day

It was the festival of St. John; there was a pause in the fierce cannonade which had so long thundered in the ears of the inhabitants of Malta, and the bright midsummer day shone over the waves, whose dancing brightness told no tale of the ghastly procession they had borne on their surface the night before. The morning had been ushered in with a religious ceremony,—the solemn burying of the martyrs of St. Elmo, as the people loved to call them; and over the grave La Valette addressed his followers, and bade them keep true to so bright and noble an example. "What more can we desire than to die for the faith of Christ? in His service we are omnipotent."

Then, turning to the women, he bade them dry their tears, and keep St. John's day with their accustomed joy. And so they did, flocking to the churches, and kindling through the streets those huge bonfires that in every Christian land, from Norway to Spain, light up the night which celebrates the Precursor's birth.

On the 16th of June, the same day on which the first assault-general had been made on St. Elmo, four galleys had set sail from Messina, having on board the force designated by the Maltese historians as the "little succour." Certainly, after its despatch had been so long talked of, it might seem little enough, consisting as it did of only 700 men and forty knights; not enough to replace those who had fallen in the siege. However, it arrived on the 29th; and little as it was, it numbered some of the first warriors of the day, among others Parisot, the grand master's nephew. They had no small difficulty in passing the Turkish fleet, and landing at Citta Vecchia, and were heartily welcomed, though, as La Valette again wrote to the viceroy, nothing less than 12,000 men would suffice for the necessities of the siege. Meanwhile a Greek slave was despatched as envoy to the grand master from the *pasha*, proposing conditions of honourable capitulation; but La Valette desired him to be conducted through the fortifications, and shown the deep ditch that surrounded the counterscarp. "This" said the knight who escorted him, "is the place we intend to surrender to your master; but there is room enough to bury him and his *Janizaries*."

Disappointed in his attempts at negotiation, Mustapha prepared to push the siege with all vigour. Not a moment had been lost in pursuing the necessary operations; and the blockade was soon complete both by sea and by land. Early in July the encircling batteries, mounted with sixty or seventy heavy pieces of cannon, poured their converging fire on the towns and fortresses and the shipping that lay at anchor in the Port of the Galleys, and the roar of that artillery sounded like the mutterings of distant thunder on the coast of Sicily; but the chief point of attack was the castle of St. Michael, situated on the promontory, or island, as it is often termed, of La Sangle.

The *pasha* determined to assault it not only by land but by sea. To effect this, without exposing his vessels to the guns of St. Angelo, it was necessary to carry boats overland across the peninsula on which St. Elmo had stood. The manoeuvre was successfully accomplished; and no less than eighty vessels were thus transported across the heights in the sight of the astonished Christians, and launched on the waters of the basin. But La Valette was equally prompt in adopting measures of defence; and to oppose the passage of the Turkish flotilla, erected with almost incredible labour,—for the work could be carried on only by night,—a strong palisade at the southern extremity of the harbour. This led to bloody combats, half on land and half on water, nay, often in the water itself, in which the dexterous Maltese swimmers, stripped naked and armed only with a short sword, at length completely routed the bands of Turkish axemen who were sent to destroy the works.

Not to weary our readers with the repetition of the same bloody details, it is enough to say that St. Michael proved as hard a task for the besiegers as St. Elmo. Dragut, as has been said, had fallen in the former conflict; but his place was supplied by the corsair Hassan, Beyler Bey of Algiers, who had landed at the head of 2500 men. As son of the famous Barbarossa, and son-in-law of Dragut, he claimed the honour of leading the assault against St. Michael. The *pasha* placed 6000 men at his command, and with these, early on the morning of the 15th of July, he assaulted the fortress from the land; while the old corsair, Candelissa, a Greek renegade, with the Algerine squadron, attacked the inner harbour of the galleys.

With the sound of tambours and blasts of trumpets he directed his course towards the palisades; before him, in a shallop, going the *imaums* and the *marabouts*, clad in their dark-coloured robes, reciting aloud passages from the Koran, and screaming out prayers to heaven and curses on the Christians. But these soon dropped aside, and the flotilla of boats came on, the chiefs conspicuous in the midst, with their gaily-streaming mantles and glittering arms. The struggle was long and obstinate: it continued for five hours, during which the Turks made incessant attempts to scale the parapets, and at one moment succeeded in planting their standards on the ramparts. But, fired at the sight, the Christians rushed upon the foe with redoubled vigour; the Admiral Monté put himself at their head; their long swords swept the ranks of their assailants; with pikes and poniards they threw themselves into the thick of the fray;—there also might be seen Brother Robert, a sword in one hand and a crucifix in the other, exhorting the Christian combatants to fight for the faith of Jesus Christ and die in its defence.

But even valour desperate as theirs might have been fruitless against such overwhelming odds, had not the grand master, whose eye nothing seemed to escape, by means of a floating bridge which he had thrown across the Port of Galleys, despatched reinforcements at the very moment of need. Then, too, was beheld a strange and an inspiring sight: a troop of boys, 200 strong, issued from the town, armed with slings; shouting "A rescue—rescue, victory!" they let fly a shower of stones on the heads and in the faces of the foe; at the same instant De Giou, commandant of the galleys, charging at the head of the new succours, drove everything before him, and forced back the infidels with frightful slaughter. The wildfire glared over their falling masses, and there was a hurried scramble to the boats, and plunge after plunge into the water; but even then the batteries played on them without ceasing; the port was filled with dead and dying, and crimsoned with blood.

In vain they who could not reach the boats begged for mercy on their knees; the terrible shout rang in their ears, "Remember St. Elmo!"

To all their cries for quarter the only answer was, "St. Elmo's pay!"

Ere this victory was accomplished the *pasha* had despatched a powerful reinforcement, which, avoiding the palisades, steered its course more northernward; but here it became exposed to one of the batteries of St Angelo, which, sunk low down, almost beneath the level of the water, had remained concealed; and now, as the enemy advanced within range of its shot, suddenly opened a terrific discharge upon them, which shattered nine out of the ten barges in which the troops were being transported to the scene of action; and in an instant the surface of the harbour was covered with splinters of wood, severed limbs, mutilated bodies, and such few of the survivors as were still left to struggle in the waves: the remaining boat turned and fled back to shore.

Meanwhile Hassan had fared no better at the breach than had Candelissa at the bastion. Again and again he strove to pierce the barrier of mail that defended the chasm in the walls; his troops threw themselves upon the little host of warriors only to recoil with thinned and disordered ranks; and when their bastion was cleared of assailants, and the defenders were at liberty to succour their comrades at the breach, the infidels were swept as by a whirlwind from the raised wall, and the victory of the Christians was everywhere complete. Of the six or seven thousand Moslems who had taken part in the two attacks not more than half that number returned to camp. The besieged had to lament the loss of 200 fighting men, among whom were the brave commander Zanoguerra, and Frederic de Toledo, son of the Viceroy of Sicily. But their confidence rose with their success; and La Valette, with all has knights, and the entire population of the *borgo*, went in procession to the great church of St. Lawrence, to adore the God of armies, and to suspend above the altar the banners of the infidels in token of thanksgiving.

Mustapha, now at last understanding the determined valour of the men with whom he had to deal, resolved to level the defences to the ground before attempting a renewal of the assault. After still further extending and strengthening his batteries, he opened a tremendous fire on the bastion of Castile, as well as on that part of the *borgo* which was nearest to it; and such was the crushing effect of the ponderous balls discharged from the Turkish mortars that the quarter of the town exposed to that unintermitting storm of stone and metal was speedily reduced to ruins, and numbers of the inhabitants were killed. La Valette, however, was as inventive of resources as was the *pasha* of engines of attack: his eye and hand were everywhere; no man knew when he took repose; by night as well as by day he might be seen, now superintending the operations he had ordered, now himself performing many of the most laborious duties of the common soldier, exhibiting the while the same unchanged tranquillity in his countenance and mien, which inspired all who beheld him with like resolution and courage.

Yet, amidst his indefatigable toils, he never failed every day to betake himself to the church of St. Lawrence, there to implore the blessing of Heaven on the Christian arms, and its protection of these to whom all human aid appeared to be denied. Forcing the Moslem slaves to aid in the work of defence, he caused a barrier of masonry to be thrown across the streets so broad and solid as to serve for a protection to the citizens; while on the side of the port he rendered all approach impossible by sinking barges laden with heavy stones not far from shore. Nor were the inhabitants less active on their part, but in all things showed themselves worthy of their beloved commander; Men, women, and children were continually engaged in constructing gabions, manufacturing fireworks, preparing stones and other missiles to hurl upon the besiegers' heads, and, above all, in repairing the breaches and fortifying the shattered walls. Nor all this time did they neglect to avail themselves of the aids which religion offered, but cultivated in themselves those pious dispositions which should enable them to gain the plenary indulgence which the Pope had granted to all who took part in this holy warfare.

Among other warlike devices the *pasha* at length contrived a sort of raised bridge by which the troops should be enabled to reach the battlements safe from the destructive fire of the garrison. Alarmed at the sight of this structure, the Christians endeavoured to set fire to it by night; but, after two failures, were obliged to defer their attempts till day. The enterprise was full of danger, and was entrusted by the grand master to his nephew Henry de la Valette, or, as he is elsewhere called, the Commander Parisot, from his lordship of that name. Parisot was accompanied by his dear friend and brother-in-arms Polastra, and a small number of soldiers. Throwing cables round the bridge, they endeavoured by main force to pull it to the ground; but being wholly exposed to the enemy's view, a severe fire was soon directed on the spot.

The two young knights, observing their men beginning to falter under the heavy cannonade, sprang intrepidly forward, and advanced alone to the foot of the bridge; but scarcely had they reached the spot when a volley of musketry laid both dead upon the ground. Instantly the *Janizaries* rushed forward to secure their bodies, in the hopes of gaining the reward offered for the heads of the Christian knights; but the soldiers, guessing their intention and reproaching themselves for their cowardice in not following the knights, rallied at the sight, and advanced to dispute the possession of the bodies. After a violent conflict the

Christians succeeded in carrying off the remains of the two gallant officers, and bearing them to the fort, whence messengers were sent to La Valette to acquaint him with his nephew's death. Parisot was a favourite with the whole order,—the *beau ideal* of a young cavalier,—but to none dearer than to the grand master himself. Nevertheless he received the news with that high and generous spirit which always distinguished him, and only raised his eyes to heaven and thanked God for granting his nephew so glorious an end, and himself a sacrifice to offer which had cost him something

Some of the brethren would have condoled with him on his loss, but he stopped them: "Every one of my knights," he said, "is equally dear to my heart, for all are my children: the loss of Parisot does not move me more than that of Polastra. And, after all, what does it matter? they have but gone a little while before us. So now to your duty, and let me hear no more about it:" nor was he ever heard to speak of his loss again to mortal ear. Nevertheless he bade them take him to the spot where the two young knights had fallen; and, after inspecting the bridge and its position, he planted a cannon on the wall opposite to it, which opened so effectual a fire as entirely to destroy the dangerous erection.

The besieged had now to sustain a double attack; for whilst the *pasha* and the Bey of Algiers continued the attempt on the fortress of St. Michael, Piali, the admiral of the fleet, led the assault on the bastion of Castile to the eastward of the *borgo*; and at the same time eighty of the largest armed galleys kept the sea, to prevent the landing of the daily-expected succours from Messina. The assault of the 2nd of August was among the most desperate yet attempted: the *pasha* animated his soldiers by his presence and his threats, and with his own hand slew two *Janizaries* who had retreated before the swords of the knights. But he fought against men resolved to conquer. Even women and children presented themselves to defend the breach, and rendered no contemptible assistance to the garrison. While the knights and men-at-arms poured withering volleys of musketry on the assailants as they rushed forward to the breach, the Maltese launched down heavy stones and pieces of timber, and discharged torrents of scalding pitch and streams of wildfire on their heads; and when the storming columns had scaled the ruined walls they found themselves opposed by an inner barrier of newly-raised entrenchments, behind which stood a living and still more impenetrable rampart in the persons of the brethren of St. John.

Great was the confusion and slaughter among the infidels: stunned by the incessant and increasing violence of the fiery hurricane that beat upon them, and entangled among the sharp-pointed spikes with which the ruins had every where been thickly planted, their disordered ranks reeled and broke as though the earth were quaking beneath their feet, and, in spite of all their leaders could do, turned and fled precipitately to their trenches, leaving the breach encumbered with their dead. Again and again, refreshed and reinforced, the Turks returned to the assault, and as often recoiled before the terrible prowess of the Christian chivalry, until at length, as the day wore on, and all his resources had been tried in vain, the *pasha* gave the word to retire; and from both bastion and fortress his baffled hosts withdrew in discomfiture and dismay.

Assaults again upon the morrow, and on each succeeding day, but with the same result; and then came the intelligence that 160 vessels and 15,000 troops were assembled in the ports of Sicily and about to sail. Mustapha was well-nigh in despair; but knowing that a failure and abandonment of the siege would entail certain disgrace at the hands of Solyman, he resolved on an extraordinary effort—an assault-general, made by relief-parties of his troops, and kept up without cessation till the physical strength of the exhausted garrison must perforce be worn out; and this was accordingly fixed to commence on the 7th of August.

He chose the hour of noon, when, in that burning climate, the knights would, he judged, be unfit for great exertions. The morning, too, passing in comparative quiet, was calculated to throw them off their guard. Suddenly, in the midday stillness, the explosion of a mine, and the cries from the wall of "Castile! Castile!" drew all eyes to the spot thus indicated. Floating over the bastion, they beheld a huge red banner, with its gilded pole and black horse-tail; and the alarming rumour spread rapidly through the city that the bastion was in the possession of the enemy.

A few moments more and the infidels would have been in the heart of the town. Brother William, a chaplain of the order, ran instantly to seek the grand master, whom he found standing, as was his wont, in the great square manned. "My lord," he exclaimed, "Castile is lost! and the *borgo* will soon be in the hands of the enemy; you will surely retire to St. Angela."

La Valette, without a gesture of surprise, took his helmet from his page's hands, and a lance from the nearest soldier: "Come, gentlemen," he said to the knights surrounding him, "we are wanted at the bastion; let us die together:" and, regardless of the entreaties of his followers that he would not needlessly expose his person, he hurried to the spot. The alarm-bell was rung, a crowd of citizens rallied round him, and at their head he fell upon the Turks.

A terrific struggle ensued, and the life of the grand master seemed in momentary peril. Mendoza, who stood by his side amidst a heap of slain, implored him to retire; he even knelt at his feet, conjuring him not to expose a life, on the preservation of which hung the only hopes of the city and the order; but La Valette answered him by a gesture of his hand: "Do you see those banners," he said, pointing to the Turkish standards, "and ask me to retire before they are trampled in the dust?"

Then, heading the attack, with his own hand he tore them from the ramparts, and planting himself among the pikemen who defended the breach, remained there till, after a long and bloody contest, the enemy had retreated. So soon as all immediate danger was over he bade his attendants prepare him some accommodation in this bastion, which he intended thenceforth to make his residence. He believed that the enemy had withdrawn only to return under cover of the night; and in reply to the knights who opposed his design he only answered, that at seventy years of age he had nothing better to hope for than to die in the midst of his children, and in defence of the faith.

The Christians kept strict watch and ward; and, as La Valette expected, darkness had no sooner fallen than the infidels, knowing that no time had been given for throwing up new entrenchments, ran swiftly to the breach, white the whole scene was suddenly lighted up by incessant discharges of artillery, and by thousands of fiery missiles that came flaming and darting through the air. They had hoped to surprise the garrison exhausted by the day's encounter, and sunk in profound repose; but they found the walls ready manned to receive them, and were met by such volleys of well-directed musketry, and by such a renewal of those deadly showers, the effects of which they had so well learnt to dread, that neither the threats nor the blows of their infuriated chiefs could urge them to the charge; and the broken routed columns rushed back as they had come, and abandoned the attempt. The Christians, in their joy at the hard-earned victory, forgot not Him from whom it came: in the morning a *Te Deum* was sung in public thanksgiving; and, if it were not performed with all the solemnity usual in the order of St. John, at least it was accompanied (says the chronicler) with tears of grateful devotion and of true contrition from the eyes of many a man as well as woman in the assembled crowd.

During the bloody assaults of the long days that followed, La Valette and his pike were ever in the front of the defence; severely wounded, he concealed his hurt, and by his words and example inspired soldiers and citizens with the same ardour that animated the knights themselves. The fight became too close for musketry; it was hand to hand, with pike and poniard, renewed every day, and scarcely ceasing even during night: for the design of the *pasha* was to do by the whole city as he had done by St. Elmo, and make himself master of the place simply by the annihilation or all its defenders. Proclamations went through the Turkish camp that the city was to be sacked, and every living soul destroyed, with the exception of the grand master, who was to be carried in chains to Constantinople. La Valette heard of this boastful threat:

> "Yet," he said to his knights, "it will hardly be as the *pasha* thinks; sooner than suffer a grand master of the order of St. John to appear before the sultan in chains, I will take the dress of one of my own pikemen, and die among the battalions of the infidels at their next rush upon the breach."

Meanwhile the condition of the besieged grew every day more desperate; their numbers reduced by half, and the survivors wounded, and well-nigh dying of fatigue; powder failing, and the ramparts all ruined and shattered by the cannon; breaches everywhere, and some so large that thirty men abreast could ride through them, dismount and mount again with ease; whilst in many places there rose over the walls enormous mounds, erected by the Turks, and furnished with cannon, which entirely commanded the quarters of the city against which they were directed. Every invention of military skill known to Turkish science was tried in turn by the *pasha*, and failed: his mines were countermined; his movable towers were burnt and destroyed; a huge machine which he caused to be constructed, capacious as a hogshead and filled with all manner of combustibles, and which was launched by engines on to the rampart of the bastion, was thrown back upon its constructors, and, bursting in its fall, dealt terrific havoc around.

At length, on the 20th of August, a letter was thrown into the *borgo*, and brought to the grand master, who opened it in the presence of his council, and found but one word, "Thursday;" which he rightly interpreted to be a warning from some friendly hand to prepare for a new assault on the 23rd. In fact, it was the last effort of Mustapha, who found that, whatever might be his own resolution, the spirits of his troops were fast giving way under their repeated failures; and it was only when the *emirs* and chief officers of the army offered to make the assault alone, that the *Janizaries* and inferior troops could be induced to move.

La Valette, who foresaw that a great struggle was at hand, and felt that he had no means of meeting a general attack with his reduced numbers, proceeded to the infirmary, and addressed the wounded knights.

"I am likewise wounded," he said, "yet I continue on duty; so also do others who have never left the walls. It remains to be seen whether you whom I see around me are content to be massacred in your beds, rather than to die like men upon the parapets; for to that crisis are we come."

Such an address had the effect he intended. "Death on the breach!" burst from the lips of all. La Valette answered their shout with a pleased and approving smile; and distributing them among the various quarters where their presence was most needed, he felt well assured that the sense of wounded honour would wring; from them a resistance so long as life remained.

The walls during those three days were strangely manned: wounded men, with arms and heads bound up in bloody cloths; women, with *casque* and *cuirass*, assumed to deceive the enemy with the appearance of a garrison, the skeleton of which alone was left; guns worked by feeble children,—sometimes the strongest and best fit to fight of all the forces that were there. The assault one day lasted twelve hours,—the bloodiest and fiercest that had yet been made; the enormous platform, or "cavalier," as it was called, which rose above the parapet afforded such a position for the Turkish musketeers, that no one appeared on the walls but he fell instantly under their deadly aim.

Nothing silenced their fire; and night alone brought a brief respite, which was employed by the grand master in assembling a council of his knights to determine what steps should be taken in the deplorable condition to which they were now reduced.

The majority of the grand crosses and dignitaries of the order were for abandoning the outworks, and retiring with what strength they had left to the castle of St Angelo, where they might hope to hold out till the arrival of the succour; but to this plan La Valette would not for a moment consent. He rejected it with as much horror as though he had been required to surrender the city to the infidels; for, good and Christian veteran as he was, he well knew that St. Angelo, though capable of receiving the troops and fighting men, could offer no protection to the women and defenceless citizens, who, in case of such a resolution being taken, must be given up to the fury of the enemy: St. Michael and its brave defenders must also be abandoned to their fate.

"No, brethren," he said, addressing the assembly, "we will all die together, and on our walls, as becomes our profession, if first, by God's blessing, we do not drive these Turkish dogs from thence."

So the day dawned on a fresh scene of battle; the Turks, maddened to frenzy, seemed callous to musketry and stones and boiling oil, and raining rampart after rampart, stood at length with nothing to separate them from the Christians who held the city but a stockade of wood, behind which the garrison was drawn up; but beyond that they could not pass. As to the bastion of Castile, La Valette had declared his resolution of remaining in it to the last; and calling in almost all the forces which garrisoned St, Angelo, he caused the wooden bridge which connected it with the *borgo* to be sawn asunder, thus cutting off the possibility of retreat.

On the last day of August, the *pasha* made an attempt on Citta Vecchia, leaving Piali to continue the assault on the *borgo* and St. Michael. Mesquita, a brave Portuguese, commanded there; and on the news of the enemy's approach, dressed up his walls with banners and pikes, women again assuming their *casques* and muskets, and crowding to the ramparts; for indeed the place was almost wholly without defenders, yet a warlike aspect was so well sustained, that no real assault was attempted. In fact the siege was drawing to its close: ammunition was foiling; twenty-five days' provision was all that remained in the Turkish camp; a dysentery, the result of the great heat, bad food, and constant exposure, was carrying off large numbers everyday; the troops were disheartened, and the garrison, as it seemed to them, invincible; and when, on the 4th of September, the sails of the Sicilian galleys were seen on the broad horizon, nothing more was needed to complete the discomfiture of the infidels.

The succour so long promised consisted of about 11,000 men, 900 being knights of the order, with whom were associated a number of volunteer adventurers of the best blood of Spain, Italy, and France, eager to join in a defence whose fame had now spread through Europe, and bade fair to surpass in glory even that of Rhodes. At the first news of their approach a kind of consternation seized the two *pashas*, and they resolved on a hasty embarkment of their troops. Without waiting to ascertain the strength of the force opposed to them, they made every preparation for retiring; the garrison which had been posted at St. Elmo was called in, the artillery was abandoned, and a precipitate retreat commenced. As morning broke on the 8th of September, the festival of Our Lady's Nativity, the weary watchers once more dragged themselves to the walls.

Taught by bitter and repeated disappointments, they had put no trust in the reported sight of those distant sails, and treated the talk of the Sicilian succours as a delusive dream; no news had yet reached them of the landing of the troops, which had, indeed, taken place on the preceding evening, in a distant part of the island, the forces being then in full march upon the town. Nothing, therefore, was looked for by the garrison, now reduced to six hundred feeble men, but a renewal of the long struggle which had lasted without interruption for so many weeks. Yet, though exhausted in body, their confidence and courage were unshaken; leaning from the ramparts, they even defied their enemies to the assault, shouting to them to come on, and do their worst, without waiting for the sunrise. There was no answer, only a clang of arms that seemed dying away in the distance.

"Heard you that?" suddenly exclaimed one of the men; "surely those were the *Janizary* trumpets sounding from the shore. And down there yonder, beneath the walls, what can be the meaning of those marshalled troops defiling from the trenches towards the camp? Either my eyes are blinded by long watching, or the infidels are in retreat."

The strange news spread quickly from mouth to mouth, and La Valette, as soon as he was convinced to its truth, ordered a sortie to be made from the walls and the entrenchments of the enemy to be destroyed, as a precaution in case of their return; for indeed the whole thing seemed inexplicable, and, as he suspected, might be nothing but a feint to conceal some deep design, Women and children worked with right goodwill at the task of destruction: and before nightfall the complicated works of the Turkish engineers presented a spectacle of utter confusion. A party was also despatched to take possession of the abandoned fortress of St. Elmo, and the infidels, from the decks of their vessels, had the chagrin of seeing the banner of St. John floating once more over those hardly-contested walls.

They could hear, too, the sonorous peal of the church-bells, silent for three months, except to give out martial signals or notes of alarm; but which now burst merrily forth from every tower and steeple, to celebrate at once the birthday of the Mother of God and the unhoped-for deliverance of her clients; Never sounded sweeter music to human ears than that which once more summoned the faithful to Mass; and doubtless the Rhodians. who might be found among the population were not slow in attributing their happy fortune to the intercession of Our Lady of Philermos.[1] La Valette headed the people in a procession to the great church of St. John, where with hearts flowing over with joy, they gave thanks to God and His blessed Mother for the mercy so signally vouchsafed. Nor was it long before the certainty of the good news was ascertained, and its cause explained by intelligence of the arrival of the Sicilian troops.

Meanwhile the *pasha* had scarcely entered his vessel when he

---

1. Von Hammer says that both Turks and Christians declared that at the last assault they suddenly beheld upon the ramparts a lady and two men whom they had never seen before; that the Christians devoutly believed that it was the Blessed Virgin herself, accompanied by St. Paul and St. John Baptist, the patron of the order, and were animated in consequence to perform prodigies of valour; while the infidels, on the other hand, were seized with consternation.

was overwhelmed with shame at the thought of having abandoned the city at the first rumour of relief. The whole Christian forces scarcely numbered half his own; and it seemed as though by an able movement he might easily crush the newcomers, and regain his position before the town, which he well knew was at its last extremity.

To land again, after having but just completed so hurried an embarkment, had certainly a foolish look about it; but the council of war agreed it was the only measure that could retrieve the honour of their arms; and so, despite the unwillingness of the troops, they were once more put on shore, and marched in the direction of the Christian forces. The two armies came up to one another in the neighbourhood of Citta Notabile, and an engagement immediately took place. The Sicilians were commanded by Ascanio de la Coroña; while the knights who accompanied them were led by Alvarez de Sandé, who led the attack with characteristic ardour.

The Turkish soldiers, dispirited and fatigued, scarcely made a show of resistance; but at the first charge turned and fled to the Port of St. Paul, where the Bey of Algiers, with 1500 men, was waiting to cover their retreat to the boats. The unfortunate *pasha*, endeavouring in vain to rally the fugitives, was hurried along with his cowardly troops, and twice narrowly escaped falling into the hands of the Christians.

The Sicilians followed the pursuit as though it had been a stag-hunt; and in then thoughtless impetuosity threw off their *cuirasses*, and broke their ranks, to enable them the more speedily to overtake the flying enemy,—an imprudence which was near costing them dear: for on arriving at the place of embarkation, they were met by the Bey of Algiers, who charged them with great fury, and would have carried off a number of prisoners but for the timely arrival of De Sandé.

Then the Turks no longer preserved even the form of a retreat; there was a general rush to the boats, the Christians pursuing the infidels even into the sea, where great numbers of the enemy were slain, or perished in the waters. This victory put the last stroke to the discomfiture of the *pasha*, and before sunset the sails of the Moslem fleet were seen sinking on the eastern horizon.

Such was the end of this memorable siege, which had lasted four months; the last of which may be said to have been little else than one continuous battle.[2] It is said that when the news of the result was brought to Solyman, he tore the letter to fragments and trampled it under his feet, repeating the exclamation of Mahomet after the failure of his Rhodian expedition,—

My arms are invincible only in my own hands,

—and swearing to return in person the ensuing year, and put every Christian in the island to the sword. Nevertheless he thought it prudent to adopt a different policy to that usually practised by Ottoman sovereigns towards their officers, with whom failure was the certain forerunner of a disgraceful death.

Following the precedent he had set himself after the retreat from Vienna, he proclaimed through Constantinople that Mustapha had met with a brilliant success, that he was bringing captive all the knights who had survived the slaughter; but that, as the Maltese rocks were unfit to maintain a garrison, the Ottoman clemency had been content with the destruction of the fortifications; so that should the Christian corsairs have the audacity to return, they would be at the mercy of his fleets, and would not fail to be again speedily "exterminated."

Whatever may be thought of the truthfulness of the sultan's proclamation of victory, there can be but little question that Malta, after the raising of the siege, resembled nothing less than a fortified city, and rather bore the resemblance of one which had been dismantled and destroyed. Full 200 knights, and more than 9000 soldiers and citizens, had perished during the three

---

2. The last knight who fell was Giovanni Malespina, and his death happened under curious circumstances. He was standing at the bastion of Castile, from whence he watched the embarkation of the Turks, and, full of joy and thankfulness, sang aloud the *Te Deum*. Whilst doing so, a chance shot struck him to the ground, but without interrupting his devotions; and he expired as he pronounced the words, "*In te, Domine, speravi.*"

months of conflict; and at the moment when the enemy retired not 600 men of all ranks or classes were to be found within the city walls. On the other hand the loss of the Turks was computed at 30,000 men amounting to nearly three-fourths of the original besieging army.

There was a joyful meeting between the Christian forces; for the chief and officers of the newly-arrived troops lost no time in proceeding to the *borgo*, where they were received by La Valette and his companions as their deliverers. Yet a proud and honest satisfaction was felt by the gallant defenders of the city, as they thought that they had won the victory for themselves; for the enemy's fire had slackened, and his assaults had grown feebler every day, and he had fled from the walls ere certain intelligence had reached him of the landing of the succours. It was an affecting scene which was then witnessed in the ruined streets of the *borgo*.

"The knights," says Vertot, "embraced one another with a loving tenderness: but when they called to mind the loss of so many brave and illustrious men; when they looked around them and beheld the shattered state of the city, the walls and ramparts all shaken and destroyed, guns dismounted and houses overthrown, and saw, moreover, the pale and emaciated countenances of the inhabitants, the knights, and the grand master himself, with matted hair and beards, their dress dirty and disordered,—for many had never laid aside their clothes for months,—and the greater part of them covered with wounds, and with arms and heads bound up and bandaged, and the traces of suffering and privation on the races of all,—none could restrain their tears at the touching spectacle; and while some wept in remembering their misfortunes, others shed tears of joy to think that Malta had at any rate been saved at last."

The *borgo* received the new name of Vittoriosa; and a plan already occupied the mind of La Valette for securing the island against any fresh attacks, by laying the foundations of a new city whose defences should be impregnable. As to the joy which the news of the Christian success spread through Europe, it was of a nature impossible to describe.

> "At Rome," says Vertot, "the day on which the news was announced was kept as a high festival; all public business was suspended; the courts of justice and the shops were closed; only the churches were open, and the people ran in crowds to thank God for the happy event."

As Innocent VIII. to D'Aubusson, so Pius IV. to La Valette made offer of the *cardinalate*; but the grand master in his humility declined the dignity, begging it might rather be bestowed on his brother, the Bishop of Vabres, for that he had himself grown old in the profession of arms. But, indeed, honours poured in upon La Valette on every side; and money too, to help forward the erection of the new capital. There was need of expedition, for rumours thickened fast of another armament in preparation at Constantinople for the last trial at "extermination;" and a singular dispensation for continuing work on all Sundays and festivals was granted by Pope Pius V. for the rapid completion of a city which was to be the bulwark of the Christian world. The first stone was laid on the 28th of March 1566, by the grand master in person, and bore the impress of a golden lion on a bloody field, which was his family device.

> "But," says a modern writer, "it was Europe rather than the order, which gave to the young city the name of *La Valetta*.[3]

Every year, on the 8th of September, the memory of the great deliverance was renewed by a solemn religious ceremony within the church of St. John: the victorious standard of the order was borne to the altar by a knight in the helmet and armour of the

---
3. Taaffe. It was, however, the custom at that time to give every city an epithet as well as a name. That chosen by the grand master was intended to express the modesty of an order whose only pride was to be in the Cross of Christ: it was *Humilissima*.

ages of Crusade,—for to Jerusalem was the lingering look of the Hospitallers still directed with a fond and sorrowful regret,—and by his side were carried the sword and poniard of La Valette, whose portrait was on that day publicly exhibited to the people. As the procession passed into the church, and the standard was laid at the foot of the altar, the action was proclaimed by flourishes of trumpets and salvoes of artillery from the forts. Mass was said by the prior of the order; and while the gospel was being read the grand master held aloft the hero's sword unsheathed, as though to notify to all Christendom, and to all the enemies of the faith, that the Knights of St. John were ever ready to do battle for the Cross.

The grand master did not long survive his triumph, or live to see the completion of his city; he received a stroke of the sun on a hot day in July, while engaged in his favourite diversion of hawking, and expired on the 21st of August 1568, retaining his consciousness to the last.

"O my God!" he was heard frequently to exclaim, "send me one of Thy blessed angels to help me in this last hour."

A cloud of darkness gathered for a while over his soul, and he seemed wrestling for the first time in his life with the emotion of fear: he, who had met so many dangers with such serene intrepidity, and who slept with a pet lioness in his bedchamber, trembled for a moment before the approach of death; but very soon the trouble passed, and a sweet tranquillity again appeared upon his countenance, as, devoutly pronouncing the names of Jesus and Mary, he departed without a struggle. He was buried in the chapel of Our Lady of Philermos within the church of St. Lawrence; but his body was afterwards removed to the new church of Our Lady of Victories, whose foundations he had himself begun as an offering of thanksgiving to the holy Mother of God.

With the siege of Malta our sketch of the order of Hospitallers, or rather of its struggles with the power of the Moslems in defence of Europe and of Christendom, must conclude. Its galleys continued to maintain their supremacy over the infidels on all the coasts of the Mediterranean, and bore a distinguished part in the victory of Lepanto, a notice of which will be given in another page. After an existence of six centuries the order of St. John still preserved its sovereign character, up to that period when, in common with almost every other of the ancient institutions of Europe, it was swept away before the conquering' arm of Buonaparte. Even now it may be styled dethroned rather than extinct;[4] and its restoration at some future day is at least no more visionary a dream than that which looks forward to the recall of other exiled and abeyant dynasties.

As a religious order it has one great claim upon our respect, namely, in having preserved to the last hour of its existence the spirit of its original institute unchanged and unabated. In 1606 we find the knights on the shores of Tunis still faithful to their old instinct of hospitality. A terrible tempest was destroying their galleys, and as they beat upon the rocks the Moors were on the watch to massacre those who escaped from the waves. Then did the Provençal, Vaucluse de Villeneuf, uphold the glory of his ancient name, and that of his order:

> "for," says Goussancourt, "though he might have escaped in the galleys among the first, yet he chose to remain with the sick and wounded, carrying them on his shoulders, which was the cause of his being taken."

---

4. At the dispersion of the Knights, upon the occupation of Malta by the French, some took refuge in Russia; where, in the year 1801, a council met to deliberate on the election of a grand master. It was resolved that, as the elements of a general chapter could not be assembled at St. Petersburg, the different grand priors should be invited to convene their chapters for the purpose of forming lists of such knights as were worthy of succeeding to the sovereign dignity. These lists the council proposed afterwards to submit to the Pope, for him to choose a grand master out of them. Accordingly (Feb. 9, 1805) his Holiness Pius VII. nominated Tommasi, an Italian knight, grand master. In 1814 the French knights taking heart at the humiliation of their arch-enemy Napoleon, assembled at Paris in a general chapter, under the presidency of the prince Camille de Rohan, grand prior of Aquitaino, for the election of a permanent capitulary commission. Under the direction of this commission a formal but fruitless application was made to the congress of Vienna for a grant of some sovereign independency, in lieu of that of which the order had been so wrongfully despoiled. (continued next page)

Down to a very late date we find the record of many whose noble confession of the Christian faith whilst in captivity won them the crown of martyrdom under most cruel tortures. The religious spirit was never wanting; and perhaps no more beautiful account of a Christian deathbed could be found than that given in a letter from the Père de la Croix, rector of the Jesuit College at Malta, in which he describes the last moments of two knights who died of their wounds received in a sea-fight off Saragossa in the year 1635.

One of these, whom he calls "my good penitent the Chevalier Serviens," was reckoned the most accomplished gentleman of his day. Such a term had unhappily in the seventeenth century a far different signification to that which would have attached to the words in earlier times; and yet the old meaning had not been forgotten among the Hospitallers of the Cross. Before departing on the enterprise in which he met with his death, Serviens had prepared himself by a general confession; "and his death," says the good father, "was one which the most austere religious might well have cause to envy."

The other knight, who was wounded in the same fight, and died in the same room with his comrade, was La Roche Pichelle.

"He was truly a saint," writes the rector; "and to my

In 1823, when the Greek cause began to wear a prosperous aspect, the same chapter entered into a treaty with the Greeks for the cession of Sapienza and Cabressa, two islets on the western shore of the Morea, as a preliminary step to the re-conquest of Rhodes; to facilitate which arrangement an endeavour was made to raise a loan of 640,000*l.* in England, but the speculation completely failed. The formalities of the order are still maintained with some degree of splendour in the French capital, and it continues to reckon a number of distinguished members; but the utter dilapidation of its revenues, and the total annihilation of its political influence, have reduced it to the position of an obscure association. (*Sutherland*, vol. 2. pp. 326-328.) It is interesting to learn that when the knights abandoned Malta they took with them, stripped of the jewels with which they were ornamented, the hand of St. John the Baptist, which had been presented to the grand master D'Aubusson by the Sultan Bajazet II., and the miraculous image of Our Lady of Philermos.
(Since the foregoing was written, a rumour has been prevalent that it was the wish of the Holy See to restore the order, for the protection of Rome and the Papal States.)

knowledge had studied the interior life of perfection for four years, and that to such good purpose that he had outstripped many a Capuchin and Jesuit father in the progress he had made. These two friends lay side by side, assisting and consoling one another: they agreed together that whichever survived the longest should offer all his pains for the relief of his companion's soul; and that the one who died first should in like manner offer all his prayers that the other might make a happy death.

"A little before his departure, Serviens called to his comrade, and asked him if he were ready to go, saying several times, 'Let us go, let us go together;' then he repeated the *Salve Regina,* and saluted his good angel; and at last took the crucifix in his hand, and repeated the prayer *Respice* as it is wont to be said in Holy Week. When he had ended, he grasped my hand," continues the rector, "saying, 'Farewell, my father;' but I told him he should try to expire with the holy names upon his lips; whereupon he kissed his scapular, and ejaculating the names of Jesus and Mary gave up his soul to his Creator."

Nor could the religious spirit of the order have been as yet decayed, when we find the edifying spectacle it presented in 1637, bringing back to the bosom of the Church a descendant of St. Elizabeth of Hungary, in the person of Prince Frederic of Hesse. In the course of his travels through Italy he arrived at Malta, where he took such delight in the sight of so many young knights of all nations gathered together and living in perfect harmony and religious discipline one with another, that, returning to Rome, he implored the holy Pontiff, Urban VIII., to receive him into the true fold; after which he solicited and received the habit of St. John.

Again, in 1783, we find the Knights of Malta exhibiting their unalterable constancy to that sublime vocation which made Goussancourt declare, that

> this order containeth within itself the perfection of all

kinds of charity.

During the horrors of the great earthquake which destroyed the city of Messina, their generous and extraordinary exertions on behalf of the sufferers earned them a higher title to fame than was ever won on battle-field or on breach.

In the regret, therefore, with which we view the extinction of an institution whose name has been illustrious for so many ages, there mingles nothing of the contempt sometimes called forth by the fall of a dynasty which has derogated from its ancient fame. It was high-minded and chivalrous even amid the anarchy and confusion of the reign of terror. La Brilhane, the last ambassador of Malta at the court of France, was warned that his life was in danger.

"I am under no apprehensions," he loftily replied; "the moment is come at last, when a man of honour who faithfully performs his duty may die as gloriously on the gallows as he could ever have done on the field of battle."

We can find no fitter words in which to give the epitaph of his order.

Chapter 11

The Battle of Lepanto

The sixteenth century was drawing to its close,—a century marked by the ravages of religious revolution, and destined to be forever honoured or deplored according as men may think of it as the age of reformation or of decay. Among the many social changes which arose out of the new order of things, we can scarcely fail to notice the growth of that exclusive nationality which has lasted until our own time. The great tie of religious unity was broken which had given the nations of Europe a common interest even in the midst of the continual warfare in which they were engaged, and which had inspired them with so many generous enterprises in defence of the faith. But when that bond of brotherhood was lost, there was no longer a common cause to fight for: a profound selfishness may thenceforward be discovered in the whole history of Europe, and the chance alliances of one power with another had no nobler basis than the political interests of the hour.

This change began to be felt immediately after the separation of the northern nations from the unity of the Church, and the circumstance was not unobserved by the great infidel power of the East. The enormous progress of that power was almost coeval with the period of the Reformation; and the distractions and divisions among the Christians that followed that event were so many gains to the Turks, who pushed their victorious arms further and further, till the dreaded Crescent,— which the long struggle of the crusades and of the heroic ages of Christendom had kept at bay,—was displayed under the very walls of Marseilles and the port of Rome by the corsair-fleets which roved at large over the waters of the Mediterranean, and scarcely found an enemy to oppose them in their course. The republic of Venice, indeed, was still master of many of the island-fortresses of the Levant and the Archipelago; but as the power of that state was now gradually declining, the eyes of her foe were fastened with a bolder ambition upon the dominions which she seemed helpless to defend. The rich and beautiful island of Cyprus in particular excited the cupidity of Selim II.,[1] who had succeeded his father, Solyman the Magnificent, in the empire of the East; and the report of a sudden disaster which befell the republic in the explosion and destruction of her arsenal, encouraged him to seize the occasion of breaking, in the face of solemn treaties, a peace which had remained undisturbed between the two states for nearly thirty years.

When the hostile intentions of the Turkish sultan became known, the republic was little prepared to recommence the desperate struggle. Her utmost efforts were spent in the equipment of a fleet which, when assembled, was found wholly inadequate to meet the enemy; and in her distress, crippled as she was by the loss of her vast magazines, and drained of all resources, she implored the assistance of the Roman Pontiff, and, through him, of the other powers of Christendom. Pius V. then filled the chair of St. Peter; and his sagacious eye had long foreseen the danger; nor had he spared any efforts to provide the necessary defences. But the times were against him.

A famine was ravaging the fair fields of Italy; the government of France was too busy with the Huguenots to have time or strength to bestow on a quarrel with the Turks; and as to England —to use the expression of a writer of the time—its ruler was Elizabeth, "a greater enemy to Rome than the Turks themselves."

---

1. Known in history as "Selim the Sot." It is said he was instigated to the conquest of the island by a Jew, his boon companion, who represented to him how easily he could make himself master of the soil on which grew the grapes which produced his favourite wine.

Nevertheless, in spite of all discouragements, the zeal of the Roman Pontiff was manifested by an extraordinary activity. Every court of Europe was visited by his ambassadors, who vainly tried to rouse the spirit of the Christian princes against a foe whose conquests were as rapid as they were bloodstained. One after another they excused themselves on the plea of domestic troubles and exhausted treasuries; and in the month of May 1570, when Pius had fondly hoped to have seen his noble appeals as nobly responded to by the universal voice of Christendom, he found himself supported by the king of Spain alone out of all the potentates of Europe.

Meanwhile the fall of Cyprus, attended by barbarities which rivalled in cruelty and atrocity the torments inflicted on the early Christian martyrs, signalised the opening of the war, and gave to the Turkish arms the prestige of the first success. A slight notice of that terrible event may give our readers some idea of the sort of adversary by whom Christendom was at this time threatened.

Already the sultan had ordered the seizure of all merchant-vessels that chanced to be at anchor within the ports of the Turkish empire, and the closing of all the avenues by which relief could be afforded to the doomed island; and yet in Venice itself counsels were still divided: the *doge* was just dead, and the senate was occupied with the nomination of his successor. To the last no vigorous measures were taken by the republic to throw a sufficient force into Cyprus, and the commanders of the allied Venetian and Spanish fleets strove in vain to convey the necessary succours. Sickness and famine made fearful ravages among the troops, and many thousands perished.

The ships which had on board Count Jerome Martinengo and 3000 men were overtaken by a tremendous storm; an epidemic broke out which carried off more than a third of the number, and among them their renowned commander himself; and they who, from the shores of the island had long watched for the reinforcements, of which they stood in such desperate need, saw at length but a few shattered vessels come into harbour, bearing with them the dead body of the man on whose bravery and skill they had rested all their hopes of deliverance. To add to the general consternation, Nicholas Dandolo, who had but just taken on himself the office of governor, was one in whose capacity and judgement neither soldiers nor people felt they could place any reliance. Lala Mustapha, a renegade already infamous for his foul and treacherous practices, was the commander of the Ottoman forces, numbering, as some historians have computed, 80,000 men; to oppose which vast armament the Christians could not muster more than 500 or 600 Horse, a small body of local Militia, and 2000 Foot-Soldiers fit for active service.

The city of Nicosia, the first object of attack, was taken by storm, on the 9th of September 1570, after an heroic resistance of seven weeks, during which the inhabitants had again and again repulsed the assaults of the Turks with a valour which struck such terror into the besiegers, that more than once they all but abandoned their attempts on the town. The ammunition had failed, the fortifications were demolished, most of the distinguished leaders had been slain; the devoted bishop, who had given up all he possessed for the support of the soldiery and people, had himself fallen in a *mêlée* ; the Count de Rochas, who ranked next in command to the governor, was killed in defending one of the ruined bastions, and the Turks, after grossly outraging his body, thrust it into a mortar and launched it into the town. Dandolo retreated into his palace as soon as the enemy penetrated into the town, and the wretched inhabitants were given up as a prey to their infuriated assailants. In vain they threw themselves on their knees before their vanquishers; they were massacred without pity: for seven hours the horrible carnage proceeded.

The palace still held out. The *pasha* offered the garrison their lives on condition of their laying down their arms: they did so, and every soul was put to the sword. The Bishop of Baffo, who, in the estimation of his countrymen, was as capable of commanding an army as of governing a *diocese*, was butchered among the rest. The unhappy Dandolo, after suffering frightful tortures at the hands of the infidels, was decapitated, and his head sent to the governor of Cerino, the third principal town of the island, as a token of what he might himself expect if he did not instantly surrender the place. The atrocities committed by the Turks defy description. Mustapha, it is related, ordered the children and old men, and all whom it was not worth the victor's while to preserve, to be piled one upon another in the great square of the town and burnt alive; at the same time, to show his hatred of the Christian name, he directed numerous carcases of swine,—for which the followers of Mahomet entertain a religious abhorrence,—to be heaped upon his victims, and consumed together with them.

For three days the town was given up to pillage, and every barbarity which an infernal malice could suggest was perpetrated upon its despairing population. Women threw themselves from the house-tops to escape from their pursuers; mothers slew their daughters with their own hands rather than that they should fall into the power of the brutal foe. More than 20,000 human beings were slaughtered on the day of the assault: in the first paroxysm of their rage the infidels spared neither sex nor age; 2000 alone were reserved for a slavery more terrible than death.

One fearful act of vengeance marked the close of this memorable siege. The Turks had collected in a single galleon the most beautiful youths and maidens of the place, together with the most precious portion of the booty, with the intention of conveying them as presents to the sultan, his eldest son, and the grand *vizier*. One of the captives, a lady of noble family, knowing but too well the wretched fate that awaited herself and her companions, set fire to the powder-magazine, and blew the vessel high into the air. Two others loaded with the spoils of the town were involved in its destruction; great numbers of the enemy perished, and among them many Christians of distinction, and the flower of the youth of either sex.

Mustapha now led his troops, flushed with victory and outnumbering by thousands their Christian opponents, under the walls of Famagosta. For eleven months the brave Bragadino, with a scanty garrison and a few thousands of armed citizens, withstood the Moslem hosts. [2] In vain had they sought relief from Spain and their own republic. The Spanish admiral weakly held aloof; the Venetians succeeded only in throwing a handful of men into the place. The besieged fought with all the strength of despair: women not only laboured in supplying arms and ammunition to the soldiers, but combated by their side upon the walls, throwing down stones and boiling-water on the assailants, or precipitating themselves with deadly effect into the masses of the foe, and causing many a Moslem warrior to bite the dust. The bishop of the place, a Dominican by profession, contributed not a little in reanimating the spirits of the garrison, whose ranks were being everyday rapidly thinned by famine and the sword: his exhortations, say the chroniclers, elicited prodigies of valour.

In the very heat of the assault he might be seen for hours upon the ramparts, surrounded by his clergy, holding aloft the crucifix, and calling on the people to resist unto death fighting for the faith. [3] All in vain: on the 1st of August 1571, the walls were nearly levelled to the ground; the defences consisted only of bags of earth and bales of cotton; the Italian and Greek auxiliaries, whose prowess had done such execution on the Turks, were all annihilated; there were left but seven barrels of powder, and of food there was none remaining; the combatants, emaciated by want and incessant toil, could scarcely hold their weapons in their hands. Further resistance was impossible, and Bragadino, yielding at length to the piteous entreaties of the townspeople, consented to sue for terms.

But as the intrepid governor bade the white flag be unfurled, he exclaimed, "Officers and men, I call Heaven to witness that it is not I who surrender this town to the infidels, but the senate of Venice, who, by abandoning us to our fate, have given us

---

2. For a short but spirited account of this heroic defence and its fatal catastrophe the reader is referred to *The Four Martyrs,* by M. Rio.
3. On one of the last days of the siege he was struck by a ball and killed, while praying in the garden of his palace.

up into the hands of these barbarians." A capitulation was concluded, by which the inhabitants were to remain in possession of their goods, and to have the free exercise of their religion; all who chose might quit the town, and sell or carry off their effects; the garrison were to march out with their arms and with all the honours of war, and to be transported in Turkish vessels to Crete.

The terms were ratified; and on the morning of the 15th August, the Feast of the Assumption, Bragadino, according to agreement, proceeded with two of his officers and a small escort to the tent of the Turkish general to deliver up into his own hands the keys of the town. But no sooner had he entered the pavilion than he and his attendants were treacherously seized on some frivolous pretence; new conditions were imposed; and on the governor's remonstrating against the injustice of such proceedings, Mustapha ordered his companions to be beheaded on the spot before his eyes. Bragadino himself he condemned to a like fate: three times he compelled the noble Venetian to bow his head to receive the murderer's stroke, and as often,—as though he would make his victim drink the bitter cup of torment drop by drop,—arrested by a sign the executioner's arm.

The tyrant had another and a more terrible death in store for one who had so long defied his most furious efforts; and he contented himself for the present with ordering his captive's nose and ears to be cut off in his presence; which done, he had him loaded with chains, and cast, bleeding as he was, into a dungeon, tauntingly bidding him call now upon his Christ, for it was time that He should help him.

Three hundred Christians who were in the camp were butchered in cold blood; the rest of the garrison and the unhappy townspeople, who were already on board the Turkish transports, were reduced to slavery; while the hostages sent into the Turkish quarters before the treaty was formally signed, among whom was Henry Martinengo, nephew of the count, were subjected to barbarous mutilation.

The fortifications were now ordered to be rebuilt; and the

Turk compelled his noble prisoner to carry loads of earth upon his shoulders for the repair of the walls, and to kiss his feet each time he passed before him; and not yet satisfied with the indignities he heaped upon him, he had him hoisted up aloft on the yard-arm of a vessel in the harbour, where he kept him exposed for hours to the gaze and scoff of the infidels, and then suddenly plunged him into the sea.

At last, after trampling him under foot, he doomed him to be flayed alive in the public square. The indomitable commander, who united in himself the resolute courage of a chivalrous soldier with the supernatural patience of a Christian martyr, amidst his untold agonies betrayed not a sign of pain, uttered not a murmur or a complaint against his torturers, but, as they stripped the skin from his quivering flesh, calmly prayed and recited aloud from time to time verses from the *Miserere* and other Psalms.

When the Christians in the crowd heard him breathe the words, *Domine, in manus tuas commendo spiritum meum*,[4] they thought he was rendering up his life to God; but there followed in tender accents,—as if to show Whose sufferings in that hour of agony were most present to his thoughts, and Whose meek and loving spirit then filled his inflexible and dauntless soul,— *Pater, dimitte illis; non enim sciunt quid faciunt*;[5] and with this prayer for mercy on his tormentors the brave soldier of Christ passed to receive the martyr's palm.

But Turkish malice was not even yet exhausted, Mustapha caused the brave man's body to be cut into four quarters, and each to be attached to the muzzle of the largest guns. His skin was stuffed with straw and, together with a representation of our Divine Lord in His adorable Passion, paraded through the camp and through the town fastened on the back of a cow. Finally, he despatched both figures as trophies to the sultan his master, with the head of Bragadino and those of the two murdered commanders.

At Constantinople the skin of the heroic martyr was hung up

---

4. "Lord, into Thy hands I commend my spirit."
5. "Father, forgive them; for they know not what they do."

as a spectacle for the Christian galley-slaves.[6]

After the fall of Famagosta further resistance was impossible; indeed (to their everlasting shame be it written) the Greek population of the island sided actively with the invaders, and, in their obstinate blindness, not knowing what they did, delivered themselves up to the degrading domination of the Turks. Everywhere the most frightful scenes were enacted: the Mussulman soldiery broke into the wine-cellars, and, maddened with drink, indulged in orgies too revolting for description. By the command of the renegade Mustapha the tombs of the dead were opened, and their contents scattered to the winds; the images and pictures of the saints were demolished; the churches defiled with abominations so loathsome that the pen of the historian refuses to record them.

Friday the 17th of August, the day on which the noble Bragadino suffered, was set apart for the deliberate perpetration of horrors which rivalled in foulness and atrocity the infamous mysteries of Venus, and the bloody rites at which pagans offered sacrifices of human victims to the devils whom they worshipped. A few days after, Lala Mustapha made his triumphal entry into Constantinople with the spoils of a conquest which had cost him 50,000 men.

During the dreadful scenes which accompanied the fall of Cyprus, there were not wanting many who displayed a spirit worthy of the best days of Christendom. F. Angelo Calepius, a member of the Dominican order, has left an interesting and valuable narrative of the taking of Nicosia, of which place he was a native. He himself played a distinguished part in its defence; for during the seven weeks of siege which preceded the entrance of the Turks, he was unwearied in his efforts to rouse the inhabitants to an heroic resistance in the cause of liberty and faith. In spite of the continual fire of the enemy, Calepius was to be seen everywhere, attending to the wounded and dying, and

---

6. It was afterwards stolen by a Christian slave and taken to Venice, where it was deposited in an urn in the church of St. John and St. Paul; the martyr's bones were also carefully collected, and buried in the church of St. Gregory.

encouraging the harassed and disheartened combatants.

When at length the place surrendered, and was abandoned for three days to pillage and slaughter, the zeal and devotion of this excellent man displayed itself under the very swords of the infidels. The streets were flowing with blood; yet wherever the danger was greatest and the heaps of dead and dying lay the thickest, Father Angelo might be seen, regardless of the ferocious soldiery who surrounded him, administering the consolations of religion to their victims, and endeavouring to comfort them in that dreadful hour by the power of his words and of his very presence.

Among those whose murder in cold blood he was forced to witness, was his own mother Lucretia Calepia and almost all his relatives, with numbers of the clergy and his fellow religious; yet the thought of flight or concealment never seemed to suggest itself to him amid scenes which, with all their horrors, offered him a field for his labours in defence of the faith and in aid of his brethren.

"He was," says Echard, "a constant champion and defender of the Christian faith."

But at length his own turn came: he was seized, stripped of his religious habit, and placed, loaded with chains, among the other captives. After passing through many hands, he was finally purchased by Osma, the captain of a Turkish galley, and carried by him to Constantinople. Before long, however, Angelo so far won the good graces of his master, that he was no longer treated as a slave: he was even suffered to sit at the same table, and permitted to go through the city wherever he desired without restraint, the only condition exacted from him being, that he should not leave the walls. He had no temptation to do so; for the sole use he made of his liberty was to visit his fellow-captives, to console them in their sufferings, and strengthen them in the faith.

There are some men who find their apostolate everywhere, and such was Calepius. True to the great instinct of his order, he was ready, like his great *patriarch*, "to save souls anywhere, and as many as he could." In those days the chains and scourges of the Moslems were a less terrible danger to their captives than the temptations to apostasy, with which they were careful to surround them.

Men needed a living and a lively faith to be able constantly to persevere in the most appalling sufferings, when a few words would purchase for them ease, liberty, and often the highest rank in the sultan's service,—for many of the most distinguished commanders were Christian renegades; and Calepius, who knew this, felt that no more fitting field of missionary labour could have been granted to him than he now found in the dungeons and *bagnios* of Constantinople, confirming his weak brethren, and sometimes winning back those who had strayed, to the profession of their faith.

Meanwhile his order had not forgotten him; his name had long been known in Rome, and Seraphin Cavalli, the general of the Dominicans, who had his liberation greatly at heart, succeeded at length in despatching four hundred gold crowns to Constantinople as the price of his ransom. Calepius was therefore free.

He might have returned to Cyprus, or made his way to Rome, where he was sure of an honourable reception; but ease and honour were the last things of which he thought. He had chosen the damp vaults of the slave-prisons for the scene of his ministry, and without hesitation he determined on remaining at Constantinople, and sacrificing liberty, advancement, nay, life itself if need were, for the salvation of his brethren.

So there he stayed, a beggar at the doors of the ambassadors and Christian merchants, carrying the alms he collected to the miserable objects of his charity, some of whom he was even enabled to set at liberty, rejoicing as he did so rather at the deliverance of their souls than the emancipation of their bodies. Many renegades were by his means recalled to the faith, and a far greater number preserved from falling.

At length, however, his unwearied labours drew on him the jealousy of the Turks: he was forbidden to visit the slaves; but continuing to do so by stealth, he was at length formally accused of being a spy and an enemy to the Prophet. The charge was a capital one; and on the 3rd of February 1572, he was again seized and thrown into a wretched dungeon. Calepius had never looked for any other result; and joyfully hailing what he trusted was the approach of martyrdom, he prepared for death with his usual calmness.

It was not so ordered, however; he had many friends, both among the ambassadors and even among the infidels themselves, and his release was at length procured, on the condition, not a little flattering to his influence and character, that he would instantly quit the Turkish dominions. It was useless to resist; and since he could no longer assist his captive brethren by his presence, he determined not the less to devote himself to their deliverance in another way. He passed over to Italy, and became there what he had already been in Constantinople—a beggar for the Christian slaves. Naples, Bologna, Florence, Milan, and Venice, and every other city whither the Cyprian refugees had retired, was visited by him in turns.

He pleaded the cause of their poor countrymen with all the skill of an advocate and all the tenderness of a father, and represented their sufferings with so touching an eloquence, that be effectually roused everyone to give according to his means. Another Dominican, by name Stephen de Lusignan, of the royal house of Cyprus, joined him in his work; and together these two men were enabled to ransom great numbers of the captives, devoting their entire energies to this undertaking for many years.

It is at the end of De Lusignan's *Universal History* that the two narratives of Calepius on the taking of Nicosia and Famagosta are inserted; and it is said that the publication of these memoirs became the means of exciting many to liberal alms on behalf of the sufferers. Some years afterwards Angelo was nominated by Gregory XIII. to the bishopric of Santarini, as a reward for his zeal and perseverance.

So was lost the fair isle of Cyprus to Venice and to Christian Europe: it passed under the dominion of the Mahometan, and to this day it remains subject to the same evil sway;[7] a monument alike of the treacherous cruelty of the Turk and of the disastrous dissensions and faithless jealousies of Christian states and princes.

The horror inspired by this catastrophe determined the Catholic League to prepare for more vigorous measures than had yet been attempted; and it is from this period that we shall endeavour to take up the narrative, and lay before our readers the details of a struggle whose result has been found worthy of commemoration not only in the pages of history, but in the office of the Church.

And first, let us see what was the relative strength of the parties about to enter into the combat. A fleet of about 160 vessels, thinly manned, was furnished by the Venetian states, under the command of Sebastian Veniero, who had as his lieutenant Agostino Barbarigo, a man of distinguished merit and courage. The pope had no naval force at his disposal, but undertook to furnish and equip twelve of the Venetian galleys; Mark Anthony Colonna, Duke of Paliano, was appointed to the command; and, besides the regular forces in the papal service, a considerable number of the Roman nobility volunteered to join the enterprise. Everything had been done to give a character of religious solemnity to the enrolment and departure of these troops.

The venerable Basilica of the Apostles had witnessed a function of singular character and magnificence in the June of the previous year, when after High Mass, sung by the Cardinal Colonna, the pope solemnly implored the Divine benediction on the Christian arms, and blessed the crimson standard, emblazoned with the crucifix and with the figures of the two apostles of Rome, which was committed to the Duke of Paliano; whilst

---

7. Dr. Newman thus describes the effects of Turkish domination: "As to Cyprus, from holding a million of inhabitants, it now has only 30,000. Its climate was that of a perpetual spring, now it is unwholesome and unpleasant; its cities and towns nearly touched each other, now they are simply ruins. Corn, wine, oil, sugar, and the metals are among its productions: the soil is still exceedingly rich; but now, according to Dr. Clarke, 'in that paradise of the Levant, agriculture is neglected, the inhabitants are oppressed, population is destroyed.'" *The Turks*, p. 149.

the words embroidered as a legend on the damask folds were given to him as his watchword and assurance of success,—

In hoc signo vinces

Nor was another kind of assurance wanting to encourage him and his followers. When, attended by all his officers and by the crowd of noble volunteers who had joined his company, he presented himself to receive the parting benediction of his Holiness, it was given to them accompanied by words which from the mouth of such a speaker had something in them of a prophetic character: "Go, my children," he said, "and fight in God's name against the Turks; it is in His name and on His part that I promise you the victory."

Similar to this had been the message sent by him to the Spanish leaders by the hands of his *nuncio* Odescalchi, as well as to the other princes who had joined in the enterprise; and to the Count de Carillo, as he knelt at his feet, the holy pontiff again repeated, "It is in the name of the Most High that I promise you a certain victory."

Yet this assurance could scarcely be thought to arise from the extent of the martial preparations. So far as the co-operation of the European governments was concerned, the embassies and negotiations of his ambassadors had almost utterly failed. Nevertheless we must remember that the influence of the Roman Pontiff over the heart of Christendom rests on something deeper and more powerful than the success of a political negotiation. And so, notwithstanding the coldness and backwardness of the Christian princes, the appeal of the pope had been loyally and warmly received by many in every nation whither his *nuncios* had been despatched. Besides the regular armaments of Spain and Venice, and the forces contributed by Genoa and the Duke of Savoy, by the Knights of Malta, and several of the lesser Italian states, the volunteers who joined the troops of the allies, to the number of more than two thousand, were of all nations, and included some of the most distinguished soldiers of the day.

But, more than this, it cannot be doubted that the confidence which filled the heart of St. Pius had another and a surer foundation. He could not command the arms of Europe, but the prayers of Christendom at least were at his disposal. Up from every church in every country that owned his obedience there had been arising for months a swell of fervent and united supplication. The religious order to which he himself belonged had been foremost in the use of this great weapon of intercession; and every Confraternity of the Rosary throughout Europe attached to the Dominican body had been unwearied in their processions and devotions for the success of the Christian arms.

How strong a feeling had been excited by the efforts of the Pope may be judged by one fact: it was the period of so-called reformation, when throughout a vast portion of Europe the devout practices of former ages were sinking into contempt; and yet we are told Loretto had never seen such a year of pilgrimage. Every road to the Holy House was crowded by devotees of all nations; and all crowded thither with but one object—to place the cause of the Christians under the patronage of Mary.

The Spanish fleet had been hitherto commanded by John Andrew Doria,[8] and some symptoms of jealousy had arisen in the first movements of the allies between him and the Roman leader, Colonna. These were, however, happily placed at rest by the appointment to the chief command of one whose rank as well as his reputation raised him far above all the subordinate generals of the league. This was Don John of Austria, the natural son of the emperor Charles V., and the captain-general of the navy of Spain. Colonna was, with the consent of all parties, declared his lieutenant; and his arrival was anxiously expected at Messina, where the various squadrons of the allied powers had assembled towards the close of the month of August.

It was the 25th of the same month when he arrived at the place of rendezvous; and his entrance into the city seemed rather the triumph given to a conqueror than the reception of one whose victory was yet to be hardly earned. All the showy magnificence of the times was displayed in the preparations made for

---
8. Nephew of the great admiral of the Emperor Charles V.

welcoming him. The city was filled with arches and triumphal columns, and the shores covered with the gaily-emblazoned banners of the various chiefs, whose martial appearance recalled to the eye the costume at least, if it did not represent something also of that chivalrous spirit which was fast expiring before the progress of modern civilisation and the eager pursuit of material interests. And indeed there was much in this, almost the last of the Christian leagues against the infidel, which was worthy of the best days of chivalry.

A great principle, even when it has received its death-blow, is long in dying; and the embers of that generous fire blazed up in many a bright and flickering flame before they were wholly quenched in darkness. We can scarcely fail, for instance, to admire the generosity evinced by the Spanish government; for, apart from the religious considerations of the war, its main object was undoubtedly the relief and protection of the Venetian states,—those very states which but a short time previously had refused to assist the Spaniards against the Turks, and by their refusal had been in great part the cause of the fall of Rhodes. Yet Philip II.,[9]—a monarch whose traditional unpopularity in England, as the husband of Mary the Catholic, has obscured the memory of his many great qualities, —never seems to have given a moments place to the petty yet not unnatural feeling of resentment which might have led him to seize so favourable an opportunity for retaliating on a humbled rival. No sooner did the appeal of the Pope reach him than he gave orders to Doria to render every assistance to the Venetian fleet, without the exaction of any condition, or a symptom of any sentiment but that

---

9. In 1587, when the armada was in preparation. Queen Elizabeth tried to draw Sultan Amurath III. into an alliance with her against Philip and the Pope. Von Hammer gives the letters written on the occasion. With characteristic astuteness she appealed to the religious sympathies of the Turk, making common cause with him as the "destroyer of idolatry," and declaring that together they could "strike down the proud Spaniard and the lying Pope with all their adherents." Such were the representations made by the English envoy as to the religious belief of his queen and nation, that one of the Turkish ministers remarked to the Austrian ambassador, that "nothing more was wanted to turn the English into good Mussulmans than that they should lift a finger and recite the Eshad." (or creed of Mahomet).

of hearty and devoted adherence to what he deemed the cause of God. There was, moreover, a deeply religious feeling among those now gathered on the shores of Messina.

Many of the most distinguished leaders in their ranks had earned their laurels in the defence of the Catholic faith; not a few of the most renowned of the French volunteers, such as the Count de Ligny, and others, like the two Sforzas, had gained their military reputation in the Huguenot wars; whilst that of Don John himself had been in great part acquired in long and successful struggles with the Moors of Africa. But above all, a distinct religious character was given to the enterprise by the presence of Odescalchi, the papal *nuncio*, whose mission in the Christian camp was not merely to bestow the apostolic benediction on the soldiers, and to animate them to the combat by the assurance of the favour of Heaven, but, as we are told, to drive away all bandits, assassins, thieves, and other public sinners, who might have enlisted from the hope of booty, and who, unworthy of fighting in a holy cause, might rather draw down the anger of God by new crimes.

The chief appointed to lead the Christian forces, whose arrival was being welcomed with such enthusiastic manifestations of joy, was one every way worthy of a great command. His German biographer thus describes him:

> He was of sanguine temperament and lordly presence; in stature somewhat above the middle height; of a frank and generous nature, possessing a strong sense of justice, and gifted with a ready wit and a retentive memory. He was remarkably vigorous and strong; so much so, that he could swim in his armour as if he had nothing on him. He was agreeable and courteous in manner, a great respecter of letters and arms, and an excellent horseman. He had a noble, clear, and spacious forehead; his blue eyes were large and bright, with a grave and kindly expression; his countenance was handsome; he had little beard, and was of a light and graceful figure.

By the terms of the league the squadron was to consist of 300 vessels and galleys, and 50,000 men. The actual combatants, however, were not more than 29,000, although there were more than 80,000 altogether in the fleet that was now assembled under the eye of its commander. The council of war having determined on seeking battle with the Turks without loss of time, only a few days were given to the marshalling of the armament, which then sailed out of the port of Messina, presenting a spectacle of naval magnificence which in those days had rarely been equalled. One by one each vessel passed in its allotted order out of the harbour, and fell into its appointed place, whilst the *nuncio* Odescalchi stood on the pier-head, blessing each in turn.

The vessel which bore the Spanish prince was conspicuous for its beauty and decorations; it was the royal galley of Spain, ornamented after the fanciful taste of the day with "delicate carving and ingenious allegories." The order of battle, which was to be inviolably preserved during the whole time of the expedition, was as follows: Doria led the right wing, having fifty-four galleys under his command, with orders to keep about six miles in advance of the main body, so as to give the ships plenty of sea-room. The left wing was under Agostino Barbarigo, and consisted of an equal number of galleys.

The main body of sixty vessels was under the personal command of Don John himself; whilst the reserve of thirty more was entrusted to Don Alvaro di Bazzano, Marquis of Santa Cruz. Don John of Cardona was despatched with some Sicilian galleys a few miles in advance, with orders to reconnoitre the enemy, and fall into his place at the extremity of Doria's wing, so soon as he should have discovered him. The hoisting of the consecrated standard was to be the signal for the whole fleet falling into line and presenting a single front; whilst a number of galleys were selected to form a circle around the leading vessels of the three chief divisions of the armament to act as a support. Besides the advanced galleys of Cardona, Andrada, a Spanish knight, had previously been sent by Don John, in a light and swift vessel, to make secret observations on the position and preparations of the

Turks; whilst the Christian squadrons meanwhile proceeded to the harbour of Gomenizza, where the whole fleet was reviewed by the commander in person, not without symptoms of jealousy and opposition on the part of the Venetians.

But there was little time for the settlement of mutual disputes; and the intelligence brought by the Spanish spies soon induced all parties to lay aside their rivalries, and prepare for the combat. The tidings of the fall of Famagosta were now fully continued; Cyprus was lost past recall; and the Turkish fleet, under the command of Ali Pasha, was drawn up in the bay of Lepanto, with orders from the sultan to seek and fight the Christians wherever they might be. Some, indeed, were found who, even at this juncture, advised defensive measures; but their votes were overpowered by the ardour of the Colonna and of Don John himself who, we are assured, had such faith in the sanctity of Pius, and in the assurance of victory which he had received from his mouth, that he relied more on his words than even on the number and valour of his soldiers. But it seemed as though his purpose of giving battle must perforce be deterred.

A sudden, obstacle presented itself; an adverse wind arose, which rendered the advance of the armada all but impassible. For two days it had kept steadily blowing from the same quarter, and there seemed no indication of a change; nevertheless (to use the words of the Spanish historian, Rosell)

> on the morning of the 7th of October, a little before daybreak, Don John, defying, the opposition of the elements, and as though impelled by an irresistible power, to the astonishment or all gave the signal to weigh anchor.

It was obeyed; and labouring against the contrary wind, the vessels began to make their slow and difficult way, tossed and beaten by the waves, as the morning light was breaking over the horizon. Just as the sun rose over the glorious coast of that island-group, anciently known as the Echinades, the watchman on board the prince's galley made signal of a sail. It was quickly repeated by the lookers-out in Doria's squadron, and many who eagerly ascended the rigging plainly discerned not one sail alone, but, like so many dark specks on the flashing surface of the western sea, the distant array of the whole Turkish fleet. A battle was therefore felt to be close at hand; and whilst the crimson folds of the consecrated banner, to which a blessed rosary was affixed, were displayed aloft on the royal vessel, and the signal-gun gave notice for all to fall into position, loud acclamations burst from every part of the Christian host in token of their enthusiastic joy.

The Turkish fleet consisted of upwards of 400 vessels of all sizes,[10] manned by not fewer than 120,000 men; in strength, therefore, the Moslems far surpassed the Christians, and they had the prestige of their late conquests in their favour. As the fleets were still distant, the interval was spent by the leaders of both parties in encouraging their followers and preparing for hostilities. Some of the Spanish generals, who still doubted the prudence of provoking the contest, appeared on board the royal galley to learn the final decision of the prince.

They received it in a few words: "Gentlemen," he replied, "you mistake; this is not the time for council, but for combat;" and turning from them, he continued issuing his orders; Then, taking a small and swift galley, he went the rounds of the fleet, animating their crews with a few of those brief and heroic phrases which fell with.such powerful effect from the lips of a great commander. He had an appropriate word for all. The Venetians he reminded of their injuries, and of the slaughter of Famagosta. Sebastian Veniero, whose irritable and stubborn temper had, at the first departure from Messina, betrayed him into excesses which banished him from the prince's council, still bore himself morose and sullen under his disgrace; but the judicious and courteous kindness of Don John so won upon him,

---

10. Von Hammer makes the Turkish fleet consist of 240 galleys and sixty vessels of smaller size, just 300 in all. His account of the Christian fleet is as follows: seventy Spanish galleys, six Maltese, three Savoy, twelve Papal, 108 Venetian; in all 199 galleys, to which he adds six huge *galeasses* contributed by Venice; making the sum-total 205 vessels.

that he laid aside his angry feelings and distinguished himself in the subsequent battle among the most valiant and devoted of the combatants.

His address to the Spaniards has been preserved:

"My children," he said, "we have come here to die—to conquer, if Heaven so disposes. Give not occasion to the enemy to say with impious arrogance, 'Where is now your God?' Fight, then, in His holy name; fallen, a victorious immortality will be yours!"

Now might be seen other galleys passing from vessel to vessel on a different mission these conveyed the religious appointed to attend the armada by the pope, who went through every squadron publishing the indulgence granted by his Holiness, hearing the confessions of the soldiers, and preparing all for death. Their labours were crowned with abundant fruit. So soon as the prince had returned to his vessel the signal throughout the squadrons was given for prayer; all the soldiers, fully armed for the combat, fell upon their knees, the crucifix was upraised on the deck of every vessel, and for some minutes, as the two hosts drew rapidly nearer to each other, every man on board the Christian fleet was engaged in humbly imploring the Divine blessing on its arms.

Gradually the whole battle-front of the enemy displayed itself to view; and the sun, now risen high above the horizon, shone over a spectacle as terrible as it was magnificent. Three hundred and thirty large Turkish vessels were to be seen, disposed in the form of a vast crescent, and far outflanking their opponents' line; but the courage of the Christian leaders remained unmoved by the terrific sight. Although it became evident that the reports of the Spanish spies had greatly underrated the numbers and strength of their opponents, yet, as Rosell relates, the heart of Don John was unappalled; and placing his hopes in God, and fixing his eyes upon the crucifix he ever carried with him, he gave thanks aloud for his victory as already won. No sooner were the words uttered than a token seemed to be given him to assure him that his trust was not ill-founded.

We have said that hitherto the wind had been all in favour of the Turks, whose enormous crescent was bearing rapidly down on the Christian host, like some fierce bird of prey with outstretched wings, when suddenly the breeze fell, and the sails flapped idly on the masts; there was a dead and profound calm. The sea, but a moment before crested with foam, became motionless and smooth as a sheet of glass: it seemed as though they were going to fight on land rather than on water, so still and quiet lay the ships but just now tossed and beaten by the angry waves. Presently a soft rising breeze was heard sighing among the cordage; by and by it gathered strength; but this time it filled the Christian sails, blowing right against the prows of the Turkish ships, and the whole state of things was changed.

The Turkish line, which but a minute previously had seemed to extend its wide arms as if to enfold its helpless foe in a deadly embrace, was thrown into some confusion by this sudden and extraordinary veering of the wind; while the Christian vessels, carried forward by a brisk and favourable breeze, bore down with impetuous gallantry on the foe, and thus gained all the advantage of attack. The Turks, however, fired the first shot, which was quickly answered by the Spaniards; then, placing himself in full armour on the prow of his galley, Don John ordered the trumpets to sound the charge; whilst in every vessel the crews and soldiers knelt to receive the last general absolution, and this being given, every thought was turned to the approaching struggle.

It was noon before the fight began; the brilliant sun rode aloft in the clear azure of the Grecian sky, and flashed brightly on the *casques* and armour of the warriors. The Moslems received their assailants with loud and horrible cries, which were met on the part of the Christians by a profound silence. The flag-ship of Ali Pasha commenced the cannonade; but the fire of the Venetians opened on the Turks so suddenly, and with such overwhelming violence, that at the first discharge their advancing vessels recoiled as though from the shook of a tremendous blow, and at the second broadside two of their galleys were sunk.

In addition to the discouragement produced by this first incident in the fight, the adverse wind carried all the smoke of the Christian artillery right upon the decks of the Turks, who were thus blinded and embarrassed; whilst their enemies were able to direct every movement with facility, and fought in the clear light of day. After this first encounter the battle became general; Don John eagerly made his way towards the *pasha's* galley, and Ali, on his part, did not decline the challenge. To form anything like a correct idea of a sea-fight in those days, we must remember the nature of the vessels then in use, propelled as they were by rowers seated on several tiers of benches, and defended less by artillery than by the armed combatants, who strove to grapple hand to hand with their opponents. The galleys of war were armed with long beaks, or pointed prows, with which they dashed against the enemy's vessels, and often sunk them at the first shook.

Terrible was the meeting of the leaders of the two armaments; the long beak of Ali Pasha's galley was forced far among the benches of the Christian rowers: his own rowers, be it said, were Christians also,—slaves chained to their posts, and working under the threat of death if they shrank from their task, and the promise of liberty if the Turks should gain the day. Then there rose the clash of arms; the combatants met face to face, and their swords rang on the armour of their opponents, whilst the waters were lashed into fury by the strokes of a thousand oars.

Wider and wider the conflict spread: the Bey of Alexandria, at the head of his galleys, made a furious attack on the Venetian squadron; but he was met by Barbarigo and his men with the most eager and determined courage; for the memory of the cruelties practised on their countrymen at Famagosta was fresh in their minds, and animated them to vengeance. A shower of darts rained around them, but they seemed regardless of all danger. One of these deadly weapons struck Barbarigo himself in the eye whilst in the very front of the battle; he was carried to his cabin, where, after lingering three days, he expired of his wound. The slaughter on both sides was terrible, though the Venetians were finally successful in repulsing their enemies; the galley of

Contarini, the nephew of Barbarigo, narrowly escaped being taken, from the fact of almost every man on board of it being slain, Contarini himself among the number.

Whilst matters proceeded thus in the left wing, the right was engaged in an equally desperate struggle. To the Spanish commander, Doria, was opposed, on the side of the Turks, the famous renegade corsair Ouloudj Ali, who, from the rank of a poor Neapolitan fisherman, had risen, through his apostasy from the faith and his extraordinary and ferocious valour, to the sovereignty of Algiers, and had become one of the most distinguished admirals of the day. In the course of the preceding year be had surprised a large squadron of galleys belonging to the Knights of Malta, three of which he succeeded in capturing, whilst others, including the admiral's vessel, were severely injured and run aground off the coast of Sicily.

This circumstance had for the time so crippled the squadron of the order, that it was able to contribute no more than [11]three galleys to the Christian fleet. They were commanded by Peter Giustiniani, grand prior of Messina, one of that illustrious race which was ever foremost when the cause was that of the Church, and the enemy was the Mussulman, and whose boast it was, to reckon the names of fifty saints among its lineage. Giustiniani's own vessel, the *Capitana di Malta,* was posted in the very centre of the fine of battle, the place of honour being granted without opposition to the banner of St. John; but the other galleys were attached to Doria's division, and received the first attack of Ouloudj Ali

In spite of their heroic defence, they were overpowered by numbers; the *St. Stephen* was assailed by three Turkish vessels at once, and was in the utmost danger of being taken, when Giustiniani, perceiving the danger of his knights, hastened to their assistance, and forced two of the enemy's vessels to strike. The third was on the point of doing the same, when Ouloudj Ali brought up four other galleys, and then ensued one of the most desperate and bloody combats that was witnessed throughout

---

11. Vertot. Von Hammer, as has been said, mentions six.

the day. Every man on board the prior's vessel was slain, with the exception of himself and two knights, who were all, however, severely wounded. One of the knights fought till he could no longer stand, and fell, as was supposed, dead; yet he afterwards recovered, and lived for several years, with the loss of an arm, a leg, and an eye, and was looked on in the order as one of their trophies of Lepanto. Giustiniani himself was wounded in fourteen places; and his galley, now without defenders, fell into the hands of the Turks, who immediately brought up their seven shattered vessels, and towed her off in triumph.

It was with inexpressible grief that the Christian fleet beheld the fall of the Maltese standard and the capture of its chief galley; but the success of the infidels was of short duration. The knights inspired with fresh courage by the spectacle of their admiral's misfortune, attacked the vessel of the corsair-chief with redoubled fury. He defended himself with extraordinary obstinacy; but at length, after the loss of all his bravest men, the banner of the Hospitallers was once more seen to float over the *Capitana di Malta,* and Giustiniani and his two wounded comrades were rescued from the enemy's hands.[12] No less than seventy-three knights fell in this struggle. Among those who most distinguished themselves was the Gascon hero, Maturin de Lescat, better known as "the brave Romegas." In his own day he enjoyed a kind of romantic celebrity; for it was said that in all his combats with the Moslems they had never been known to gain a single advantage over him.

In the course of five years he is said to have destroyed more than fifty Turkish vessels, and to have delivered one thousand Christians from slavery. Many of his most daring exploits had been performed on the coasts of Sicily, where he was so great a favourite, that, as Goussancourt informs us, whenever he entered any city of that island, the people would flock out of their houses only to behold him; not knowing which to admire most,

---

12. Von Hammer says that Ouloudj Ali struck off Giustiniani's head with his own hand. Contarini, on the contrary, writes that he was "so badly wounded that he was all but killed."

so much courage adorned with such rare graces of person, or those graces sustained by so undaunted a valour. Much of the old chivalrous spirit was to be found in his character, defaced, indeed, by an ambition which afterwards obscured his fame; but at Lepanto that fame had as yet lost nothing of its brilliancy, and Romegas was never higher in estimation than when he led on the galleys of his order to the rescue of the admiral.

Before the battle began he made a solemn vow that the first Turkish captain who might fall into his hands should be offered to God: it chanced that his first prisoner was a most ferocious Turk, who had lost the use of his right arm, as was said, in consequence of the violence he had used in inflicting the torture on his Christian slaves. This man was given by Romegas, in fulfilment of his vow, to the church of St. John at Malta, and had good reason to thank the brave Gascon for his happy fortune: for his heart changed in his captivity, and he learnt to weep over the actions wherein he had formerly placed his glory; so that, embracing Christianity, he solicited baptism from his masters, and died happily in the true faith. The gallantry displayed by the Hospitallers in the engagement forced the Venetian Contarini to acknowledge that, in spite of their insignificant numbers, their part in the victory almost surpassed that of Venice herself; and in feet, when we remember that Don John of Austria was himself a member of the order,[13] we are bound to admit that their share in the honour of the day has not been sufficiently acknowledged by historians.

Among the combatants in Doria's division, whose courage equalled any of those engaged in the battle, was one whose celebrity, great as ever in our own day, jests, strange to say, rather on the wit, whose ridicule gave the last blow to the chivalry of the middle ages, than on the valour which made its owner himself worthy of the highest chivalrous renown: it was Miguel Carvantes, "brave as the bravest." He lay sick of fever in the cabin

---

13. All the members of the order did not live in community; some were scattered about, and were liable to be called in, in case of emergencies—*e. g.* we find several Knights of St. John among the early governors and settlers of Canada.

of his ship when the tumult of the battle began; but he could no longer endure to remain inactive. In spite of the entreaties of his friends, he arose, and rushed into the hottest of the fight. Being covered with wounds, his companions again urged him to retire; but he replied, "Better for the soldier to remain dead in battle than to seek safety in flight. Wounds on the face and breast are like stars to guide others to the heaven of honour." Besides other less important wounds, Cervantes lost in this battle his left arm;[14] his right hand was destined to gain him another kind of immortality.

The combat soon became too general for the different divisions of the two armaments to preserve their respective positions. Every portion of the hostile fleets was engaged; but the most desperate fight was that between the galleys of the rival generals, Ali Pasha and Don John of Austria. Both commanders fought in the thickest of the fray, regardless of their rank, and with the bold temerity of simple men-at-arms. By the side of the prince's galley were those of Colonna and Sebastian Veniero; and in them, and in the other vessels that surrounded them, were assembled the very flower of the Christian host. Here for the most part were the noble French and Roman volunteers; hardly a great house of Italy but had its representative among the combatants: two of the Colonnas; Paul Orsini, the chief of his name, with his brothers, Horace and Virginius; Antonio Carrafa, Michel Bonelli, and Paul Ghislieri, nephews of the Pope; and Farnese, prince of Parma, who played a very hero's part in the flag-ship of the Genoese republic.

The battle in the centre, led on by such men, and met with equal valour and determination on the part of their adversaries, lasted more than two hours. Already had the Christians made two gallant attempts to board the vessel of the *pasha*, and each time they were driven back with loss so soon as they reached his decks. The burning midday sun added to the heat of the engage-

---

14. "A trifling price to pay (he says in the Preface to the second part of *Don Quixote*) for the honour of partaking in the first great action in which the naval supremacy of the Ottoman was successfully disputed by Christian arms."

ment, and the thirst of the soldiers was almost intolerable. The decks were heaped with dead, and those still living were covered with wounds, and wellnigh exhausted from loss of blood, and still they maintained the conflict with unabated courage.

At length the signal was given for a third charge. It was obeyed with an impetuosity nothing could resist; and whilst Ali Pasha vainly strove, as before, to drive back his desperate assailants, a shot from an *arquebuse* struck him in the forehead. Staggering from his wound, he fell, and his head was instantly cut off by a blow from one of the galley-slaves, and thrown into the sea. The event of the battle after this was no longer doubtful; Don John with his own hands pulled down the Turkish flag, and shouted, "Victory!" whilst Santa Cruz, profiting by the confusion, pushed forward with the reserve, and completed the discomfiture of the foe. At this critical moment the corsair Ouloudj Ali, seeing that the whole Turkish centre was broken, and the day irretrievably lost, hoisted all sail, and with forty galleys, the only vessels that escaped out of that bloody battle, passed safely through the midst of the Christian fleet.

The Turks struggled long and desperately before they finally gave way. It was four in the afternoon ere the fight was over; and the lowering sky betokened the gathering of a tempest. The remains of the Turkish fleet fled in all directions, pursued, though with difficulty, by the allies, whose wearied rowers could scarcely hold the oars; whilst their numbers were so thinned by the slaughter, that it was as much as the commanders could do to find crews for their vessels. Crippled as the Christians were, however, the infidels were seized with panic, and ran their vessels madly against the shore of Lepanto. In their terrified efforts to land, many were drowned; whilst the galleys were broken by the waves, or fell an easy prey to the conquerors. The whole sea for miles presented most terrible tokens of the battle; those clear waters, on which the morning sun had shone so brightly, were now dark and discoloured by human blood. Headless corpses and the fragments of many a wreck floated about in strange confusion; while the storm, which every moment raged in wilder fury, added to the horror of the scene, lit up as the night advanced by the flames from the burning galleys, many of which were found too much disabled to be of any use to their captors.

Twelve [15] of those belonging to the allies were destroyed; but the extent of their victory may be estimated by the fact that eighty vessels belonging to the Turks were sunk, whilst 130 remained in the hands of the Christians. The *pasha's* galley, which was among those taken, was a vessel of surpassing beauty. The deck, says Knolles, was of walnut-wood, dark as ebony, "chequered and wrought marvellously fine with divers lively colours and variety of histories;" and her cabin glittered with ornaments of gold, rich hangings, and precious gems.[16]

The enemy's slain amounted to 30,000 men; and 15,000 of the Christian slaves who had been compelled to work the Ottoman galleys were liberated. Yet the victory, complete as it was, was dearly bought; the loss of the allies was reckoned at about 8000 men; and their ships, riddled with balls, and many of them dismasted, presented a striking contrast to the gay and gallant trim in which but a few days previously they had left the harbour of Messina.

The conduct of Don John of Austria after the battle justifies us in ranking him among the true heroes of chivalry. He had been foremost in the day's conflict, where he had been seen, sword in hand, wherever the danger was greatest and the blows hardest. He was now equally conspicuous for his care of the wounded, his generosity towards his prisoners, and his frank and noble recognition of the services of a rival. Sebastian Veniero, the disgraced leader of the Venetian forces, had distinguished himself in the fight by a valour that had made his gray hairs the centre round which the most gallant of the young volunteers of France and Italy had rallied during that eventful day. The prince sent for

---

15. Von Hammer says fifteen; and that the Turks lost 224 vessels, of which 94 were burnt or shattered on the coast; the rest were divided among the allies. But this calculation leaves thirty-six vessels unaccounted for, after reckoning the forty which Ouloudj Ali succeeded in saving. The number of prisoners he estimates at 8468.
16. *Sutherland*, vol. 2. p. 244.

him as soon as the confusion of the victory had subsided, and (adds Rosell in his history of the battle).

> to show him that he harboured no resentment for past offences, he advanced to meet him as far as the ladder of his galley, embraced him affectionately, and, calling him his father, extolled, as was just, his great valour, and could not finish what he would have said for the sobs and tears that choked his utterance. The poor old man, who did not expect such a reception, wept also, and so did all who witnessed the scene.

Whilst this interview was taking place, the two sons of Ali Pasha were brought prisoners into the prince's presence.

"It was a piteous sight," says the same historian, "to see the tears they shed on finding themselves at once prisoners and orphans."

But they met with a friend and comforter in their generous captor; he embraced them, and expressed the tenderest sympathy for their misfortunes. The delicacy of his kindness showed itself in more than words; he treated them rather as his guests than as captives, lodging them in one of his own cabins, and even ordering Turkish clothes to be provided for them at his expense, that they might not be pained by being obliged to adopt the European costume. Neither was he less forward in returning thanks to God for the victory granted to his arms than he had been in commending to Him the event of the day's conflict. Thus the night closed: the vessels cast anchor amid the wreck of battle, and the wearied combatants took a short and necessary repose. So soon as day again broke, the sails were hoisted, and, securing their prizes, they proceeded to the port of Petala, to repair their damages and provide for the necessities of the wounded;

Such was the celebrated battle of Lepanto, whose results were in one way insignificant, owing to the losses incurred by the Christian allies, and the limitation put on the power of Don John by the cautious policy of the Spanish king. Yet we should be wrong to estimate the worth of any victory by the amount of its territorial conquests, or its lists of killed and wounded. The moral enacts of the day of Lepanto are beyond calculation: it was the turning point in the history of the Ottoman Turks; from it may be dated the decline of their dominion; for though indeed, during the following century, the terror of Europe was still constantly excited by their attacks on the frontier of the empire, yet their naval power was never again formidable, and the long prestige of continual success was broken.[17]

Moreover, whilst it is impossible to deny that the advantages of the victory were never followed up, and that in consequence of the desertion of the Venetians, the league itself was soon dissolved; yet it is also certain that the further progress of the Ottomans westward was checked from the hour of their defeat; whereas every campaign during preceding years had witnessed their gradual advance.

It only remains for us to speak of the manner in which the news of the success of the Christian arms was received by those who were so anxiously awaiting the result of the expedition at the courts of Rome and Madrid. Pius V., who may be considered as the originator of the whole enterprise, had, from the first departure of the fleet, ordered continual fasts and prayers for its success. On the memorable 7th of October on which the battle took place, and which fell that year on a Sunday, all the confraternities of the Rosary had assembled in the Dominican church of the Minerva to offer their devotions for victory under the intercession of Mary. All Rome was in prayer that day, and her prayer was the *Ave Maria*.

The pope himself had attended the procession; and on returning to the Vatican after the conclusion of the ceremony, he was walking to and fro through the long suites of rooms in the pontifical palace, in conversation with some of the cardinals and Baffotti, the treasurer, on various matters of business. Suddenly

---

17. Cervantes calls it "that day so fortunate to Christendom, when all nations were undeceived of their error in believing the Turks to be invincible at sea." *Don Quixote,*

he stopped as if listening to a distant sound, then, leaving his companions, he approached one of the windows, and threw it open; whilst those who watched his movements observed that his eyes were raised to heaven with the expression of one in ecstasy. They themselves also listened, but were unable to catch the faintest sound that could account for his singular behaviour; and whilst they gazed at one another in astonishment, unable to comprehend the scene, Pius (says his biographer Maffei),

> whose eyes had been fixed upwards for a good space, shutting the window again, and seemingly full of great things, turned graciously to the treasurer, and said, 'This is no time for business; let us go and give God thanks, for our fleet has fought with the Turks, and in this very hour has conquered.' He knelt down as he spoke, and gave thanks to God with great fervour; then taking a pen, he wrote down the day and the hour: it was the decisive moment at which the battle had turned in favour of the Christians.

The actual intelligence of the victory did not reach Rome until the 21st of October, owing to contrary winds which delayed the couriers of Colonna; so that the first news was brought by a messenger from the republic of Venice. It was night when he arrived; but when word was brought to the holy father of the happy realisation of his hopes and of the Divine assurance he had received, he sprang from his bed, and bursting into tears, exclaimed, "There was a man sent from God, whose name was John;" then, hurrying to his private chapel, he summoned all his attendants and officers to meet him there, to offer their thanksgivings for the great event.

A more solemn function was performed on the following morning in the Basilica of the Apostles, and none of those who had joined in the previous and reiterated prayers by which the patronage of Mary had been invoked on the Christian arms, failed to ascribe the success which had been granted, to the power of her intercession, especially as invoked in the holy devotion of the Rosary, under whose banner, as it were, the battle had been fought and won. The emotion displayed by St. Pius was in accordance with the simplicity and tenderness of his character. Not less characteristic, nor less religious, though possibly less calculated to engage the sympathy of our readers, was the calmness with which the same intelligence was received by Philip of Spain. He was at Vespers when the news was brought him, and heard it without the smallest manifestation of joy or surprise. When the office was concluded, he desired the *Te Deum* to be sung; and on the following day proceeded to Madrid, to be present at a solemn Mass offered in thanksgiving for the victory.

An entire and rigid self-command was at once the virtue and the cause of the unpopularity of this singular man. As a virtue, it was the effect of natural impulse subdued and annihilated; but along with this there doubtless mingled much of constitutional reserve and coldness. As to the Venetian republic, the charge of insensibility could not certainly be brought against either its senate or its people. The religious emotion of St. Pius, and the austere self-restraint of King Philip, were there exchanged for the tumultuous expressions of popular rejoicing. The great *Piazza* of St. Mark was like a fair, where *doge* and senator, nobles and citizens, all met to congratulate one another; whilst the shouts and *vivas* of the crowd rang far over the waters of the Adriatic; and by an edict of the senate the prisons were thrown open, and none of those whose relations had fallen in the battle were allowed to wear mourning, or show any outward demonstrations of grief; for their loss was rather counted to them as glory.

We shall not dwell on the tokens of gratitude showered on the victorious chiefs,—on those revivals of the classic triumphs which filled the streets of Rome on the entry of Colonna,—nor on all the laurel-wreaths and orations, the poems and painted galleries, and other similar memorials of the great event, which the gratitude and the genius of the day presented to the conquerors of Lepanto. There was another kind of gratitude owing, and to a different victor; and the Church well knew how to pay her debt. The voice of Catholic Christendom agreed in attributing the victory to the intercession of Mary; and the invocation,. "Help of Christians," was introduced into the *Litany* of Loretto in memory of the feet. But St. Pius was scarcely content with so slender an acknowledgement as this.

"In the revelation granted to him of the victory," says Maffei, "it had been also made known to him that the prayers of the brethren of the Holy Rosary had greatly contributed to the same. Being therefore desirous of perpetuating the memory of this, he instituted a feast, appointed for the 7th of October, in honour of 'Our Lady of Victories'. But Gregory XIII., admiring the modesty of his predecessor, who, being a religious of the Order of Friars Preachers, had not chosen to make mention of the Rosary, for fear he should be thought rather to have sought the honour of his order than that of truth, desired that in future the feast of our Lady of Victories should be kept on the first Sunday in October in all Dominican churches, and wherever the Confraternity of the Rosary existed, under the new title of the 'Festival of the Holy Rosary,' which was thence forward no longer to be celebrated on the 25th of March, as in time past it had been. This was finally extended to the whole of the Church by Clement XII., who changed the wording of the Roman Martyrology to its present form: The 'Commemoration of our Lady of Victories', which Pope Pius V. ordained to be observed every year, in memory of a famous victory gained at sea this day by the Christians over the Turks, through the help of the Mother of God; and Gregory XIII. likewise ordained the annual solemnity of the Rosary of the same most Blessed Virgin to be kept on the first Sunday of the month for the same came."

Baronius, in his notes on the Martyrology, has commented on these words, saying they are but the confirmation from the hand of Clement of that which had been already declared by Gregory XIII, namely, that by the common consent of the Catholic world the victory of Lepanto was due to the intercession of Mary, invoked and obtained by the prayers of the brethren of the Rosary, and of the Dominican Order; not only the prayers offered up before the battle, but those especially which were rising to Heaven at the very moment when the tide of victory turned in favour of the Christian league.

On one of the northern hills of Rome may be seen another monument of the Church's gratitude to her mother and protector: it is the Church of our Lady of Victories. There, upon walls dazzling with the rich colours, of their jaspers and marbles, hang the tattered and discoloured banners of the infidels. The church was raised to receive them, and to be a witness to all ages of the omnipotence of prayer.

Nor, considering how slight were the immediate and apparent results of the victory of Lepanto,—so slight, indeed, that historians have spoken of them as null,— will the pious mind fail to note and admire how, with prophetic eye reading futurity, the Church saw in that event the crisis in the fortunes, and the incipient decay, of that monstrous anti-Christian power, whose advances, so far from being arrested, seemed only to be accelerated by any check it might chance to encounter. The commemorations of the Church are not only preludes of victory, but triumphs already accomplished and secured.

CHAPTER 12

Vienna: The Siege

On the evening of the 7th of July 1688 the city of Vienna presented a strange and melancholy spectacle. The road leading out of the Rothenthurm Gate was crowded by a dense mass of carriages and other vehicles, as well as by a vast multitude of foot-passengers, who, by their anxious and terrified looks, seemed to be flying from a pressing danger. Hour after hour you might have watched the stream of fugitives, and still it flowed on without intermission, till you would have thought the city emptied of its inhabitants, or at least of all those of the noble and wealthier classes. Had you sought the reason of so strange a spectacle, the red glare of the distant horizon, lit up by the flames of burning villages, and nearer still, those that enveloped the Carmelite Convent on the heights of the Kahlenberg, would have furnished you with the answer. Those fires were the tokens that Vienna was surrounded by the dreaded forces of the Turks.

Every post, for weeks past, had brought the intelligence of some fresh disaster. Hungary was in open revolt; and 400,000 Turks, under the command of the *vizier*, Kara Mustapha, had poured into the territories of the empire, invited by the treachery of the insurgents. Then came the news that Emerick Tekeli had accepted the investiture of the Hungarian kingdom at the hands of the infidels, and basely acknowledged himself and his countrymen *vassals* to the Porte. At last, on that very morning, the city had been thrown into a very panic of alarm by the hasty entrance of fugitives of the imperial cavalry; and the rumour quickly spread that the forces of the Duke of Lorraine had been surprised and totally defeated at Petrouel by the Tartar house, and that the remains of the imperial army were falling back in disordered flight upon the capital.

This, as it afterwards proved, was a false report; as Lorraine, although surprised by the enemy, had succeeded in repulsing them, and was effecting his retreat in good order. But the Emperor Leopold did not wait for the confirmation or contradiction of the intelligence; and at seven o'clock on the same evening the imperial carriages were seen hastily passing over the Tabor Bridge on their way to Lintz, thus giving an example of flight which was quickly followed by the greater portion of the wealthier citizens. It is calculated that upwards of 60,000 persons left the city during that memorable night, the confused masses being lighted on their way by the flames of the burning convent.

A great number of these having no conveyances fell into the hands of the very enemy from whom they sought to escape; and the roads leading to Styria were covered with unhappy fugitives, whom the Turks are even said to have hunted down with bloodhounds: some perished of hunger in the woods; others met a cruel death from their barbarous pursuers; the rest succeeded in reaching the Bavarian dominions, where Leopold had already found refuge, after narrowly escaping the Tartar cavalry, who occupied the very line of route which had been originally proposed for him to take.

Our present business, however; is rather with the story of the few who, resisting the infection of terror, remained at their post, and prepared, as best they could, to offer a determined resistance to the besiegers. Their numbers were fearfully small One regiment of troops only was within the walls, and the citizens capable of bearing arms were reckoned at no more than 1200 men. Ernest Ruchjer, Count of Stahremberg, was the heroic governor to whom the defence of the city was entrusted; and if his scanty forces, and the utter want of all preparation for a warlike emergency, might well have made his heart sink at the task before him, yet his own gallantry and the active co-operation of some of his followers and of the *burgher* authorities almost supplied for the want of other resources.

The works necessary for the defence of the city were not yet begun; for even the ordinary engineering tools were wanting. The supplies of fuel, water, and provisions requisite for sustaining a long siege were still unprovided; and all this had to be done, and was done, by the astonishing exertions of a few men within the space of a single week. The spectacle which their courage and activity presented formed a striking contrast to that which had been displayed only a few days previously by the flight of the court and of so many of their fellow-citizens. Men of all classes, priests, and even women, were to be seen labouring at the fortifications: the *burgomaster*, Von Liebenberg, was foremost with his wheelbarrow among the workmen, cheering them on by his example and words of encouragement; some carried loads of wood from the suburbs to the city stores; whilst the circle of flames from the burning villages, denoting the advance of the enemy, drew nearer and nearer, so that by the 12th of July they were working under the very eyes of the Turks.

Before proceeding to the story of the siege, it may be necessary to say a few words on the position of the two parties in the struggle about to commence, so as to give some idea of their relative chances of success. The hostilities between the Turks and the Empire had been interrupted only by occasional truces, from the first occupation of Constantinople by the former two centuries previously. The present invasion had been brought about mainly through the means of the Hungarian insurgents; and however much we may be disposed to allow that the severity of the Austrian government to a conquered country provoked the assertion of national independence on the part of its oppressed people, yet we cannot but withhold the title of "*patriots*" from those who, in their hatred to Austria, were ready to sacrifice the very safety of Christendom, and whose notions of national independence consisted in exchanging subjection to the Austrians for a far more degrading *vassalage* to the infidels. When the news of the vast preparations of the Ottomans reached Vienna, it found the imperial government almost without defence. The day was past when Christian Europe could be roused to a crusade in defence of its faith, or even of its freedom; nay, in the history of this contest we are met at every page by the details of secret negotiations and most unworthy intrigues, by which the emissaries of the "Most Christian King," Louis XIV., encouraged and assisted the invasion of the infidels to gratify his personal jealousy against the House of Hapsburgh.

In the day of his distress and humiliation Leopold was compelled to seek for assistance from one whom till then it had been the policy of his government to slight and thwart on all occasions, and from whom, according to the calculations of a selfish policy, he had certainly nothing to expect. This was John Sobieski, the elective King of Poland, whose former exploits had rendered his name a very watchword of terror to the Turks, but on whom the Austrian sovereign had but little claim. The interests of the Polish king were all opposed to his taking any part in the hostilities.

After years of civil war and foreign invasion, his surpassing genius had but just obtained for Poland a profound and honourable peace. An alliance with the House of Hapsburgh was at variance with the close and intimate connection existing between himself and the court of Versailles; and the favour and protection of the French king was of no small importance to the distracted councils of Poland; whilst the contemptuous and unfriendly treatment he had ever received from the Austrian sovereign might very naturally have prompted him to refuse the sacrifice of his own interests in that monarch's behalf. But none of these considerations had any weight in the noble heart of Sobieski, who looked on the question simply as one involving his faith and honour as a Christian king.

> "For thirty years," to use the words of Pope Innocent XI, "he had the bulwark of the Christian republic—the wall of brass against which all the efforts of the barbarians had been broken in pieces!"

Indeed, if we may so say, he had come to look on war with the infidel as his special vocation: the victories of Podhaiski and Choczim, and that other wonderful series of achievements, to which history has given the title, adopted from the gazette of Louis XIV., of the "Miraculous Campaign," had, as it were, installed him in his glorious office; and when the same pope called him in council "the lieutenant of God" he did but give expression to the feeling with which all Christian Europe looked to him as her hero and protector. It is not a little striking that the greater number of the semi-infidel historians of the eighteenth century, while doing full justice to the gallantry and genius of this extraordinary man, have condemned his enterprise against the Turks as proceeding only from a religious and chivalrous impulse, undirected by any views of sound state-policy.

Whether the policy which saved Europe from the horrors [1] of an Ottoman invasion can rightly be termed unsound, our readers may determine; it was doubtless unselfish, and probably its very generosity has been the principal cause of its condemnation by these writers; but we refer to their criticism as an unquestionable testimony in proof of the real character of this campaign, and of the motives from which it was undertaken; and we think, on their own showing, we can scarcely be wrong in representing this war as purely a religious one, entered on in defence of the Christine faith, and without any mixture of these political motives, the want of which is so deplored by the historians of that sceptical age, but which renders its history so glorious in the eyes of the Christian student.

The treaty between the two sovereigns, signed on the 31st of March 1688, was confirmed by the solemnity of an oath administered by the *cardinal-legate*, the obligation of which on the conscience of Sobieski will be found to have exercised a marked influence on his future conduct. At the time when the treaty was concluded the invader had not yet set foot in Hungary. To ap-

---

1. It was calculated by contemporary writers of credit that, in this very expedition, the Turks carried off into slavery from Austria 6000 men, 11,000 women, 19,000 girls—of whom 200 were of noble extraction—and 56,000 children.

proach the Austrian capital they would have to pass a number of strongly fortified towns, which, according to the ordinary course of military proceedings must first be reduced before pushing further into the enemy's country.

Nevertheless, the intelligence which reached Sobieski from his secret spies and envoys in the Turkish dominions all pointed to Vienna, itself as the object of attack. But in spite of his representations to Leopold, that monarch could not be induced to believe himself in danger, or to prepare for an emergency; and thus, when the heights of the surrounding hills blazed with the camp-fires of the Tartars, the city, as we have seen, was taken by surprise; and the inhabitants of the surrounding country were quietly at work in the harvest-fields, when the hosts of the enemy came on them like some sudden inundation. Indeed, the march of Kara Mustapha was without a precedent. To advance from the borders of Hungary to the walls of Vienna, leaving in his rear all the fortresses of the imperialists, was the affair of a week; before another had closed, his trenches were opened and the siege begun; and this extraordinary rapidity must account, both for the defenceless state of the capital and for the time which necessarily elapsed before the Polish king could come to its relief.

An incident may here be related which will show the nature of the warfare waged by the infidels, and the treatment which the Viennese might expect at their hands. In the neighbourhood of the city was the small town of Perchtoldsdorf; and as one of the first objects of the invaders was to secure all the places capable of being fortified within a short distance of Vienna, a detachment was sent to take possession. The inhabitants under the direction of their bailiff, at first endeavoured to hold the town; but owing to the superior numbers of the enemy and the failure of ammunition, they were soon compelled to abandon it, and to betake themselves to the tower of the church and its precincts, which, on its approach of the Turks, they had diligently fortified, as their forefathers had done 150 years before. Small hope, however, was there that they should be able to keep the enemy at bay; and when a horseman, bearing a flag of truce, summoned them to surrender, with the offer of security to life and property in case of immediate compliance, they did not hesitate to accept the terms.

On the morning of July 17th a *pasha* arrived from the camp, and, seating himself on a red carpet opposite the church, announced to the besieged the conditions of surrender; which were, that the inhabitants should pay a contribution of 6000 florins, and, as a token that they had not yielded up the place, but had honourably capitulated, the keys were to be delivered by a young maiden with her hair flowing and a garland on her head. These terms concluded, the citizens left their stronghold; and the daughter of the bailiff, arrayed as described, bore the keys of the place on a cushion, and presented them to the *pasha*.

The latter now required that all the men capable of bearing arms should be drawn up in the market-place, on pretence of ascertaining what number of troops were needed for the occupation of the town. It was too late to retreat, and the order was obeyed. As the inhabitants came out, the Turkish soldiers closed about them, and deprived them of their arms; such as hesitated were overpowered, and those who paused in the gateway, reluctant to proceed, were dragged out by the hair of their heads. The unfortunate people were no sooner all assembled than their persons were searched; and everything they had about them was taken away. At the same time the entrance-gate was strongly guarded. Some of the townsmen; seized with alarm; endeavoured, with the bailiff at their head, to regain the church; but the Turks rushed upon them with drawn sabres, and the bailiff was cut down on the threshold.

At that instant the *pasha* rose from his seat, flung down the table before him, and gave the signal for a general massacre; himself setting the example by cutting down with his own hand the trembling girl at his side. The slaughter raged for two hours without intermission; 3500 persons were put to the sword, and in a space so confined that the expression "torrents of blood," so often a figure of speech, was fully applicable to the case. The women and children, who still remained within the church, together with the parish-priest and his coadjutor, were dragged into slavery, and never heard of more. Among the victims, numbers of whom were inhabitants of adjacent places who had taken refuge in the town, some, it is conjectured, were people of condition; for, in the course of excavations which lately took place on the scene of the massacre, valuable rings set with precious stones have been discovered.[2] To this day the Holy Sacrifice is offered every year for those who perished on the fatal 17th of July by this act of savage treachery.

But to return. Thirteen thousand regular troops from the army of Lorraine were assembled within the walls of Vienna by the evening of the 13th; and at sunrise on the following day a dusky moving mass appeared on the heights of the Weinerberg, which was the main body of the enemy. Scarcely could the most practised eye distinguish one object from another in the confusion of the crowd. Men, horses, camels, and carriages, formed a mixed multitude, which from the ramparts of the city seemed like some swarm of locusts, and extended for miles along the plains of the Danube and the surrounding hills. The formation of the besieging camp was immediately begun, and within a few hours 25,000 tents had risen as if by magic out of the ground.

Luxury and magnificence formed the very tradition of an eastern army; and since the days of Xerxes perhaps no such host had been seen, either for numbers or for splendour of equipment, as that which now spread around the walls of the devoted city of Vienna. We should form an imperfect notion of the spectacle presented to the eyes of its defenders, if our idea of the Turkish camp were modelled on the usual military equipages of European nations. The pavilion of the *vizier* and his principal officers blazed with a wealth which the imperial palaces could hardly rival. That of Kara Mustapha was a town in itself: the canvas walls formed streets and houses and included within one enclosure baths, fountains, and flower-gardens, and even a menagerie stocked from the imperial collection of the Favorita, which had

---

2. *Two Sieges of Vienna,* pp. 95-98.

fallen into the hands of the invaders. Within the mazy labyrinth of these luxurious alleys stood the pavilion of Mustapha himself. The material was of green silk, worked in gold and silver, and it was furnished with the richest oriental carpets and dazzling with precious stones. In a yet more magnificent sanctuary, forming the centre of the whole, was preserved the sacred standard of the Prophet, which had been solemnly entrusted to the care of the *vizier* by the sultan's own hands. The display of the inferior officers was on a corresponding scale.

Whilst these preparations were going on outside the walls, Stahremberg was busy in his arrangements for the defence. Among his most able coadjutors was one whose name deserves to be remembered among the noblest ranks of Christian patriots. This was Leopold von Kollonitsch, Bishop of Neustadt, on whom the spiritual care of the city had devolved; the Bishop of Vienna having accompanied his royal master in his flight. It could scarce have fallen on one better fitted to hold it at such a time.

In his youth he had served as a Knight of Malta in many campaigns against the infidels; and in the Cretan war had exerted the wonder and admiration of the Venetians, before whose eyes he boarded several Turkish galleys, killing many unbelievers with his own hand, and tearing down and bearing away as a trophy the Moslem standard of the horse-tail. The military experience of such a man was of no small use in the present crisis; yet we should be in error if we attached to the name of Kollonitsch the prejudice which has against the character of a military prelate. If he was daily on the ramparts, and by the side of Stahremberg in the posts of greatest danger, it was to console the wounded and administer the last rites of religion, to the dying. His talents and scientific knowledge were directed towards securing the safety of his fellow-citizens, and mitigating the sufferings of the siege.

It was he who suggested, and, indeed, by his exertions supplied the necessary means for provisioning the city; regulated the tariff; and even provided for the extinction of the fires which might be caused by the shells of the besiegers. Yet, extraordinary as were the services he rendered, in discharging them he never seems for one moment to have stepped beyond the line assigned to him by his clerical character. The hospital was his home; women, children, and the aged and infirm, were the only forces whose command he assumed; and by his ingenuity they were organised into a regular body, and rendered efficient for many services which would otherwise have necessarily taken up the time of those whose presence was required on the walls.

Let us now place ourselves on these walls and watch the scene before us. A week ago there was a pleasant prospect over the *faubourgs* of the city, where in the midst of vineyards and gardens might be seen the white walls of costly public edifices, or the villas of the nobility and richer citizens. All this is now gone; for, as a necessary precaution of public safety, the suburbs, whose proximity to the city would have afforded a dangerous cover to the invaders, have been devoted to the flames. Beyond the blackened ruins, which gird the ramparts of Vienna with a dark line of desolation, stretches the camp of the Ottomans, in the form of a vast half-moon. The bright July sun is shining over its gilded pavilions, and you may see the busy caravans of merchants with their trains of camels and elephants, which carry your fancy back to the gorgeous descriptions of an Arabian tale.

It seems like the work of some of its own fabled *genii* when you see the landscape, but a day or two age rich in the civilisation of an European capital, now suddenly transformed into an Oriental scene, and mark the picture of mimic domes and minarets, and the horse-tail standards waving in the breeze, every breath of which brings the echo of a wild and savage music from the cymbals and trombones of the Tartar troops.

Now let us turn our eyes on the city itself. The first object which meets our gaze is the smoking ruin of the Scottish convent. On the first day of the siege it caught fire, and was reduced to ashes; and you may hear from the lips of any citizen you meet how but for the protection of God and our Lady that first day of siege bade fair to have been the last: for the fire spread rapidly to the imperial arsenal, which contained the whole store of powder belonging to the garrison. It seemed to defy every effort to extinguish it; and an explosion was each moment expected, which, had it taken place, must have destroyed the whole northern quarter of the city, and laid it open for the entrance of the enemy. Two windows were already on fire, and the heat prevented the workmen from approaching the spot. But the people, who watched the scene with terrible anxiety, prayed, even as they worked, and invoked the patronage of that fond Mother whose ear is never closed to her children's prayers: and then, what historians call a favourable chance happened, which saved the city.

The wind suddenly changed; the flames went out of themselves, or spread in a contrary direction. Though posterity may laugh at their superstition and credulity, the foolish people of Vienna are contented to believe that they have been preserved by the providence of Him whose ministers are the winds and His messengers the flaming fire. Nor indeed had this been the only instance of what was naturally deemed a providential intervention in behalf of the besieged. The first shell fired by the Turks into the town fell near the church of St. Michael; and before it had time to burst, a little child of three years old ran fearlessly up to it and extinguished it. A second struck through the roof of the cathedral; and fell among a crowded congregation; but one woman alone was slightly injured by the explosion; and a third was thrown right into an open barrel of powder, but no mischief ensued: and the citizens were accustomed to collect the fragments; and; after having them blessed by a priest; to redischarge them at the enemy. In vain did the besiegers try every combustible weapon which ingenuity could suggest; Vienna seemed at least insured against conflagration; and the fireballs; and arrows wrapped with combustible materials; fell on the roofs and in the streets as harmlessly as a shower of leaves.

Now let us look up to the tall and graceful spire of St. Stephen; whose tapering summit; surmounted by the crescent; bears witness to the former presence of the infidels. Within those fretted and sculptured pinnacles, beyond the reach of the most piercing eye, is the stone-chair whence the governor Stahremberg overlooks the whole camp of the enemy. There he sits, hour after hour; for a wound in his head, received from the bursting of a shell, has disabled him for the present from taking his usual position on the ramparts; though not a day passes but you may see him carried in a chair to the defences which are being completed under his direction. There are others whom you encounter at every turn, whose names and services are almost as memorable as his. There is the Baron of Kielmansegge, who is ready for anything, and will carry a private's musket in the ranks, if need be; while his mechanical and scientific ingenuity have supplied the garrison with a powder-mill and a handgrenade of his own construction.

Or there is Count Sigbert von Heister, whose hat was pierced through with the first Turkish arrow shot into the town: and both arrow and hat are still to be seen in the Ambrose Museum of the city. Or you will come across singularly accoutred members of the various volunteer-corps of the city, whose patriotism has taught them to shoulder a gun for the first time; while the name of their companies may perhaps account for their awkwardness in their new profession: they are members of the gallant *burgher* companies,—of the butchers, or the bakers, or the shoemakers,— and they render good service on the walls, and never shrink from fire.

But a more trimly equipped body may be seen, neither *burghers* nor yet of the regular force, there is a fanciful oddity in their costume, and a certain recklessness in their very walk and gestures; you see at once they are the students from the university, commanded by their rector Lawrence Grüner. Lastly, wherever the shots are thickest and the danger greatest, wherever blood is flowing and men are dying or suffering, you may see the form of the excellent Kollonitsch, not a quiver of whose eyelid betrays that the balls whistling round his head are any objects of terror to his soul, while he stoops over the prostrate bodies of the wounded, and tenderly bears them on his shoulders to the hospital which is his home.

A month has passed; and the siege has rapidly advanced, and brought many a sad change to the position of the defenders. There have been assaults and sallies, mines and countermines, without number: the bastions are in many places a heap of ruins, smashed with shot and by the explosion of mines. There are some where the fire is so thick and continual, that to show yourself for a moment on them is certain death. The city lies open in many places to the enemy; but in vain have the *Janizaries* led their best men to the breach; each time have they been met by the heroic defenders, whose own arms hare proved a surer barrier than the most skilful fortifications, and over and over again have they been compelled to retire to their trenches with loss.

The progress of the Turkish miners, the most skilful of their day, has been rapid and alarming. Their excavations have reached the very heart of the city; and each house has its sentinel day and night to prevent a subterraneous surprise. In every cellar there is a large vessel of water and a drum covered with peas, that the possible presence of the enemy underground may be betrayed by their vibration. These mines were indeed extraordinary works of art, and excited the admiration of the German engineers when they inspected them at the close of the siege. They were vast excavations, often themselves fortified; for the countermines of the besieged sometimes broke into them, and then a deadly contest was carried on hand to hand in the bowels of the earth. Frequently did the brave defenders succeed in destroying not only the works but the workmen, and many hundredweights of powder were thus seized and carried off. The trenches were divided into chambers for the accommodation of the officers, and some prepared for the use of the *vizier* were perfectly carpeted and cushioned. He himself divided his time between the inspection of the trenches and the luxurious enjoyments of his camp.

Every third day he caused himself to be carried to the works in a litter made shot-proof by strong plates of iron, and might be seen urging on the men with his words, and sometimes striking the idlers with the flat of his sabre. But the fire of the enemy was not the only danger that now threatened the defenders. The usual consequences of a siege began to show themselves in disease, brought on by bad food and the infection from the dead bodies. Among its victims were the brave Burgomaster Liebenberg, and many of the highest functionaries and ecclesiastics of the city.

The hospitals were crowded as well with the sick as with the wounded; and if the pestilence at length subsided, it was in great measure owing to the exertions of Kollonitsch, whose sagacity suggested, whilst his prompt and untiring activity carried out, every precaution that the urgency of the case required. You might see him everywhere: he was constantly in the hospitals, nursing the sufferers with the tenderness of a woman; and an hour after you would find him superintending the construction of drains and kennels, and working with his own hand to teach and encourage his men. His name became so familiar in people's mouths as the chief protector of the city, that the fame of his services reached the *vizier's* camp; and Kara Mustapha is said to have vowed his head to the sultan as a revenue for his success in checking the ravages of that pestilence on which he counted as his best ally.

Meanwhile every man in the city was employed in his own way: the citizens were busy with carts and horses; the Jesuits had two of their number constantly perched on the tower of St. Stephen, making telescopic observations of the hostile movements. Such men as Kielmansegge turned their amateur ingenuity to account by manufacturing handmills to grind the flour; and, spite of their sufferings, no abatement of courage or spirit was observable among the ranks.

Still there was no sign of relief. Sobieski, besieged by messages from the pope and the emperor, was indeed making prodigious efforts to raise the necessary forces; but many had to be armed and disciplined before they could be ready to meet the enemy. The small army of Lorraine maintained its position at Crems, and even showed itself on the offensive against Tekeli, whom it compelled to retire from Presburg; but its numbers were wholly inadequate to an encounter with the Turks. The alarm of Europe grew every day greater, and showed itself in generous contributions towards the expenses of the war. Every town in Italy sent its list of voluntary subscriptions; whilst the cardinals of Rome sold plate and carriages to offer everything to the cause.

Once more, as in the days of Lepanto, the devout hearts of the faithful were roused to prayer; and before every Catholic shrine were to be seen crowds of pilgrims and daily processions to invoke the protection of the God of armies. Something like the old enthusiasm of the crusades revived in Europe, and volunteers from all nations enrolled themselves under the banners of Lorraine. France alone was chained back by the will of her "*grand monarque*," whose conduct on this occasion must remain a perpetual disgrace upon his name.

The brave Conti, who had secretly set out to offer the services of his sword to the Austrian commander, was followed and arrested by the order of his royal master, who preferred the triumph of the infidel to the success of a rival. Two princes of the house of Savoy, who had accompanied Conti in his flight, succeeded, however, in making their way to the scene of war; these were the Prince of Carignan Soissons and his younger brother, known then by the name of the little *Abbé* of Savoy. The news of their departure was brought to the minister Louvois, who received it with an expression of contempt. "So the *abbé* has gone," he said; "so much the better; he will not come back to this country very soon." Nor, indeed, did he return till he came with arms in his hands; and then "the little *Abbé* of Savoy" was better known as the Great Eugene,

Thus, by degrees, the imperial camp of Crems became the rendezvous for all the gallant spirits of the time; but, no means had yet been found of communicating with the city, which was closely hemmed in on all sides by the besieging forces, and thus cut off from all knowledge of the chances of its relief. At length, on the 6th of August, a trooper of Lorraine's succeeded in the daring enterprise of swimming across the Danube in the face of the enemy, and making his way into the city, bearing despatches from the duke, secured from the water in a thick envelope of wax.

On his return, however, he fell into the hands of the Turks; and, on being questioned concerning the state of the city, saved his life by a cunningly invented tale of the despair of the besieged and their approaching surrender. After this, a great number of others were found to imitate his exploit; and, in spite of the vigilance of the Turks, the communication between the city and the camp was continually carried on; the safe arrival of their respective messengers being announced by a shower of rockets. Many are the stratagems and hair-breadth escapes which the annals of the siege record. There we read of the brave Pole, Kolschitzki, attended by a countryman as daring as himself, strolling in disguise through the Turkish camp, and singing gaily as he goes; drinking coffee at his ease in an *aga's* tent, and entertaining his host the while with many a song and careless jest, telling him he had followed the army of the *vizier* from sheer love of fighting and adventure; and dismissed with a caution to beware of falling into Christian hands: so pursuing his perilous journey, and returning unscathed, with precious despatches from the duke.[3]

We read, too, of his intrepid attendant twice repeating the hazardous exploit alone: how, on his second return, with an autograph letter from the emperor, after having all but passed the enemy's lines, he is joined by a Turkish horseman, and, unable to shake off his unwelcome companion, he suddenly turns upon him, strikes off his head at a blow, and springing on the now riderless steed, reaches the city gates in safety.

Meanwhile deputies from all the imperial dominions were sent to hasten the preparations of the Polish king, to whose warlike spirit the delay he was forced to endure was as painful as it was to them. Once the apostolic *nuncio* and the imperial minister surprised him alone, and, throwing themselves at his

---

3. Kolschitzki was rewarded for his extraordinary services during the siege by a permission to set up the first coffee-house in Vienna; and "to this day," says the authority from whom we have taken the above, "the head of the corporation of coffee-providers is bound to have in his house a portrait of this patriarch of his profession." It was in consequence of the enormous stores of coffee found in the abandoned camp of the Turks, after the raising of the siege, that it became from that day the favourite drink of the Viennese.

feet, embraced his knees in a very agony of distress. Leopold condescended to the most extraordinary promises, in case he should succeed in delivering him and his capital The kingdom of Hungary was to be his; his eldest son should form an alliance with the imperial family; he was to name his own conditions, only he must come, and come quickly. Sobieski's reply to these offers was worthy of himself: "I desire no other reward than the glory of doing right before God and man."

At last, on the 15th of August,—a day he had chosen as being the Feast of the Assumption of the glorious Mother of God, to whom he had consecrated his arms and his enterprise,—the royal lance of Poland, surmounted by a white plume, was displayed in the streets of Cracow; the usual signal for the gathering of the forces destined for war. Sobieski commenced the day by performing the stations on foot to the different churches of the city; then, without waiting for the troops expected from Lithuania, he set out at the head of the Polish forces for the frontier of Germany. Caraffa, the Austrian general, pushed forward to meet him, impatient to know if the report of the king's presence with the army were indeed true; for so extraordinary was the power of his name, that—as Lorraine expressed it— that one man was an army in himself, He was instantly introduced to Sobieski, who eagerly inquired from aim the disposition of the Ottoman troops, and the ground they occupied.

"They occupy every space and height around the city," replied Carafe, "the Kahlenberg alone excepted."

"Then the Kahlenberg will be the point of attack," replied Sobieski; and in the rapid conception of genius the whole plan of the campaign was before him in that single phrase. In fact, the neglect of the Turks in leaving these important heights unguarded forms an unaccountable blunder in the otherwise skilful dispositions of the *vizier*.

They commanded the whole of the adjacent plains, and in their present state offered a cover for the approach, and a strong post for the occupation, of the relieving army. This the quick eye of Sobieski at once perceived. Had it been otherwise, the event of the coming struggle might have been very different; and the singular oversight of the Turkish commander was felt in the hour of the Christian success to be explained only by the superintending influence of that God to whom the cause had been so solemnly committed.

August, therefore, is now closing in; and far away on the frontier the warriors of Poland are making their way to the scene of combat over the rocky heights of the Carpathians. The fast-crumbling walls of Vienna are now no longer the defence of the city, but the rough battle-ground on which the besieged and their enemies meet daily hand to hand. Strange sights may be seen in those deadly combats: musket and matchlock are laid aside, for there is scarcely room to use them; and the keen Turkish *scimitar* is met on the side of the besieged with battle-axe and *halberd*, and with uncouth and frightful weapons fashioned for the purpose. There is the morning-star, a hideous club covered with spikes of brass; long scythes fixed to the ends of poles, like the Lochaber axes of the Highlanders; and in every street in the city you may see huge fires, over which there boil cauldrons of water and pitch, which the women and children carry to the battlements, and which, dashed in the faces of the advancing squadrons, prove a deadly means of offence. What cries of pain and baffled rage, what wild shouts and imprecations, rise from those savage Tartar tribes! They fall by hundreds into the ditch, pushed back by the strong arm of their opponents; and the scalding, blinding deluge from above pours down on them, like the brimstone tempest of Gomorrah!

But the daring defence is not kept up with impunity; the air is darkened with the shower of Turkish arrows, whose poisoned wounds are almost certain death. They have for days past kept off the enemy from the shattered ravelin of the Burg by wooden palisades erected in the very face of their fire. Now the whole work is in flames; the Turks press hard behind the burning timbers, and threaten to overwhelm the scanty troop of defenders, rendered helpless by the scorching heat. But in another moment the tide of fortune has turned again; for the soldiers, tearing off their steel head-pieces, fill them with water, and rushing into the midst of the blazing mass, extinguish it, and drive back their assailants.

Still they advanced step by step,—slowly, yet with a terrible certainty. Above, the ruined bastions became in turn the batteries for the guns which they turned against the town; whilst still the war was carried on underground between the desperate combatants, and no less than 16,000 of the Turkish miners were slain in these subterranean conflicts. Famine was beginning to show itself; and he who could succeed in getting a shot at some wandering cat was considered a fortunate speculator with his prize. The chase of these poor animals, indeed, became a regular trade; and, keeping up their spirits in the midst of their sufferings, the Viennese bestowed on this new game, which they hunted over the roofs of the houses, the truly German appellation of *dachshase*, or roof-hare.

At length, the *vizier* prepared for a vigorous assault; and had it been conducted by the mass of the besieging force, there can be little doubt that the result would have been fatal. As it was, a portion only of his troops were despatched to the breach. This want of energy at the very crisis of the siege proceeded from a covetous fear on the part of the Turkish chief, that, in the license of a general assault, he should lose the enormous plunder which he promised himself, could he reduce the city by less violent measures.

Nevertheless, on the morning of the 4th of September, a column of smoke rising from the Burg bastion announced an enormous explosion, and 4000 Turks rushed to the breach. They were met by Stahremberg and his whole staff, who, hopeless of success, prepared to die at the post of honour. On came the Moslems, carrying baskets of earth on their backs, to form a way for those who followed, and the horse-tail standards were even planted on the rampart crest; but again and again they were driven back with loss. Then came a breathing space of a single day; and the interval was occupied by the heroic defenders in filling up the yawning breaches in their walls with mattresses, sandbags, and every imaginable material they could supply. A yet more furious assault followed on the 6th; But still the result was the same, and 1500 bodies of the infidels remained heaped on the summit of the strange barrier. Alas, this was almost the energy of a death agony; and, nobly as they fought for faith and fatherland, each one well knew, if relief did not quickly come, the fate of the city might be delayed from day to day, but must be sealed at last. Every night, fires from the spire of St. Stephen's, and the graceful fall of those beautiful rockets,—the sad signals of distress,—were to be seen, notifying to the distant army of the Imperialists the urgency of the danger.

The evening of that day, which had witnessed so obstinate a repulse of the last assault, closed in more sadly for the victors than for the defeated infidels. The bodies of 117 brave men of their little army were lying among the corpses of their enemies; the town was crumbling into ruins; and the hearts of the besieged were at last giving way under exhaustion and despair. Kollonitsch might be seen going from house to house, striving to reanimate the courage of the citizens with the hopes of speedy succour; but he was met with a moody and dispiriting silence. Suddenly there was a cry from the ramparts, a signal from the watch-tower of the Jesuits, and thousands hurried to the shattered walls, expecting some surprise from the enemy. What did they see? and why did men cast themselves into one another's arms, and weep like women; and women kneel by their side, as they gazed on the distant horizon, giving thanks to God and to the Mother of God for their answered prayers?

There was the clear starlit sky of a summer's night, and the far outline of the Kahlenberg cutting the sapphire canopy overhead with its deep dark mass of shadow; and there, on the very summit of its rocky height, rising into the air and floating in its glorious vault, like a string of jewels, were the gleaming tracks and the fiery stars of five signal-rockets from the advanced guard of the Imperial army. They had, then, crossed the river; the outposts were already in possession of those rampart hills; and, as the blessed truth came home to the hearts of the beholders, they were filled with a fresh courage; and, cheered on by their noble leader, they prepared to prolong a yet more obstinate resistance, till the hour of their deliverance should arrive. Nor were theirs the only eyes who had marked those signal-rockets; and the preparations for a street-fight within the walls of Vienna were accompanied by redoubled preparations for hostilities in the Ottoman camp.

Chapter 2

The Relief

Sobieski and his army were on the borders of Silesia within a week from their departure from Cracow. His eldest son, Prince James Louis, the youth of many a hope and many a bitter disappointment, marched by the side of his heroic father. His queen accompanied him to the frontier, where they were obliged to separate; and the letters which passed between them during the remainder of the campaign form a singular and most valuable portion of the documentary history of the day. His march revived the hopes of Europe, and the malice of the *"grand monarque;"* and whilst the intelligence of the approaching crisis was received in Rome by solemn prayers for the success of the Christian arms, by exposition of the Blessed Sacrament in all the churches, and by processions in all the streets, Louis XIV. could see in it nothing but an opportunity for surprising the Austrian provinces of the Low Country by a *coup-de-main:* and Brussels saw a French army at its gates without even a declaration of war.

Such are the tactics of that state-policy which the French writers of the succeeding century deplore as so deficient in the enterprise of Sobieski. We leave our readers to draw their own comparison between the conduct of the Christian hero and that of the "Most Christian king." The events of the march followed one another in rapid succession. It lay through a rough and mountainous country, beset with wandering tribes of Tartars and Hungarians. As they drew near the head-quarters of the Imperialists the ardour of Sobieski would not allow him to delay; but setting forward with a few cavalry, he pushed on in advance of his army,

> "that he might the sooner taste the waters of the Danube and hear the cannon of Vienna:" these are his own words in his letter to his wife.

Lorraine hastened to meet them. Destiny had hitherto matched them as rivals, both in love and in war; but each was too great to remember past jealousies at such a moment. By the 5th of September the junction of the two armies at Tuln was completely effected; and the supreme command was unanimously made over to the Polish king.

There was still a doubt about the practicability of crossing the river; but Sobieski had a way of his own for settling such questions. He went down to inspect the bridge, which the Imperialists were still engaged in constructing in the very face of the Ottoman batteries:

> "The man who suffered this bridge to be built under his very beard is but a contemptible general, and cannot fail to be beaten," he said. "The affair is settled; the army will cross tomorrow."

Even as he spoke, a messenger from Stahremberg, dripping with water,—for he had swum across the river,—was ushered into the presence of the generals. He bore a despatch of few words, yet they told all the agony of suspense which was then reigning in the city: "No time to be lost! —no time to be lost!"

The affair was therefore settled as Sobieski had said, and none ventured a remonstrance.

The next day was that memorable 6th of September of which we have spoken. Whilst the besieged, still ignorant of the near presence of their deliverers, were making that gallant and despairing stand against the assault of their opponents, the Christian host were passing over the Danube and making their rapid advance upon the Kahlenberg. The Polish cavalry marched first, their costume mingling something of oriental magnificence with the European character of their arms; the infantry followed, less brilliantly equipped; one regiment, indeed, and that one of the bravest of the whole force, showed so ragged and dilapidated an exterior, that Sobieski's pride was hurt.

He turned to Lorraine, as the ranks defiled before them, saying, "Look at these fellows; they are invincible rascals, who have sworn never to clothe themselves except out of the enemy's spoils." It was a glorious and inspiring sight; and never had Sobieski found himself at the head of so numerous or powerful an army. He who had beaten the Turks over and over again at the head of a handful of armed peasants, felt it pusillanimous to doubt of victory with a force like the present, and the favour of heaven on his side: 70,000 men were passing in brilliant order before his eyes.

There were the troops of Saxony, with their elector at their head; and those of the Bavarians, just arrived in time to join the main body, with their young and gallant Elector Maximilian, burning with military ardour, and destined to celebrity, as well in his achievements as in his misfortunes, who now entrusted the command of his people to abler hands, and served himself in the ranks as a volunteer. There was a crowd of illustrious names in the battle-roll of that army; and the "little *Abbé* of Savoy" was not missing among them. The river crossed, there yet remained the Kahlenberg to be scaled and secured. They did not yet know if the summit were still unoccupied; and the dangerous task of reconnoitring was undertaken by Sobieski himself.

Let us place the scene before us, to estimate the difficulty of the task. The Kahlenberg mountain, which now stretched like a huge curtain between the hosts of the infidels and the advancing bands of the allies, was a wild range of rocky hills and precipices, covered on one side by a vast forest, whilst the other descended abruptly to the waters of the Danube. Its crest was crowned with a fortress and a little chapel; and these were still untouched. Kara Mustapha, in his gilded pavilion, lay buried in profound and luxurious security in the plain below, all unconscious that on the other side of those rugged peaks, struggling among the rocks and in the mazes of the tangled forest, wearily dragging their guns over the rough roads, and casting away baggage and accoutrements in their eagerness to press on to the longed-for goal, were the scattered forces of his enemies, whom a handful of determined men might have annihilated whilst they were in the pails of that terrible ascent. But a blindness had come over the judgement of the Turks.

Some of their wandering Tartar bands even encountered the outposts of the enemy, and, with singular simplicity, are said to have inquired what all this bustle meant "It means that the King of Poland is behind," replied the soldiers.

"The King of Poland!" answered the Tartar, with a sneering laugh: "we know very well that he is far away from here."

This scrambling weary march lasted three days. They climbed the rocks like cats, and threw themselves down the crags, clinging to the bushes. A few must have reached the summit, by means of incredible exertions, the very evening of the passage of the river, as we have already seen that signal-rockets from the top of the mountain gave warning to the citizens of their approach so early as the night of the 6th; but it was not until the 10th that the main body succeeded in taking up a position on the heights.

The ascent of the Kahlenberg must be reckoned amongst the most brilliant achievements of the Polish king. Its difficulties were such as could be surmounted only by determined courage and a surpassing genius. The Imperial troops were fearful and discouraged; and when the cry of "*Allah!*" from some of the outposts of the infidels first broke on their ear, they were all but taking to flight, in the extremity of their terror. The heavy pieces of artillery were obliged to be left below; for there were no means of transporting them through the savage passes they had to cross. Neither chiefs nor soldiers had encumbered themselves with provisions, and during their three days' march their food was oak-leaves. A few who gained the summit before the others, terrified by the first prospect of the infidels, came back, leaping over the rocks in wild confusion, spreading fear and disorder wherever they appeared. Sobieski's own voice, and the might of his heroic presence, his gay and cheerful words, and the memory of his past victories, which seemed to surround him as with a glory, were necessary to restore the courage of his men.

The soldiers of his own guard showed symptoms of discontent. He advanced to them, and proposed that they should return to the baggage-wagons; and, at those few words, they cast themselves at his feet, and exclaimed, with tears, "We will live and die with our king, Sobieski!" All this time, amidst the incessant anxieties and fatigues of his post, he could find leisure to write an incredible number of letters to his wife, in which the hearty expressions of generous affection, and the thoughtful simple tenderness with which he tells her "to be sure not to rise too early in the morning," would fill us with feelings of more unmixed pleasure as we read them, could we forget the unworthy and vexatious character of the woman on whom he lavished so devoted an attachment.

It was on the morning of the 10th that the Turks, perceiving at length the importance of the Kahlenberg position, made a hasty movement of their troops to occupy it. But it was too late to repair their error. A few Saxon squadrons were forced forwards into line, and three guns brought to the summit. The Turks instantly retired; and the roar of those three pieces of artillery proclaimed to the ears of the distant citizens that their deliverance was at hand. The echo of that sound drew them to the walls; and the sight that met their eye on that distant ridge revived all their hopes.

The morning sun sparkled on a bristling forest of lances and the pennons of the Polish hussars. Every moment the armed battalions might be seen gathering in greater numbers, as they climbed the last ascent, and formed in array of battle. There was a stir too in the camp of the Ottomans; and the vast masses of the Turkish troops swayed to and fro, then broke into three divisions. One seemed to prepare for conflict with the Polish force, and faced towards the mountains; another, composed of the camp-followers and other irregular combatants, might be seen securing their baggage, and moving off, with camels and horses, in the direction of the Hungarian frontier; whilst the third advanced to renew the assault on the city. It was a day of agonising suspense.

The final struggle had not, indeed, as yet begun, but it was evidently close at hand; and whilst Kollonitsch called the women and the infirm to the churches, Stahremberg once more led the remains of his dauntless forces to the breach and the ramparts. By eleven o'clock on the morning of the 11th the main body of the army was formed into line on the ridge of the Kahlenberg, occupying the old castle and the little chapel before mentioned. Below them lay the vast plain of Austria, where stretched the enormous crescent of the Ottoman camp, sparkling with its gilded tents, and entrenched with lines of fortifications; whilst, close at the foot of the hill, and under cover of the forest and ravines, was drawn up a considerable portion of the hostile army. No movement was, however, made by either side; and both parties spent the remaining hours of the day in councils of war, and arrangements for the morrow. And so, whilst the rocket-signals of distress continued to rise from the city walls, and were answered by blazing fires from the mountain, the eve of the great day closed in. Sobieski spent it in the saddle, and before night had ridden along and inspected the entire position of his forces.

The dawn of the autumn morning was breaking in the horizon. A thin mist rested on the crest of the Kahlenberg, and gathered in dense masses on the plain and river below. The eye of the Polish sentinels could catch the spire of St. Stephen's rising above that silvery cloud, whilst the darker masses of the city-walls were still veiled within its folds; and still unceasingly from that tapering tower there rose those fiery signals, which seemed to repeat, hour after hour, the words of Stahremberg's last despatch: *No time to be lost.*

It was a Sunday morning, as on the day of Lepanto,—an association not forgotten by the Christian host; and as the sun rose higher, and raised the curtain of mist that hung over the scene, life seemed to wake in the Turkish camp, and again the roar of their artillery was heard pouring its destructive fire upon the city, whilst their cavalry and the squadrons of the Tartars faced towards the mountain. The *vizier* was thus preparing for battle on either side of his encampment. But before we endeavour to follow the course of the conflict, let us pause on the heights of the Kahlenberg, and watch the scene that meets our eye among the forces of the Christian allies. Falling sweetly and gently through the morning air, there comes the echo of a bell from the chapel of the Margrave: its little steeple rises above the masses of forest-foliage, rich with autumn tints; and as the sound reaches the lines of the Polish troops, the clang of their arms, and the long reveille of their trumpets, are hushed in silence.

Before the chapel-door is planted the Christian standard,—a red flag bearing a white cross; and as the symbol of their faith, and of the holy cause for which they are in arms, is displayed, a shout of enthusiasm bursts from the ranks, and is caught up again and again from every quarter of the mountain. But silence is restored, and all eyes turn in the direction of the old castle; and as its gates are suddenly flung open, you may see a procession of the princes of the empire, and of many a gallant and noble soldier from every nation of Christendom; moving forward to commend the cause of their arms to the God of battles.

At the head of that column walks neither king nor prince, but the form of one with the brown habit, shaven crown, and sandalled feet, of a Capuchin friar. The soldiers cross themselves as he passes, and kneel to receive the blessing which he gives with outstretched hands. It is Marco Aviano, the confessor to the emperor, and one on whom there rests the character of a saint, and the reputation of prophetic gifts. He has been with the army in all its hours of difficulty and distress; he is with them now, to bless their arms, and to remind them of the cause for which they are about to fight. Close following him in the gorgeous procession, are three figures, that rivet you as you gaze.

The first is one whose look instantly commands respect. He is past the prime of life, and there is something too much of portliness in his manly form; and yet the majesty of his bearing tells you at a glance that he is a hero and a king: that broad and noble forehead, that quick yet gentle eye, and the open look that mingles such simplicity with its command,—all bespeak no common man: it is the conqueror of Choczim and Podacksi. On his left is the young Prince James, the father afterwards of the Princess Clementina, whose marriage with the Chevalier of St. George mingled the blood of Sobieski with that of our own exiled Stuarts. His after-career was sad and inglorious; but now he marches by his father's side, a gallant youth of sixteen, armed with helmet and breastplate, the pride and darling of the hero's heart. On the right of the king is the form of Charles of Lorraine, plain and negligent in his attire; and yet, in spite of negligence, and even a slouching and unmilitary gait, you may tell, to use Sobieski's words;

> that he is no shopkeeper, but a man of note and distinction

Then follow the sovereign princes of Germany. We will not weary our reader with a list of names. As our eye wanders over the royal and noble ranks, glittering with the insignia of their rank and military command, it rests on a slender youth of middle stature, whose eye has in it the promise of a future career of glory. Yes, you have guessed aright: the prince, his eldest brother, has already fallen in the cause; but Eugene of Savoy has escaped to draw his maiden sword in the defence of the faith, and to learn under Sobieski his first lessons of that science in which he was hereafter to share the battlefields and renown of our own Marlborough.

They enter the chapel: Aviano celebrates the Mass, which is served by Sobieski himself; and during the pauses in which he is not engaged at the altar, he is kneeling on the steps, his head bowed down, his arms extended in the form of a cross, and his whole soul absorbed in prayer. It is a spectacle which revives to your imagination the days of Dominic and de Montfort, and the consecration of the crusaders' swords before the fight of Muret, as you see every individual in that princely and martial assembly kneeling in turn to receive the Bread of Life, whilst the thunder of the Turkish guns is even now sounding in their ears: they will soon be in the field, and, ere the sun is down, some of them will be lying there cold and dead. But they have fitted themselves for death; and at this moment, as you gaze on them, they seem full of that antique spirit of the elder chivalry, which has stamped its likeness on those tombs and sculptured effigies, making you doubt whether they who lie beneath were men of war or prayer.

The Mass is over. Aviano, in his priestly vestments, is standing at the chapel door, with the crucifix in his hand. Raising it on nigh, he gives his solemn benediction to the troops, saying these words:

> Soldiers, I announce to you, on the part of the Holy See, that if you have confidence in God, the victory is yours.

And then the last act of the religious ceremony is completed by a touching and beautiful incident. Prince James is led to the feet of his heroic father to receive the still honourable and sacred dignity of Christian knighthood. When this was done, the ardour of Sobieski became impatient of further delay. He sprang into his saddle, and riding forward to the front of the line, spoke to his followers in their own language:

> "Warriors and friends," he said, "our enemies are yonder in the plain, in greater numbers than at Choczim, when we trampled them under our feet. We fight them on a foreign soil, but we fight for our country; and under the walls of Vienna we are defending those of Cracow and Warsaw, We have to save this day, not a single city, but Christendom itself: the war is therefore holy. There is a blessing on our arms, and a crown of glory for him who falls. You are not fighting for any earthly sovereign, but for the King of kings. It is He who has led you up these heights, and placed the victory in your hands. I have but one command to give: Follow me. The time is come for the young to win their spurs."

A tremendous shout from the ranks was the answer to this harangue; replied to from the distant enemy by cries of "*Allah! Allah!*"

Then, pressing his horse to the mountain edge, Sobieski pointed to the plain below, to the rocks and precipices of the descent, and the moving masses of the enemy. "March on in confidence," he cried; "God and His Blessed Mother are with us!" As he spoke, five cannon-shots gave the signal for the advance. The ranks immediately commenced the descent; and Aviano turned back into the chapel to pray.

It was the original plan of the king to content himself this day with the descent of the Kahlenberg, and the secure establishment of the troops in position for battle on the morrow. Even his quick and ardent genius had proposed no such gigantic undertaking as the routing of the whole Turkish host, and the deliverance of the city, in the course of a few hours. The event of the day was scarcely so much the result of his own calculations as of the unforeseen circumstances by which the left wing of the army, under Lorraine, became engaged in a premature and desperate struggle with the right of the Turkish force, and thus brought on the necessity for a general action. The Imperial troops descended the wooded ravines, driving their opponents before them, slowly but surely; for though the Turks obstinately defended every root of ground, they were no match for their adversaries.

The Christian army was arranged in order of battle in five distinct columns, which came down the mountainside "like so many irresistible torrents, yet in admirable order," stopping every hundred paces to enable those behind to come up to them, and preserve their ranks. Each ravine was found guarded and fortified, and was the scene of a separate conflict. The rocks, and groups of trees, and the thick tangle of the vineyards,—all formed so many covers for defence to the retreating Ottomans; but still, spite of all resistance on their parts, nothing could check the downward progress of those five mountain-torrents, which rolled on steadily and victoriously, sweeping all before them.

The descent had commenced at eight o'clock, and by ten the left wing of the army was in the plain. Lorraine halted, by command of Sobieski, to enable the Polish troops to come up; and as each squadron issued from the mountain-defiles, it took up its position in the order of battle prescribed by the king, and planted its standard in the field.

By this time, the hope of pushing the struggle to a decisive issue that day had suggested itself to the imperial commanders, and Field-Marshal Geltz, perceiving the progress of the Bavarians and Poles on the right and centre, observed to the Duke, that it would be his own fault if he did not that night sleep in Vienna. It was eleven o'clock: the burning sun had scattered all the mist of the morning, and the whole scene glittered in the noonday blaze. The heat was oppressive; and there was a pause in the movements of the imperial troops.

Suddenly a cry ran along the line, caught up from regiment to regiment, "Live Sobieski!" Out from the wooded defiles of the Weinerberg flashed the gilded *cuirasses* of the Polish cavalry; and the bay horse and sky-blue doublet of the rider at their head announced the presence of the king. Before him went an attendant, bearing a shield emblazoned with his arms. Another rode near him, bearing the plumed lance of Poland: this, as it streamed above the heads of the combatants, always showed Sobieski's place in the battle; and round it the fight always gathered the thickest; while his soldiers were accustomed to look to that white and waving signal as to the star of victory.

The rocks and broken ground in which they stood formed a vast and beautiful *amphitheatre*, carpeted with turf and dotted with noble trees. Under one of these Sobieski alighted; and, ordering his men to do the same, they took a hasty repast. It occupied but a few minutes; and then, the semicircular battle-line of the Christian columns forming in admirable order, the king rode round the whole body, speaking to each in their own language; for there were few European tongues of which he was not perfect master.

The order was given for the whole line to advance. The Turks, profiting by the halt of their enemies, had brought up large reinforcements, commanded by the *vizier* in person. They were met by a furious charge from the Polish lancers, who at first drove all before them; but, led on by their impetuosity, and surrounded by the masses of the infidels, they were for a moment nearly overwhelmed. Their officers fell thick and fast. Waldech and his Bavarians came up to their rescue; but the struggle was still doubtful, when the second line and the Imperial Dragoons, with Sobieski at their head, came down on the squadrons of the Turks with a tremendous shock. Everything gave way before them: on they went, through ravines and villages, and still, as they dashed on, they swept their foes from one outpost to another, nor drew their reins till they touched the glacis of the camp, and the gilded peaks of the Ottoman tents rose close before their eyes. Here the whole Turkish force was drawn up to receive them. The front of their line bristled with artillery; the flanks were strongly protected by fortifications hastily but skilfully raised.

It was five o'clock.

"Sobieski," says Salvandy, "had reckoned on sleeping on the field of battle, and deferring until next day the completion of the drama; for that which remained to be done scarcely seemed possible to be completed in a few hours, and with tired troops. Nevertheless the allies, in spite of the oppressiveness of the weather, were reanimated rather than exhausted by their march; whereas it was evident that consternation reigned in the Ottoman ranks. Far away were to be seen the long lines of the camels, hastily pressing forward on the road to Hungary: they might be tracked by the cloud of dust which darkened the horizon for miles."

The *vizier* alone showed confidence, as dangerous and unreasonable as was the panic of his followers. He counted on an easy triumph; and having, as a first step, ordered the slaughter of all his captives, including women, and children, to the number of 30,000 souls, he appeared on the field mounted on a charger, whose accoutrements, glittering with gold, rendered the animal equally unserviceable for battle or for flight. But flight was the last idea that suggested itself to the mind of Kara Mustapha. Dismounted from his overloaded horse, he might have been seen seated in a *damask* tent, luxuriously drinking coffee with his two sons, as if he had but to look on at his ease, and watch the dispersion of his enemies. The sight stirred the choler of Sobieski. So rapid had been his advance, that he had no heavy artillery with him, save two or three light pieces, which Kouski had dragged on by the strong arm of his artillerymen. These the king ordered to be pointed at the brilliant tent, from which the *vizier* was now giving his orders; but the ammunition soon failed, and a French officer ingeniously rammed home the last cartridge with his wig, gloves, and a bundle of newspapers.

We are not told the effect of this original discharge; bat at that moment the infantry came up under Maligni, the king's brother-in-law, and were instantly despatched to a height which commanded the position of the *vizier*. A vigorous attack soon carried them beyond the outposts, and planted them on the redoubts. Then a wavering hesitation was observed in the crowded ranks of the Mussulmans, which caught the quick eye of Sobieski and decided the fate of the day.

"They are lost men," he cried; "let the whole line advance."

As he led them in person right for the *vizier's* tent, his terrible presence was recognised by the infidels.

"By *Allah*, the king is with them!" exclaimed the Khan of the Crimea, and every eye was turned in terror towards the spot where the dancing feathers of that snow-white plume carried victory wherever they appeared. Sobieski had sent word to Lorraine to attack the centre, and leave him to finish the disordered masses in his front. Then, surrounded by his hussars, and preceded by his emblazoned shield and the plume-bearing lance which distinguished his place in the battle, he brandished his sword in the foremost rank, calling aloud, in the words of the royal prophet,

Not unto us, not unto us, O Lord God of hosts, but to Thy name

give the glory!

The enthusiasm of his presence excited his troop to prodigies of valour; his name rang through the plain; and, as the infidels quailed and gave way before the charges of his cavalry, led on by their glorious chief, a bloody token appeared in the evening sky, which struck a supernatural dread into their hearts. It was an eclipse of the moon, and the heavens themselves seemed fighting against the host of the Ottomans.

"God defend Poland!" the national cry, now sounded from the advancing columns of a fresh body of troopers. They came on at full gallop, the other squadrons joining in their desperate charge. *Palatines*, senators, and nobles, they fell with headlong impetuosity on the masses of their foes; and such was the fury of their attack, that as man and horse went down before their lances, the huge body of the Ottomans was cleft in twain, and a road, as it were, cut in their centre, formed by the passage of the Christian troops. The shock was so terrible, that nearly every lance of the Polish squadrons was snapped asunder; those lances of which one of their nobles once said, that should the heavens fell, they would bear them up upon their points.

The Turks could offer no further resistance, and there was but one thought among their ranks, and that was flight: their very numbers, instead of strengthening, only embarrassed them. The *vizier*, but an hour before so proud and confident, was borne along in the panic-stricken crowd, weeping and cursing by turns. In the *mêlée* he came across the Khan of the Crimea, himself among the foremost of the fugitives

"You, too," he said bitterly, "can you do nothing to help me?"

"The King of Poland is behind," was his reply; "there is but one thing left for us. Look at the sky, too, and see if God be not against us;" and he pointed to the bloody moon, which, close to the horizon, presented a ghastly spectacle to the eyes of the terror-stricken infidel. So the tide of night and of pursuit swept on: conquered, terrified, and not daring to raise their eyes from the earth, the Mussulman army no longer existed. The cause of

Europe, of Christendom, and of civilisation, had triumphed; the floods of the Ottoman power were checked, and rolled backwards, never to rise again.

An hour only had passed since the fight began; and when it closed, Sobieski was standing within the *vizier's* tent. The charger, with its golden caparisons, was led to him by a slave, who held its bridle, before the door of the pavilion. Taking one of its golden stirrups, the king gave it in charge to a courier to bear to the queen, as a token of the defeat and flight of its owner.[4] Then his standards were planted in the camp, and a wild and stormy night closed over the field of battle.

Meanwhile there had been an action as desperate, and as successful in its result to the Christian arms, on the breach of Vienna. The storming party was repulsed by the determined valour of Stahremberg and his shattered yet heroic followers. And when the Turks gave way, and Louis of Baden pushed on towards the Scottish Gate, the garrison, sallying from the walls, and mingling with his dragoons, fell on the main body of the *Janizaries* occupying the trenches of the enemy, and cut them all to pieces.

The king passed the night under a tree; and after fourteen hours spent in the saddle, his sleep was sound and heavy. The sunrise broke over a scene of strange and melancholy confusion. The Ottoman camp, so lately glittering in all its oriental splendour, was now deserted by its occupants, and bore in

---

4. The fate of Kara Mustapha, the leader of the Ottoman forces, although one of common occurrence in the history of oriental despotism, has enough of singularity in it to demand a notice. When tidings first reached the sultan that all was not advancing as prosperously before the walls of Vienna as his proud confidence had decreed, his fury was such, that he was hardly restrained from ordering a general massacre of all the Christians in his dominions; but to this succeeded a fit of sullen gloom, from which he was not roused even by the news of the *vizier's* defeat and flight. He seemed, however, to accept the interpretation which the commander's despatches put upon his conduct, sent him the usual marks of honour, and, to all appearance, regarded him with his wonted favour. But his rage did not so much slumber as coil and gather itself up, to spring with the more fatal suddenness on its prey. After the unsuccessful issue of the Hungarian campaign, with the silence and celerity which not inaptly represent the dread resistless force of that fate to which the haughtiest follower of the false prophet bows without a murmur, an officer of the court is sent to fetch the *vizier's* head. (Continued next page)

every direction the traces of their ferocious cruelty. As the Poles marched through it, they trod over the bodies of the Christian captives murdered in cold blood. Every woman attached to the camp had suffered a similar fate.

Nor was this all; for camels and horses were found slaughtered in great numbers, lest they should fall alive into the hands of the victors; nay, it is said, the *vizier* had beheaded an ostrich with his own *scimitar*, that it might never own a Christian for its master. The camp, with its silken pavilion, and all its riches, was one vast *charnel*-house. The horrors of the scene were heightened by the signs of luxury that every where met the eye. The baths and fountains, the tissues and gay carpetings, the jewelled arms and ornaments, with which the ground was strewn, contrasted strangely with the heaps of ghastly corpses that lay piled around.

But we will pass over the lists of the slain, and the details of a booty almost fabulous in value, to bring our readers to the walls of Vienna, where the agony of a long suspense had been exchanged for the joy of a deliverance at once so sudden and so complete. Sobieski entered the city through the breach made by the guns of the infidels, and through which, but for his speedy succour, they would themselves have passed as victors.

As he rode along by the side of Stahremberg, accompanied by the Duke of Lorraine and the Elector of Saxony, the streets

---

The affair is conducted with all due solemnity; not a point of ceremonious *etiquette* is omitted. The messengers reverently announce their mission, and present their credentials, which are as formally acknowledged. The carpet is spread; the *vizier* gravely says his prayers; then yields with calm dignity his neck to the bowstring; and in a few moments the commander of 200,000 men lies a hideous trunk on the floor of his pavilion. His head is taken to Adrianople, and thence is sent by the sultan to Belgrade, to be deposited in a mosque; but its fortunes ended not there. Ere long the latter place is captured (1688) by the Christians; the mosque once more becomes a Christian Church, and is given to the Jesuit fathers ; and the unholy relic is despatched by them to the good bishop Kollonitsch. Strange reversal of the vow which the proud infidel had made, when he swore that he would send the head of the brave *prelate* on a lance's point to the sultan his master, for daring to stay even the ravages of the plague, that was playing the part of an ally to the besieging Moslem! The skull or the *vizier* was presented by the bishop to the arsenal of Vienna, where, for aught we know, it still remains.

resounded with the acclamations of the people who crowded about his horse. They kissed his hand, his feet, his very dress; and some were heard to exclaim, as they involuntarily compared the hero who had delivered them with the sovereign who had deserted them, "Why is he not our master?" It was evident that these demonstrations of feeling were already exciting the jealousy and displeasure of the Austrian authorities; and even in his triumphal entrance, the king was made to taste something of that ingratitude and cold neglect that was afterwards exhibited in so extraordinary and disgraceful a manner by Leopold himself.

Nevertheless the people were not to be restrained by the marked discouragement of their civic rulers; they followed Sobieski in crowds to the church of the Augustines, where, finding the clergy unprepared, or hesitating, perhaps, to offer the usual service of thanksgiving, he himself, filled with impatient enthusiasm, stepped before the high altar, and commenced intoning the *Te Deum*, which was instantly taken up by his own Poles and the clergy of the church.

The sudden stillness caused by the cessation of the firing, which had been distinctly heard, not only at Neustadt, but far over the Styrian Alps, struck terror into the surrounding population, who thought that the ancient city of the Christian Caesars had fallen into the hands of the enemies of the faith. A welcome sound, therefore, to them was the boom of the three hundred cannons, the thunder of which accompanied the thanksgiving at the church of the Augustines. Ashamed of their neglect, the magistrates caused the ceremony to be repeated with something more of pomp and splendour in the cathedral of St. Stephen's; and as the echoes of the chant rolled through its glorious aisles, Sobieski knelt, as his biographer relates,

"prostrate, with his face upon the ground."

There was a sermon too; and if the text were a plagiarism from the lips of St. Pius, on the day of Lepanto, it was at least an appropriate one:

There was a man sent from God, whose name was John.

Where was Kollonitsch? for his name has not appeared in the list of those who are rejoicing in the streets, or preaching in the churches. You must look for him in the camp, where, unappalled by the terrors of the scene, he is searching among the bloody corpses for any in whom life may not yet be quite extinct; and his patient noble charity has its reward; for, hiding among the tents, or even under the bodies of their mothers, he has found more than six hundred infants, and has claimed these children as his own. Nor is this all: many of the Turkish women and Christian slaves are but half murdered; and Kollonitsch has ordered carriages from the city to transport them, at his own expense, to the hospitals. As to the children, his care of them will end but with his life.

"Like another St. Vincent de Paul," says Salvandy, "he became the father of them all."[5]

He provided them with both maintenance and education, and thought himself well paid for all his sacrifices by having gained them to the Christian faith. The pope, however, not so unmindful either of his personal merits, or of the eminent services he had rendered to religion in the hour of need, bestowed upon him the highest dignity which it was in his power to confer, by exalting him to the *cardinalate*. Of Aviano we find only an allusion to his joy at the victory, and that during the whole of that eventful day, as he watched the conflict from the chapel of the Margrave, he thought he beheld, as he prayed, a white dove hovering over the Christian host. After the return of Leopold to Vienna, "disgusted with the intrigues of the court and the license of the camp," he refused to retain the office he held in the Imperial family, and returned to Italy.

Sobieski himself soon left the city to return to the camp, and prepare for the following up of this victory by a march into

---

5. Kollonitsch, who, at the siege of Crete, had so valorously defended the Christian faith, at that of Vienna showed himself the benefactor of mankind, a second Vincent de Paul. *Von Hammer.*

Hungary. Indeed, anyhow he was unwilling to remain in Vienna; for, strange to say, Leopold would not enter his capital until the man who had saved it from destruction was at a distance from its walls. And what do our readers suppose was the pretext for so ungracious a proceeding? A scruple of ceremony; a piece of court-*etiquette*! How should the emperor receive him? Were he an hereditary monarch, courtesy would place him on the Imperial right hand; but to one who was but an elective king, how could so high a dignity be accorded When the question, how such a one should be received, was proposed to Charles of Lorraine, the Duke magnanimously replied: "With open arms, if he has saved the empire!"

But the generosity of this sentiment found but little response in hearts which a narrow jealousy and pride had closed to every noble impulse. The simple straightforwardness of Sobieski at last solved the difficult problem. Finding himself put off from day to day by clumsily invented excuses, he bluntly asked one of the imperial courtiers whether the right hand were the obstacle to the interview so long delayed; and on being answered as simply in the affirmative, he ingeniously suggested that the meeting should be one of face to face, each on horseback, the emperor, accompanied by his suite, and himself, at the head of the Polish troops. And thus it actually took place, as described in the king's own words:

> We saluted each other civilly enough. I made him my compliments in Latin, and in few words. He answered in the same language, in a studied style. As we stood thus, face to face, I presented to him my son, who came forward and saluted him. The emperor did not even put his hand to his hat. I was wholly taken by surprise. However, to avoid scandal and public remarks, I addressed a few more words to the emperor, and then turned my horse round. We again saluted each other, and I returned to my own camp.
> [6] The *Palatine* of Russia, at the emperor's desire, passed our

---

6. The king, it has been observed, does not mention in this letter the reply he made to the emperor's cold and formal thanks: "I am glad, sire, to have done you this little service."

army in review before him. But our men have felt greatly affronted, and have complained loudly that the emperor did not condescend to thank them, even with a bow, for all they had done and suffered. Since this parting, a sudden change has come over everything: they take not the slightest notice of us; they supply us with neither forage nor provisions. The Holy Father had sent money for these to the Abbé Buonvisi, but he has stopped short at Lintz.

The conclusion of the memorable campaign to which we have adverted forms no part of our present subject. It is enough for us to remember, that in spite of every insult offered him; the ingratitude shown him by the emperor, nay, the cruel insolence which denied hospitals to his sick and burial to his dead, and which formally refused all redress when the Poles were robbed of their baggage and their horses by the followers of Leopold himself; the artillerymen pillaged of their effects while on guard over the very guns they had taken from the enemy;—in spite of all this, and of the marked personal affronts which (as just related) the emperor put upon his gallant deliverer on the plain of Elbersdorf, Sobieski did not desert him; or rather, he would not desert the cause of Christendom, to which his solemn oath, as a Christian king, bound him by an obligation which he felt to be inviolable. His letters to his queen abound with the expressions of this loyalty to his plighted word:

> "I know there are many," he says, "who wish me to return to Poland: but for me, I have devoted my life to the glory of God and His holy cause, and in that I shall persist. I too cling to life," he adds; "I cling to it for the service of Christendom, and of my country, for you, my children, and my friends; but my honour is yet dearer to me. Have no fear: we shall reconcile all these things if God give His help."

If gratitude and joy were wanting where they seemed most due, Europe took the burden on itself, and paid the debt of Vienna. The news of the great event, which fixed the destinies of the West, flew from country to country, and everywhere roused the enthusiasm of the people. Protestant and Catholic states united in decreeing public thanksgiving to be offered in the churches for the great victory obtained; and every where it was celebrated with rejoicings at court and in the houses of the nobility. Even in England, severed as she was from Catholic unity, the pulpits rang with the triumphs of the Polish king.

At Rome, the feast of thanksgiving lasted an entire month. When the news of the victory reached the ears of Innocent XI., he cast himself at the foot of the crucifix, and melted into tears. The night saw the magical dome of St Peter's blazing with its fiery illumination; and within that dome, a few days later, the great banner of the *vizier*, which had been despatched to the pontiff in the first moment of victory, was solemnly suspended side by side with the captured standards of Choczim.

But it was not to Sobieski's name alone that the glory and honour of Her great deliverance was ascribed by the voice of Christendom. *Non nobis, Domine, non nobis,* had been his battle-cry in the front of the Turkish lines; and it was taken up and re-echoed by the Church, Europe, in its gratitude, gave thanks to the interceding love of Her whose image, on the shattered and crumbling walls of Vienna, had remained untouched by all the batteries of the infidels; and by order of Innocent, the Sunday within the octave of our Lady's Nativity, on which day the memorable action was fought, was thenceforward kept as a solemn festival of thanksgiving for this and all the other mercies bestowed on the Church through her gracious intercession, and has received the title of the Feast of the Name of Mary

ALSO FROM LEONAUR
AVAILABLE IN SOFTCOVER OR HARDCOVER WITH DUST JACKET

CAPTAIN OF THE 95th (Rifles) by *Jonathan Leach*—An officer of Wellington's Sharpshooters during the Peninsular, South of France and Waterloo Campaigns of the Napoleonic Wars.

BUGLER AND OFFICER OF THE RIFLES by *William Green & Harry Smith* With the 95th (Rifles) during the Peninsular & Waterloo Campaigns of the Napoleonic Wars

BAYONETS, BUGLES AND BONNETS by *James 'Thomas' Todd*—Experiences of hard soldiering with the 71st Foot - the Highland Light Infantry - through many battles of the Napoleonic wars including the Peninsular & Waterloo Campaigns

THE ADVENTURES OF A LIGHT DRAGOON by *George Farmer & G.R. Gleig*—A cavalryman during the Peninsular & Waterloo Campaigns, in captivity & at the siege of Bhurtpore, India

THE COMPLEAT RIFLEMAN HARRIS by *Benjamin Harris as told to & transcribed by Captain Henry Curling*—The adventures of a soldier of the 95th (Rifles) during the Peninsular Campaign of the Napoleonic Wars

WITH WELLINGTON'S LIGHT CAVALRY by *William Tomkinson*—The Experiences of an officer of the 16th Light Dragoons in the Peninsular and Waterloo campaigns of the Napoleonic Wars.

SURTEES OF THE RIFLES by *William Surtees*—A Soldier of the 95th (Rifles) in the Peninsular campaign of the Napoleonic Wars.

ENSIGN BELL IN THE PENINSULAR WAR by *George Bell*—The Experiences of a young British Soldier of the 34th Regiment 'The Cumberland Gentlemen' in the Napoleonic wars.

WITH THE LIGHT DIVISION by *John H. Cooke*—The Experiences of an Officer of the 43rd Light Infantry in the Peninsula and South of France During the Napoleonic Wars

NAPOLEON'S IMPERIAL GUARD: FROM MARENGO TO WATERLOO by *J. T. Headley*—This is the story of Napoleon's Imperial Guard from the bearskin caps of the grenadiers to the flamboyance of their mounted chasseurs, their principal characters and the men who commanded them.

BATTLES & SIEGES OF THE PENINSULAR WAR by *W. H. Fitchett*—Corunna, Busaco, Albuera, Ciudad Rodrigo, Badajos, Salamanca, San Sebastian & Others

AVAILABLE ONLINE AT **www.leonaur.com**
AND OTHER GOOD BOOK STORES

ALSO FROM LEONAUR

AVAILABLE IN SOFTCOVER OR HARDCOVER WITH DUST JACKET

WELLINGTON AND THE PYRENEES CAMPAIGN VOLUME I: FROM VITORIA TO THE BIDASSOA by *F. C. Beatson*—The final phase of the campaign in the Iberian Peninsula.

WELLINGTON AND THE INVASION OF FRANCE VOLUME II: THE BIDASSOA TO THE BATTLE OF THE NIVELLE by *F. C. Beatson*—The second of Beatson's series on the fall of Revolutionary France published by Leonaur, the reader is once again taken into the centre of Wellington's strategic and tactical genius.

WELLINGTON AND THE FALL OF FRANCE VOLUME III: THE GAVES AND THE BATTLE OF ORTHEZ by *F. C. Beatson*—This final chapter of F. C. Beatson's brilliant trilogy shows the 'captain of the age' at his most inspired and makes all three books essential additions to any Peninsular War library.

NAVAL BATTLES OF THE NAPOLEONIC WARS by *W. H. Fitchett*—Cape St.Vincent, the Nile, Cadiz, Copenhagen, Trafalgar & Others

SERGEANT GUILLEMARD: THE MAN WHO SHOT NELSON? by *Robert Guillemard*—A Soldier of the Infantry of the French Army of Napoleon on Campaign Throughout Europe

WITH THE GUARDS ACROSS THE PYRENEES by *Robert Batty*—The Experiences of a British Officer of Wellington's Army During the Battles for the Fall of Napoleonic France, 1813.

A STAFF OFFICER IN THE PENINSULA by *E. W. Buckham*—An Officer of the British Staff Corps Cavalry During the Peninsula Campaign of the Napoleonic Wars

THE LEIPZIG CAMPAIGN: 1813—NAPOLEON AND THE "BATTLE OF THE NATIONS" by *F. N. Maude*—Colonel Maude's analysis of Napoleon's campaign of 1813.

BUGEAUD: A PACK WITH A BATON by *Thomas Robert Bugeaud*—The Early Campaigns of a Soldier of Napoleon's Army Who Would Become a Marshal of France.

TWO LEONAUR ORIGINALS

SERGEANT NICOL by *Daniel Nicol*—The Experiences of a Gordon Highlander During the Napoleonic Wars in Egypt, the Peninsula and France.

WATERLOO RECOLLECTIONS by *Frederick Llewellyn*—Rare First Hand Accounts, Letters, Reports and Retellings from the Campaign of 1815.

AVAILABLE ONLINE AT **www.leonaur.com**
AND OTHER GOOD BOOK STORES

ALSO FROM LEONAUR
AVAILABLE IN SOFTCOVER OR HARDCOVER WITH DUST JACKET

THE JENA CAMPAIGN: 1806 *by F. N. Maude*—The Twin Battles of Jena & Auerstadt Between Napoleon's French and the Prussian Army.

PRIVATE O'NEIL *by Charles O'Neil*—The recollections of an Irish Rogue of H. M. 28th Regt.—The Slashers— during the Peninsula & Waterloo campaigns of the Napoleonic wars.

ROYAL HIGHLANDER *by James Anton*—A soldier of H.M 42nd (Royal) Highlanders during the Peninsular, South of France & Waterloo Campaigns of the Napoleonic Wars.

CAPTAIN BLAZE *by Elzéar Blaze*—Elzéar Blaze recounts his life and experiences in Napoleon's army in a well written, articulate and companionable style.

LEJEUNE VOLUME 1 *by Louis-François Lejeune*—The Napoleonic Wars through the Experiences of an Officer on Berthier's Staff.

LEJEUNE VOLUME 2 *by Louis-François Lejeune*—The Napoleonic Wars through the Experiences of an Officer on Berthier's Staff.

FUSILIER COOPER *by John S. Cooper*—Experiences in the 7th (Royal) Fusiliers During the Peninsular Campaign of the Napoleonic Wars and the American Campaign to New Orleans.

CAPTAIN COIGNET *by Jean-Roch Coignet*—A Soldier of Napoleon's Imperial Guard from the Italian Campaign to Russia and Waterloo.

FIGHTING NAPOLEON'S EMPIRE *by Joseph Anderson*—The Campaigns of a British Infantryman in Italy, Egypt, the Peninsular & the West Indies During the Napoleonic Wars.

CHASSEUR BARRES *by Jean-Baptiste Barres*—The experiences of a French Infantryman of the Imperial Guard at Austerlitz, Jena, Eylau, Friedland, in the Peninsular, Lutzen, Bautzen, Zinnwald and Hanau during the Napoleonic Wars.

MARINES TO 95TH (RIFLES) *by Thomas Fernyhough*—The military experiences of Robert Fernyhough during the Napoleonic Wars.

HUSSAR ROCCA *by Albert Jean Michel de Rocca*—A French cavalry officer's experiences of the Napoleonic Wars and his views on the Peninsular Campaigns against the Spanish, British And Guerilla Armies.

SERGEANT BOURGOGNE *by Adrien Bourgogne*—With Napoleon's Imperial Guard in the Russian Campaign and on the Retreat from Moscow 1812 - 13.

AVAILABLE ONLINE AT **www.leonaur.com**
AND OTHER GOOD BOOK STORES